OXFORD ENGLISH MONOGRAPHS

General Editors
CHRISTOPHER BUTLER   STEPHEN GILL
DOUGLAS GRAY   EMRYS JONES
ROGER LONSDALE

Joseph Conrad and the Anthropological Dilemma
'Bewildered Traveller'

JOHN W. GRIFFITH

CLARENDON PRESS · OXFORD
1995

Oxford University Press. Walton Street, Oxford OX2 6DP

Oxford New York
Athens Auckland Bangkok Bombay
Calcutta Cape Town Dar es Salaam Delhi
Florence Hong Kong Istanbul Karachi
Kuala Lumpur Madras Madrid Melbourne
Mexico City Nairobi Paris Singapore
Taipei Tokyo Toronto
and associated companies in
Berlin Ibadan

Oxford is a trade mark of Oxford University Press

Published in the United States
by Oxford University Press Inc., New York

©John W. Griffith 1995

British Library Cataloguing in Publication Data
Data available

Library of Congress Cataloging in Publication Data

Griffith, John W. (John Wylie), 1964–
Joseph Conrad and the anthropological dilemma: 'bewildered
traveller' / John W. Griffith.
—(Oxford English monographs)
Rev. of the author's thesis (Ph. D.)—Oxford University.
Includes bibliographical references (p. 231) and index.
1. Conrad, Joseph, 1857–1924—Knowledge—Anthropology. 2. Voyages and
travels in literature. 3. Society, Primitive, in literature. 4. Man, Primitive, in
literature. 5. Anthropology in literature. 6. Travelers in literature.
7. Ethnology in literature. 8. Culture in literature. 9. Travel in
literature. I. Title. II. Series.
PR6005.04Z736 1995 823'.912—dc20 94-45316
ISBN 0-19-818300-3

1 3 5 7 9 10 8 6 4 2

Typeset by Best-set Typesetter Ltd., Hong Kong
Printed in Great Britain
on acid-free paper by
Bookcraft Ltd,
Midsomer Norton, Avon

*To my Father,
and to the memory
of my Mother*

Acknowledgements

Numerous and often incalculable debts must be acknowledged here. Indeed, the opportunity to recognize those who have helped so much in the creation of this book is one of the greatest pleasures in seeing it published. Most importantly, my sincere thanks to Christopher Butler of Christ Church College, Oxford, who supervised the D. Phil. thesis from which this book has emerged, and whose support and insightful criticism have been tireless. I am also grateful to the editors of the English Monographs Series and to the Delegates of Oxford University Press for selecting and supporting this project at various stages; in particular, thanks to Dr Stephen Gill, who corresponded with me on behalf of the Oxford English Monographs Committee, and under whom I had the good fortune to study as an undergraduate. Thanks to Jason Freeman, my editor at Oxford University Press, who has been extremely patient, attentive, and supportive of this project; thanks also to the staff of Oxford University Press.

Thanks must go to Professor John Batchelor of the University of Newcastle upon Tyne and Dr John Kelly of St John's College, Oxford, for their helpful comments and encouragement when they examined the thesis. Special thanks must be given to the anonymous readers of the thesis at Oxford University Press, who offered such valuable criticism and encouragement in revising the thesis into a monograph. My gratitude also to another tutor at Oxford, Jon Stallworthy, of Wolfson College. Professors John Bertolini, Robert Price, Paul Cubeta, and Robert Hill at Middlebury College encouraged me to pursue graduate studies in English several years ago, and helped in many subtle ways to form my critical judgements and methods.

Materially, I must thank the staff of the Bodleian Library—in particular, the staffs of the Radcliffe Camera, Rhodes House Library, the Radcliffe Science Library, the Old Library, and the Law Library; the staff of the English Faculty Library; and the staff of the Lincoln College Library. I should also acknowledge the staff of the Vanderbilt University Library, where much of the revised version of this book was written.

Kevin Grogin of the Fisk University Art Gallery helped me

to obtain the image of the African figure pictured on the cover. Thanks to Mr Grogin and the Stieglitz Collection for permission to use this image from the permanent collection; special thanks also to the photographer, Vando Rogers.

Other people who must be recognized for their support and encouragement are friends in Oxford and in the States. Thanks to colleagues at Montgomery Bell Academy—particularly Wayne Batten—for invaluable reading and criticism. There are many others who undoubtedly deserve a word of thanks who go unmentioned by name here.

My grandmother and grandfather, the late Mary and Samuel Wylie, gave unfailing support over the course of my graduate studies. By far the greatest thanks, though, must go to my parents, Louis Griffith and the late Margaret Griffith, without whom no word of this book could have been written. In particular, I must acknowledge my mother, one of the greatest teachers I have known.

Since revising this book, I have learned of the serious illness of a friend and mentor, an illness which casts these acknowledgements in a more sombre light. I would like to dedicate this book with gratitude and love to Douglas Paschall, headmaster of Montgomery Bell Academy, a warm friend and a great and humane educator.

Contents

Textual Notes and Abbreviations   x

Introduction: 'Bewildered Traveller': The
Anthropological Dilemma in Joseph Conrad's
Fiction   1

1. Transcultural Identification: The Anthropological
   Dilemma in *Heart of Darkness* and Victorian
   Anthropology   13

2. Cultural Immersion and Culture Shock in Conrad's
   Fiction   46

3. 'Pioneers of Trade and Progress': Conrad's
   Civilization and its Discontents   72

4. The Rise and Fall of Empires: *Heart of Darkness*
   and Historical Cycles in the Victorian Era   100

5. 'Going Native', Coming Home: 'Decivilization' in
   Heart of Darkness and Conrad's Malaysian Novels   125

6. Nordau's *Degeneration* and Lombroso's Atavism
   in *Heart of Darkness* and 'Falk'   153

7. Anthropology's Impact on Evolution and Ethics
   in the Victorian Era   179

8. Tribes and Detribalization: *Gemeinschaft* and
   Gesellschaft   196

Bibliography   231
Index   245

Textual Notes and Abbreviations

With the notable exceptions of *Heart of Darkness* and *Last Essays*, references to Conrad's works are to the *Doubleday, Page and Company Canterbury Edition of the Works of Joseph Conrad* (Garden City, NY: Doubleday, Page and Company, 1926). Pagination is often identical to that of the Dent Uniform edition (1923, 1926). All references to *Heart of Darkness* are to Robert Kimbrough (ed.) *Heart of Darkness*: A Norton Critical Edition (New York: W. W. Norton, 1988). Kimbrough's edition offers the advantages of historical and critical essays, as well as an emended text which attempts to duplicate Conrad's original punctuation in several places. Kimbrough also notes changes from the original manuscript. The rationalization for this edition is convincingly explained in his introduction; and I will not reiterate his arguments here. The volume of *Last Essays* referred to is *Dent's Collected Edition of the Works of Joseph Conrad* (London: Dent, 1945–55).

Unless otherwise noted, all references to Conrad's works will be made parenthetically within the text. In any quotation, brackets enclosing three dots (...) indicate elisions I have made. All other elisions are textually original.

The following abbreviations for Conrad's works are used:

AF	*Almayer's Folly*
F	'Amy Foster' in *Typhoon and Other Stories*
FA	'Falk' in *Typhoon and Other Stories*
HD	*Heart of Darkness*
I	*The Inheritors*
LE	*Last Essays*
LJ	*Lord Jim*
MS	*The Mirror of the Sea*
NN	*The Nigger of the 'Narcissus'*
N	*Nostromo*
NL	*Notes on Life and Letters*
OI	*An Oucast of the Islands*
OP	'An Outpost of Progress' in *Tales of Unrest*
PR	*A Personal Record*
R	*The Rescue*
SA	*The Secret Agent*
SL	'The Shadow-Line' in *'Twixt Land and Sea*
UW	*Under Western Eyes*
V	*Victory*

Introduction: 'Bewildered Traveller': The Anthropological Dilemma in Joseph Conrad's Fiction

> If I imagined two kingdoms adjoining one another, with one of which I was fairly well acquainted, and altogether unfamiliar with the other, and I was not allowed to enter the unknown realm, however much I desired to do so, I should still be able to form some conception of its nature. I could go to the limits of the kingdom with which I was acquainted and follow its boundaries, and as I did so, I should in this way describe the boundaries of this unknown country, and thus without ever having set foot in it, obtain a general conception of it. And if this was a task that engrossed my energies, and if I was indefatigable in my desire to be accurate, it would doubtless sometimes happen that, as I stood sadly at my country's boundary and looked longingly into the unknown country, which was so near me and yet so far away, some little revelation might be vouchsafed me.
>
> Sören Kierkegaard, *Either/Or*[1]

> the age in which we are camped like bewildered travellers in a garish unrestful hotel.
>
> (V 3)

Joseph Conrad's works can usefully be placed in the context of historical and contemporary anthropology in order to demonstrate the complex manner in which cultural assumptions regarding European 'civilization' are simultaneously challenged and reinforced in the late nineteenth century. This study seeks to historicize a cluster of value-laden ideas regarding the dialectic between 'primitive' and 'civilized' cultures in the late nineteenth century, and to recuperate a body of cultural texts—especially anthropological writing, broadly defined—many of which have been overlooked.

---

[1] Sören Kierkegaard, *Either/Or*, 2 vols., trans. Howard V. Hong and Edna H. Hong (Princeton: Princeton University Press, 1987), i. 64.

The research mapped out in this book attempts to recapture a palaeontology of culture in the Victorian period; in particular, the excavation of anthropological and other scientific writing of the late Victorian period is attempted in order to explore the impact of debates regarding 'primitivism' in the work of one modernist writer, Joseph Conrad. In short, this work is as much a cultural history as it is a literary history in the traditional sense. By scrutinizing the writing of Victorian anthropology, I hope to reveal some fissures in what has been viewed as a confident melioristic age.

New historicists 'have reminded us that it is treacherously difficult to reconstruct the past as it really was, rather than as we have been conditioned by our own place and time to believe that it was'.[2] Many anthropologists recognize a similar difficulty in 'bridging conceptual gaps' to 'primitive cultures', a difficulty constantly insisted upon by writers such as Victor Turner, James Clifford, and Clifford Geertz.[3] Both Conrad and anthropologists, Victorian and modern, occupy a position similar to that of the traveller in Kierkegaard's allegory; they are borderland observers: 'And if this was a task that engrossed my energies, and if I was indefatigable in my desire to be accurate, it would doubtless sometimes happen that, as I stood sadly at my country's boundary and looked longingly into the unknown country, which was so near me and yet so far away, some little revelation might be vouchsafed me' (quoted above, p. 1). Conrad and his contemporaries who travelled in 'primitive cultures' seem to have felt robbed even of many of the little revelations of Kierkegaard's traveller. Yet, their efforts at understanding and bridging conceptual gaps are witness to the growth of a dynamic intellectual climate in the late nineteenth

  [2] Ross C. Murfin, 'The New Historicism and *Heart of Darkness*' in Ross C. Murfin (ed.), *Heart of Darkness. A Case Study in Contemporary Criticism* (New York: St. Martin's Press, 1989), 229.
  [3] Some works of interest in this regard include James Clifford, *The Predicament of Culture: Twentieth Century Ethnography, Literature and Art* (Cambridge, Mass.: Harvard University Press, 1988); J. Clifford and D. Marcus (eds.), *Writing Culture: The Poetics and Politics of Ethnography* (Berkeley: University of California Press, 1986); Clifford Geertz, *The Interpretation of Cultures* (New York: Basic Books, 1973), *Local Knowledge: Further Essays in Interpretive Anthropology* (New York: Basic Books, 1983), *Works and Lives: The Anthropologist as Author* (Stanford: Stanford University Press, 1988); Victor W. Turner, *On the Edge of the Bush: Anthropology as Experience* (Tucson: University of Arizona Press, 1985); Victor W. Turner and Edward M. Bruner (eds.) *The Anthropology of Experience* (Urbana: University of Illinois Press, 1986); another related work is Richard G. Fox (ed.) *Recapturing Anthropology: Working in the Present* (Santa Fe: School of American Research Press, 1991).

century in which the nascent science of anthropology flourished.

In many ways, historical inquiry, or penetrating the thought of another time period, is analogous to the difficulty an anthropologist encounters in interpreting another culture. As Clifford Geertz phrases this dilemma, 'it becomes profoundly unclear how individuals enclosed in one culture are able to penetrate the thought of individuals enclosed in another'.[4] This issue of bridging conceptual divides is a recurring question in Conrad's writing. The debate over transcultural or transhistorical understanding inevitably calls into question a study such as this, which will attempt to recover an historical movement.[5] The problems of new historicism and anthropology both have a profound relevance to the writings of modernists such as Conrad who attempted to 'read through' the cultures in which they travelled, and who, at the same time, recognized, as did perhaps few others in the Victorian era, the profound difficulties of such transcultural endeavours.[6] Even a modernist writer such as D. H. Lawrence, who believed fervently in the possibility of not only understanding but assimilating a 'primitive' culture, often expressed profound doubt that such an understanding was possible or desirable. In his essay on Melville in *Studies in Classic American Literature*, Lawrence wrote:

> The truth of the matter is one cannot go back. Some men can: renegade. But Melville couldn't go back: and I know that I could never go back. Back towards the past, savage life. One cannot go back. It is one's destiny inside one.
>
> There are other peoples, these savages. One does not despise them. One does not feel superior. But there is a gulf in time and being.[7]

[4] Geertz, *Interpretation of Cultures*, 149.

[5] Does this difficulty of historical interpretation mean, as Michel Foucault and others would have us believe, that we are so imprisoned in our own cultural assumptions that it is, *a priori*, impossible to enter into the past? As E. D. Hirsch has argued, this merely 'exaggerates a difficulty into an impossibility'. Hirsch, 'Back to History', quoted by Murfin in *Case Study*, 233. In other words, it is difficult for an anthropologist to understand his or her subject; it is difficult for an historian to recover the past; it is difficult for a member of one culture to 'penetrate' the thoughts of another; but difficulties should not be equated with impossibilities.

[6] Murfin writes, 'It (new historicism) is a movement that would destabilize our overly settled conceptions of what literature and history are. It is one, too, that would define history broadly, not as a mere chronicle of facts and events, but rather, as a "thick description" of human reality, one that raises questions of interest to anthropologists and sociologists, as well as to those posed by traditional historians'. Murfin, 226.

[7] D. H. Lawrence, *Studies in Classic American Literature* (1923) (Reprinted London: Penguin, 1987), 51–2.

Bridging the 'gulf in time and being' nevertheless remained a goal not only of anthropology but of a great deal of travel writing and even popular fiction in the Victorian and modernist periods. For the Victorians the idea of *going back* often had a specific, though coded, meaning. To go back was to abandon the cultural acquisitions of 'civilization'. To go back was to risk degeneration. This image of going back to the primitive leads us to the consideration of Conràd's works as 'cultural artifacts' which themselves depict the difficulty of bridging conceptual gaps to primitive cultures.

The Anthropological Dilemma

Many of Joseph Conrad's fictions on so-called primitive cultures— *Almayer's Folly, An Outcast of the Islands, Heart of Darkness,* and *Lord Jim*—seem to have been predicated upon popular Victorian debates about the degradation or development of culture. Conrad's works, like the anthropology with which they were so often allied, charted the course of cultural development literally and figuratively, geographically and epistemologically. From the Congo to Borneo, from South America to Malaysia, Conrad depicted the contacts and conflicts of so-called primitives and European peoples. If this journey traced literal wanderings, it also, perhaps more significantly, involved psychological journeys, journeys of whose implications Conrad himself does not seem to have been fully aware.[8] From its inception, anthropology was an unsettled and unsettling science. Almost by definition, anthropology traced disorienting journeys to distant lands; these voyages were also viewed as temporal wanderings, back to the ways of life

---

[8] Michael Levenson comments: 'And in the view of *Heart of Darkness* that has prevailed until recently, the fiction has been regarded as a paradigm, almost a defining instance of interior narrative. Within this conception, Marlow's journey only incidentally involves movement through physical space; in essence it represents a "journey into self", an "introspective plunge", "a night journey into the unconscious". The African terrain is taken as a symbolic geography of the mind, and Kurtz as a suppressed avatar lurking at the core of the self.' Michael Levenson, *Modernism and the Fate of Individuality: Character and Novelistic Form from Conrad to Woolf* (Cambridge: Cambridge University Press, 1991), 5–6. Martin Bock writes that 'typically, Conrad employs the convention of the disorienting journey, which leads character, narrator, and reader to a point of sensual, cognitive, or psychological derangement'. Martin Bock, *Crossing the Shadow-Line: The Literature of Estrangement* (Columbus: Ohio State University Press, 1989), 87.

of older, primitive societies. Such journeys, as anthropologists have come to realize, were fraught with moral, cultural, and epistemological difficulties from the start.[9]

Conrad's contacts with 'primitive' cultures dislocated him; and his writings of the early period up until *Nostromo* often record this dislocation. This cultural anxiety, or *anthropological dilemma*, reflected not merely a personal concern on Conrad's part, but rather a wider ambivalence in late Victorian culture. The term anthropology here is used broadly to refer to cultural interest in 'primitive' peoples, for although anthropology and ethnology were scientific disciplines, they also influenced non-scientific writing such as travelers' tales and ethnographic novels. The anthropological dilemma applies not merely to the scientific concerns of anthropology or the analysis of particular cultures, but more widely to the cultural attractions and animadversions which have become known as 'primitivism'.[10] The journeys of these Victorian writers coincided with the philosophical meanderings of anthropological writers like the founder of cultural anthropology, E. B. Tylor.

The anthropological dilemma, which arose in the light of Victorian science and travel literature concerned the ability of people of one culture (particularly 'civilized' societies) to penetrate the thought of another society ('the primitive'). Conrad, who was himself a notable cultural *émigré*, never underestimated the profound difficulties of transculturation—the understanding of another culture. Conrad's early writings reflect the prevalent Victorian anxiety that such cross-cultural contacts would prove dangerous to the members of each society. Degeneration and atavism inevitably accompanied colonization, many Victorians argued. Conrad's contacts with other cultures in his own journeys seem to have exposed a literary anxiety similar to those traced by Daniel Pick in his study of cultural degeneration in the Victorian

---

[9] For one account of these difficulties see Gísli Pálsson, 'Introduction: Going Beyond Boundaries' in Gísli Pálsson (ed.), *Beyond Boundaries: Understanding, Translation and Anthropological Discourse* (Oxford: Berg, 1993), 1–40.

[10] Anthropology was not yet a clearly defined discipline. Non-scientific writers of the late Victorian period often assimilated anthropological doctrines into their works. Anthropology was only beginning to crystallize as a science. E. B. Tylor gives a 'general acknowledgement of obligations to writers on ethnography and kindred sciences as well as to historians, travellers, and missionaries.' E. B. Tylor, *Primitive Culture, Researches into the Development of Mythology, Philosophy, Religion, Art, and Custom*, 2 vols. (London: John Murray, 1871), i, p. vi.

era.[11] Faced with 'alien' cultures, the question was raised, would Europeans be able to maintain their cultural identities, or would they degenerate in a Kurtzian manner?

Many late nineteenth-century writers explored the degeneration of individuals and societies, especially in relation to 'primitive' cultures.[12] In the Victorian era, this perceived degeneration received recognition from writers, social reformers, and politicians alike.[13] Perhaps more importantly, this perception of atavism received the sanction of the Victorian sciences—anthropology, zoology, and medicine, as well as the developing social sciences of criminology, sociology, and psychology. J. A. Symonds, a writer born in the 1860s and steeped in Darwin's theories, wrote that 'It seems to be a law of life that nothing can stand completely still and changeless. All must vary, *must progress or retrograde*'.[14] Progression or retrogression: these two antithetical movements in human societies are at the centre of many philosophical debates of the Victorian era, for stasis seemed to many thinkers unimaginable. The apparent solidification of British smugness about the high level of their civilization often conflicted sharply with ideas of cultural dissolution and primitivism introduced by anthropology.[15] Indeed, anthropology could be seen as the *locus classicus* for such paradigms of progression and retrogression.

Often underlying the Victorian interest in cultural atrophy in the nineteenth century, there is a common fear that degeneration unleashes primitivistic and atavistic desires in Europeans. Degeneration, *dégénérscense*, *Entartung*, reversion, atavism, regression,

[11] Daniel Pick, *Faces of Degeneration: A European Disorder, c.1848–1918* (Cambridge: Cambridge University Press, 1989).

[12] The term 'primitive' has always been problematic. Adam Kuper has written, 'the orthodox view is that there never was such a thing as primitive society. Certainly, no such thing can be reconstructed now. There is not even a sensible way in which one can specify what a primitive society is (. . .) Even if some very ancient social order could be reconstituted, one could not generalize it.' Adam Kuper, *The Invention of Primitive Society: The History of an Illusion* (London: Routledge and Kegan Paul, 1988), 1.

[13] See Gareth Stedman Jones, *Outcast London: A Study in the Relationship between Classes in Victorian Society* (1971) (Reprinted London: Penguin, 1984), and Pick.

[14] J. A. Symonds, *Stella Fregelius* (London: Macmillan, 1906), 289, italics mine.

[15] 'The incongruity of these pictures gives us some feeling for the incongruities of the nineties, when the middle classes had perfected both the habits of leisure and the methods of colonialism. To enjoy the delicacies of a long cultural tradition and to overstep the boundaries of that tradition, to witness civilization at its most finely wrought and to confront its rude origins, to contemplate the refinements of social

retrogression: all of these varied terms were used in late nineteenth-century Europe to describe the process through which individual men and civilizations declined and fell.[16] These terms often transcended particular cultural, scientific, and linguistic boundaries to be absorbed into a broader discourse regarding progression or regression in culture. The evidence for such anxieties was often ill-founded; however, the anxiety was still deeply felt. Degeneration, in short, as Daniel Pick has so convincingly argued, was often projection rather than reality; and its history is the history of an illusion, although a passionately perceived illusion.[17] This illusion was supported by the burgeoning science of anthropology. While anthropology provided abundant evidence for atavism, the impact of anthropology on this perceived cultural degeneration was more subtle. By challenging the accepted boundaries of cultures, anthropology itself mimicked this cultural dilemma regarding progress or regress. In the light of anthropological discoveries, as we shall see, both individual and cultural boundaries blurred and became indistinct. Anthropology became the cultural map upon which were charted the progression or degeneration of mankind; and the painful anxieties and dislocations etched on this cultural map should not be underestimated.

In exploring this theme of cultural progression and retrogression that precipitated the anthropological dilemma, the primary text I will be focusing on is Conrad's *Heart of Darkness*, though I will also make reference to other novels, particularly *Almayer's Folly*, *An Outcast of the Islands*, *Lord Jim*, and *The Secret Agent*, as well as to Conrad's short stories and essays. Obviously, Kurtz's apparent reversion to the 'primitive' has found a prominent place in criticism of *Heart of Darkness*.[18]

In light of some of these anxieties over progression, Kurtz's 'incredible degradation' in the Congo would not have been as

convention and to watch such conventions dissolve—these are concurrent historical possibilities that will allow us to locate modernist character within the expansive context that it demands.' Levenson, *Modernism and the Fate of Individuality*, 1.

[16] See Pick, 6–33 and *passim*.

[17] As Pick writes, regression 'was a process which could usurp all boundaries of discernible identity, threatening the overthrow of civilization and progress'. Pick, 9.

[18] John A. McClure has summarized these critical discussions: 'A common interpretation of Kurtz's metamorphosis is that Conrad intends it as an example of "reversion to savagery." Guerard, for instance, writes of Kurtz's "savage reversion" in *Conrad, the Novelist*, and Fleischman follows suit; Marlow, he writes, "is (. . .)

shocking to Victorian readers as might be assumed. Such readers would probably have been familiar with other works regarding reversion, degeneration, and regression. Contemporary readers of *Heart of Darkness* could also have been expected to relate the story to the larger debate concerning the direction of culture—a debate that ranged widely over the fields of archaeology, philosophy, zoology, and anthropology. Could the 'civilizing mission' in Africa regenerate culture amidst perceived savagery? Would the opposite occur, and colonists shed their civilization when confronted with primitive cultures? Conrad and his contemporaries considered these questions to be of grave concern.

Many Victorians looked at the apparently static condition of 'savages', which was becoming increasingly familiar to them through the burgeoning field of anthropology, and concluded that there was no innate progressive tendency in man—that, as Arthur Mitchell put it in his influential work *The Past in the Present*, 'a state of high civilization is difficult to keep as well as to gain'.[19] Drawing loosely upon the evidence which anthropology, archaeology and biology offered, many people concluded that degeneration must be a natural corollary to progress: 'The truth is that man's capacities of degradation stand in close relation, and are proportionate, to his capacities of improvement.'[20] Situating Conrad's writing in the centre of the discourse of progression and regression will challenge some of the false portraits of the Victorian era as a confident era in which imperialism flourished and Britannia ruled the waves.[21]

struck by the realization that the potential for regression to primitive savagery to which Mr. Kurtz had succumbed resides within himself as well."' John A. McClure, *Kipling and Conrad: the Colonial Fiction* (Cambridge, Mass.: Harvard University Press, 1981), 132. Bernard Meyer is representative of this reversion theory: 'Under such circumstances, regression to savagery can be a powerful temptation (. . .) In short, there are circumstances under which a man, even a good man, may be hard put to resist reverting to the beast which lies dormant within everyone.' Bernard Meyer, *Joseph Conrad: A Psychoanalytic Biography* (Princeton: Princeton University Press, 1967), 158. Meyer also writes: 'a strange and ominous transformation had taken place in Mr. Kurtz's personality; like a snake shedding its skin, he had cast off all his fine European habits and ideals, revealing a creature whose condition of moral degradation and animal primitivism made him indistinguishable from the savages for whom he had once expressed such touching concern.' Ibid. 156.

[19] Arthur Mitchell, *The Past in the Present: What is Civilisation?* (Edinburgh: David Douglas, 1890), 214.

[20] George Douglas Campbell, *Primeval Man: An Examination of Some Recent Speculations* (London: Straham & Co., 1869), 192.

[21] While they write convincingly, critics such as Patrick Brantlinger emphasize one facet of the Victorian cultural ethos: 'For many of its adherents, however, imperial-

Before beginning the main part of my argument, it is necessary to sketch briefly the parameters of this study. The first two chapters of this work contextualize Conrad's *Heart of Darkness* in relation to both Victorian and contemporary anthropology and travel writing. In particular, I focus on the concepts of cultural assimilation and transcultural identification, and relate Conrad's work to the participant-observer school of anthropology. Fieldwork in anthropology is investigated as a rich analogy for the process of negotiating the *terra incognita* of 'primitive' cultures. The third chapter explores the genesis of the idea of degeneracy as applied to African culture; in this chapter I also consider the implications of terms such as civilization, culture, and progress in the context of Victorian anthropology. In particular, I consider the debates in anthropology between progressionism and degenerationism. The decline and fall of cultures is explored in the fourth chapter in relation to Conrad's ideas of retrogression and relapse. In this chapter I also investigate the comparative method in anthropology, which provided Victorian thinkers with a matrix for making comparisons between their own cultures and those of 'primitives'. In the fifth chapter I attempt to contextualize the numerous examples of characters in Conrad's works who 'go native' when faced with a primitive culture; the opposite trend of natives who revert to their previous 'savagery' is again seen in a historical context. A corollary theme of acclimatization is also explored. In the sixth chapter, I consider the impact of two notorious Victorian positivists, Max Nordau and Ccsarc Lombroso, whose theories of degeneracy and criminal atavism seem to have influenced Conrad's portrayal of Kurtz. The seventh chapter situates Conrad's work (and to a lesser extent the work of H. G. Wells) in the context of the evolution of ethics in the Victorian period, and, particularly, in relation to Nietzsche's reception in England. In both the seventh and eighth chapters the theme of altruism and egoism is traced in relation to works by several anthropologists, psychiatrists, and historians of ethics, in-

ism was a compelling set of beliefs precisely because it seemed to express their interests clearly and rationally. It was good to be British and on top of the world, a member of the most enlightened, progressive, civilized race in history, and to most Victorians and Edwardians it would have seemed crazy to deny it. (...) that phase (the imperial) was the chief glory and merit of modern history, the ever-rising pinnacle of progress and civilization.' Patrick Brantlinger, *Rule of Darkness: British Literature and Imperialism, 1830–1914* (Ithaca: Cornell University Press, 1988), 14, 16. Brantlinger briefly mentions fears of regression, but his study emphasizes the melioristic imagery of British imperialism (see 32–6 and *passim*).

cluding T. H. Huxley and Henry Maudsley. Concepts of the tribe and detribalization are explored in the eighth and final chapter.

In contrast to a widely-accepted view of the Victorian era as centred in a teleological or melioristic confidence, we constantly recognize the opposite—that Victorians discovered discontinuities and schisms in the picture of their alleged cultural advance. Not coincidentally, the crisis of faith in cultural advancement coincided with the rise of anthropology and found expression in many of Conrad's works. Indeed, the words progress and civilization usually have ironic connotations in Conrad's works, as we shall see. In the late novel *Victory*, for example, Conrad writes of post-lapsarian Axel Heyst:

> He reflected, too, with the sense of making a discovery, that this primeval ancestor is not easily suppressed (. . .) There was in the son a lot of that first ancestor who, as soon as could uplift his muddy frame from the celestial mould, started inspecting and naming the animals of that paradise which he was soon to lose.

> Action—the first thought, or perhaps the first impulse on earth! The barbed hook, baited with the illusion of progress to bring out of the lightless void the shoals of unnumbered generations! (*V* 173–4)[22]

In this book, Conrad is seen not as a representative of a counter-movement against progressivism—a critic of this 'illusion of progress'; such an interpretation would cast his works in too dogmatic a light. Indeed, to argue too polemically for a sharply delineated reading of Conrad's works is to ignore Conrad's own injunction, in a letter to the *New York Times*: 'The only basis for creative work lies in the courageous recognition of all the irreconcilable antagonisms that make our life so enigmatic, so burdensome, so dangerous—so full of hope.'[23] Nevertheless, Conrad's early works can be seen as a kind of map upon which were engraved these cultural anxieties.[24] In a small way, this study attempts to counter some of the common myths which are still prevalent of

[22] See Cedric Watts, *A Preface to Conrad* (London: Longman, 1982), 77–8. Ian Watt is also relevant here. See particularly 'Ideological Perspectives: Kurtz and the Fate of Victorian Progress' in *Conrad in the Nineteenth Century* (Berkeley: University of California Press, 1980), 147–8.

[23] Letter of 2 August 1901, Frederick Karl and Laurence Davies (eds.), *Collected Letters of Joseph Conrad* (Cambridge: Cambridge University Press, 1983), i (1861–1897), 348–9.

[24] Clearly, these are paths that others have trod before me; and I am indebted to a number of critics whom I acknowledge in my notes. In particular, I should take

the late nineteenth century as a period of progressivism. Anthropology both upheld and debunked progressive ideals. Conrad remains a crucial figure in the debunking of these myths of late
nineteenth-century meliorism.[25]

note of the work of Ian Watt, whose writing probably first impelled me toward a
historical reading of Conrad's fiction.

[25] See J. B. Bury, *The Idea of Progress. An Inquiry into its Growth and Origins*
(1920) (Reprinted Chicago: Chicago University Press, 1948), and Robert A. Nisbet,
History of the Idea of Progress (New York: Basic Books, 1980). Cf. Pick, 12.

Transcultural Identification: The Anthropological Dilemma in Heart of Darkness and Victorian Anthropology

The process of fieldwork always subjects an anthropologist to an attack against his sense of self/identity because he has lost, at least temporarily, those innumerable identifications with his home world and significant others that normally sustained his sense of self-identity. The anthropologist wakes up to find himself a stranger, and perhaps a little afraid, in a world he never made, a world that is totally perplexing, mysterious, and often difficult to penetrate . . . the anthropologist begins to experience the disintegration of his sense of identity.[1]

'In leaving home one learns life. You travel. Travelling is victory! You shall return with much wisdom.'
    'I shall never return . . .'

(*OI* 131)

'Bewildered Travellers': Travel Literature and Anthropology

The subtitle of this book comes from a phrase that Conrad employs in the late novel, *Victory* (1915), to give a sense of the cultural displacement of an 'age in which we are camped like bewildered travellers in a garish unrestful hotel' (*V* 3). This image of people as 'bewildered travellers' seems particularly *apropos* as a point of departure in a discussion of *Heart of Darkness*. On one level, the novella deals with the psychological and cultural anxieties involved in travel in 'primitive' cultures. In this image from *Victory*, Conrad

[1] John L. Wengle, *Ethnographers in the Field; The Psychology of Research* (Tuscaloosa: University of Alabama Press, 1988), 153.

seems to echo a passage deleted from the final version of the novella in which he describes the fate of the colonists in an African coastal city:

They filled the dining room, uniforms and civil clothes(,) sallow faces, purposeless expressions. I was astonished at their number. *An air of weary bewilderment* at finding themselves where they were sat upon all the faces, and in their demeanor they pretended to take themselves seriously just as the greasy and dingy place that was like one of those infamous eating shops you find near the slums of cities, where everything (. . .) pretended to be a sign of progress.   (*HD* 18, note 1; italics mine)

Here Conrad identifies the disorientation and absurdity of a group of people culturally adrift as part of the haphazard 'progress' of colonialism; they are portrayed as having 'purposeless expressions' and an 'air of weary bewilderment'.[2] In short, they are the colonial *déracinés* so common in Conrad's fiction. He also hints here at the ironic meanings of 'progress', a word that occupied an ambiguous place in Victorian anthropology. Despite the distance he emphasizes from these colonists, Marlow is another of Conrad's many bewildered travellers in 'primitive' cultures. Although Conrad deleted this passage from the final version of the novella, the implication of this section to Conrad's primitivist concerns is clear. Bewilderment, displacement—these are often the psychological results of crossing the shadow-line into a more 'primitive' culture.[3]

In trying to grope toward an understanding of Conrad's place in the *mélange* of late nineteenth-century theories of culture in general, and particularly the binary opposition of 'primitive' and 'civilized', we should recognize that cross-cultural contacts are not easily made or understood. The borderland which the anthropologist occupies between his or her own culture and the 'alien' provides a rich analogy for Conrad's own experience. The anthro-

---

[2] 'Bewilderment' is a common feature of Marlow's response to his journey: 'It seems to me that I am trying to tell you a dream—making a vain attempt, because no relation of a dream can convey the dream-sensation, that commingling of absurdity, surprise, and bewilderment in a tremor of struggling revolt, that notion of being captured by the incredible, which is the very essence of dreams' . . . (*HD* 30).

[3] Bock says similarly, 'During these voyages, character and reader journey across both physical and psychological shadow-lines, away from the culturally familiar and into a heretical landscape'. Bock, 85–6.

pologist, in other words must be, to use a term Conrad applied to himself, a 'homo duplex'. Throughout his life, Conrad remained profoundly aware of the plight of the perpetual border-dweller: 'Both at sea and on land my point of view is English, from which the conclusion should not be drawn that I have become an Englishman. That is not the case. Homo duplex has in my case more than one meaning.'[4]

Critics have argued that Conrad understood little of the Congo in which he travelled; however, we must question to what extent a clear understanding would have been possible.[5] If an objective understanding of a foreign culture is virtually impossible, by what standards of transcultural identification or cultural relativism are we judging Conrad's *Heart of Darkness*? As Clifford Geertz has remarked on this subject, even in the case of modern ethnography, 'it becomes profoundly unclear how individuals enclosed in one culture are able to penetrate the thought of individuals enclosed in another'.[6] We must be careful neither to overemphasize nor underrate the problem of bridging cultural divides. This problem of transcultural identification is even more crucial to my argument in that Conrad's work is often seen to be at the centre of this dilemma in the modernist *Weltanschauung*. As Leo Gurko has written,

He was the outside man looking in, longing to participate in life but obscurely inhibited . . . He keenly understood the plight of the foreigner seeking roots in an adopted country and of the exile in the process of finding a new home. Virtually all his characters are foreigners and exiles . . . The fact of their being outsiders aggravates the difficulties under which they labor.[7]

---

[4] Quoted in Zdzislaw Najder, *Joseph Conrad. A Chronicle*, trans. Halina Carroll-Najder (New Brunswick: Rutgers University Press, 1983), 240.
[5] 'The point of all this is to suggest that Conrad's picture of the peoples of the Congo seems grossly inaccurate even at the height of their subjection to the ravages of King Leopold's International Association for the Civilization of Central Africa. Travellers with closed minds can tell us little except about themselves. But even those not blinkered, like Conrad, with xenophobia, can be astonishing [sic] blind.' Chinua Achebe, 'An Image of Africa: Racism in Conrad's *Heart of Darkness*', *The Massachusetts Review*, 18 (1977), 782–94 (Reprinted in *HD*, 251–62), p. 260.
[6] Geertz, *Local Knowledge*, 149.
[7] Leo Gurko, *Joseph Conrad: Giant in Exile* (New York: Macmillan, 1962), 36.

This theme of displacement is such a common denominator in literature from the modernist period on that Joseph Brodsky recently remarked, in a slightly different context, 'Displacement and misplacement are this century's commonplace'.[8] The same might be said of much of Conrad's fiction: displacement and misplacement are its commonplaces. The place of the atopic (foreign) in Conrad may be mapped out with reference to a lesser-known short story, 'Amy Foster'.[9]

On one level, Conrad's sense of displacement is personal, a reflection of his own plight as a cultural outsider. For example, the main character in 'Amy Foster', Yanko Goorall, a Slavic *émigré* shipwrecked on the English coast, is widely interpreted to be a stand-in for Conrad himself. Goorall, whose name means 'mountain man', 'finds himself a lost stranger, helpless, incomprehensible, and of a mysterious origin, in some obscure corner of the earth' (F 130). The description of Goorall could be applied to Conrad himself, or to many of his *déraciné* characters. Linguistic and cultural boundaries separate Goorall from those among whom he has been shipwrecked: 'He could talk to no one, and had not hope of understanding anyone. It was as if these had been the faces of people from the other world (. . .) Upon my word, I wonder he didn't go mad' (F 129). The idea of madness as a result of cultural displacement reveals a common concern in Conrad's writings; his colonists—Kurtz, Almayer, Willems—live in a state of disorientation which is a kind of madness. Interestingly, Goorall's name itself, which implies a degree of 'savagery' or 'barbarism' may be seen as a reflection of Conrad's own cultural relativity. The etymology of the word barbarian, after all, comes from the root for foreigner. The barbarian, then, by definition, is the stranger; the word itself defines otherness. Culturally sensitive to his difference, Conrad suggests that the Slav is, from the English perspective, a savage, a 'mountain man'. At the same time, Goorall expects to find savagery in the strange land: 'for him, who knew nothing of the earth, England was an undiscovered country. It was some time before he learned its name; and for all I know he might have

---

[8] Joseph Brodsky, 'The Condition We Call Exile', *New York Review of Books*, 21 January 1988, quoted in D. C. R. A. Goonetillike, *Joseph Conrad: Beyond Culture and Background* (London: Macmillan, 1990), 1.

[9] On the biographical significance of this story see Frederick R. Karl, *Joseph Conrad. The Three Lives* (New York: Farrar, Straus & Giroux, 1979), 513–14 and Najder, *Joseph Conrad*, 273.

expected to find wild beasts or wild men here' (F 111–12). Here Conrad provides one of the inversions of expectations that is so crucial a part of his writings on other cultures. The English stereotype of the 'wild beasts or wild men' which might inhabit the alien culture are reversed.

In 'Amy Foster' Conrad reminds us, as he does so often in his writing, that the foreign and the foreigner are often viewed with suspicion.[10] In his writing, Conrad constantly implies that despite our desire to believe with Menander that 'I am a man, and nothing human is foreign to me', we are constantly reminded that ethnocentricity is a cultural condition that probably applies to most of the world:

... The relations of shipwrecks in the olden times tell us of much suffering. Often the castaways were only saved from drowning to die miserably from starvation on a barren coast; others suffered violent death or else slavery, passing through years of precarious existence with people to whom their strangeness was an object of suspicion, dislike, or fear. (F 113)

Elsewhere, in *An Outcast of the Islands*, Conrad writes pessimistically of ethnocentricity as a natural, if undesirable condition of humanity: 'the accursed feeling made up of disdain, of anger, and of the sense of the superior virtue that leaves us deaf, blind, contemptuous and stupid before anything which is not like ourselves' (*OI* 253–4). 'Amy Foster' perfectly illustrates the specter of ethnocentric anxieties. The English villagers whom Conrad depicts treat Goorall with 'disdain, (. . .) anger' when confronted with this person 'not like ourselves'. In blackly comic terms, Conrad portrays Goorall's difficulty in comprehending a culture that is entirely alien, an England that is cruel and unwelcoming to strangers:

If it hadn't been for the steel cross at Miss Swaffer's belt he would not, he confessed, have known whether he was in a Christian country at all. He used to cast stealthy glances at it, and feel comforted. There was nothing here the same as in his country! The earth and the water were different; . . . Everything else was strange. Conceive you the kind of an existence over-shadowed, oppressed, by the everyday material appearances, as if by visions of a nightmare. (F 130)

---

[10] This problem of cultural assimilation clearly has political ramifications. Julia Kristeva writes: 'The difficulty inherent in thinking and living with *foreigners*, which I analyzed in my book *Strangers to Ourselves*, runs through the history of our civilization'. Julia Kristeva, *Nations Without Nationalism*, trans. Leon S. Roudiez (New York: Columbia University Press, 1993), 16.

Conrad evokes the sense of bewilderment when the familiar is replaced by the 'strange'. Even the most banal 'material appearances' are transformed into nightmarish visions. When Goorall wonders if England is 'a Christian country at all' we are reminded of the easy stereotypes of the alien as barbaric and atheistic, two stereotypes that were commonly applied in the Victorian period to Africa. Despite the adjustments which he makes to the foreign environment ('He became aware of social differences . . .', F 131), cultural immersion is never a possibility for Goorall: 'His foreignness had a peculiar and indelible stamp. At last the people became used to seeing him. But they never became used to him' (F 131–2). Just as Conrad must have retained a sense of his foreignness in England, so Goorall remains a cultural outsider.[11] The Greeks in the classical period distinguished between the *barbarous* and *metic*, the resident foreigner who despite residency possessed only a tenuous relationship to the Greek *polis*.[12] Both Goorall and Conrad occupy this *metic* status in England, the curious place of an inside-outsider.

This short story encapsulates many of Conrad's anxieties regarding the difficulty of cross-cultural contacts: 'He was different; . . . this castaway, that, like a man transplanted into another planet, was separated by an immense space from his past and by an immense ignorance from his future' (F 132).[13] Perhaps evoking the extreme dislocation of which his friend H. G. Wells had written in *The Time Machine*, Conrad depicts a man who finds himself radically 'transplanted'. Even Goorall's marriage to a local woman, the Amy Foster of the title, gives him little more than a 'precarious footing in the community' (F 134). Finally, even Amy Foster begins to see him as foreign, and deserts him while he is dying of fever: 'I wondered whether his difference, his strangeness, were not penetrating with repulsion that dull nature that had begun by irresistibly attracting' (F 137–8). In 'Amy Foster', as in so many of

---

[11] On English ethnocentricity and Conrad, J. H. Retinger writes: 'Besides, to be frank, the English, at the beginning of the twentieth century, were not very hospitable to foreigners, especially to one who was not rich, who had indeed barely enough to live on, who was not covered with titles or glory, who was a bit of an eccentric, who spoke with a pronounced foreign accent, and who did not kowtow to their foibles.' J. H. Retinger, *Conrad and his Contemporaries* (New York: Roy Publishers, 1943), 83.

[12] I am indebted to Kristeva for this analogy. See Kristeva, 18–19.

[13] In *Heart of Darkness*, Marlow speaks of the same sense of disorientation: 'We were wanderers on a prehistoric earth, on an earth that wore the aspect of an unknown planet' (*HD* 37).

Conrad's works, the interest lies in that space where cultural loyalties and identifications clash or elide, where identity is threatened by defamiliarization.

Defamiliarization is an important topic in contemporary anthropology as well. For example, in a book on the psychological hazards of fieldwork anthropology, John L. Wengle writes: 'the stability of an individual's sense of identity depends directly on the 'innumerable identifications' he has established with the familiar, personal and impersonal, concrete and abstract, animate and inanimate objects of his past and present existence. When these many identifications are threatened, as for example when an individual's social or physical environment changes rapidly, his sense of identity will be challenged.'[14] Threats to identity occur in the process of transcultural identification: 'the individual's sense of identity depends very significantly on the responses and reactions he produces in and receives back from people surrounding him'.[15] If it is true that we depend upon others for clues as to our identity, for responses and reactions, then the cultural isolation of a Goorall among a people whose reactions to him are confusing must inevitably create a sense of disorientation. In *Lord Jim*, Marlow's identification of Jim as 'one of us', though it may appear racist, squares with some anthropologists' findings regarding cultural identification: 'It is only in the eyes of our own like, of our own ilk, that we can find a mirror.'[16] For Marlow, Jim clearly serves such a mirroring function. In a passage deleted from the published novel, Marlow remarks that 'I don't know what was the matter with me that morning but . . . they all seemed to me so strange, foreign, as if belonging to some order of beings I had no connection with. It was only when my eyes turned to Jim that I had a sense of not being alone of my kind, as if we two had wandered in there from some distant regions, from a different world. I turned to him for fellowship'.[17] Conrad implies that the sense of reacting against the 'strange, foreign' and seeking refuge or 'fellowship' in like-minded

[14] Wengle, 7–8.   [15] Ibid. 8.

[16] Gary Thrane, quoted Wengle, 8. The phrase 'one of us' in *Lord Jim* is repeated several times: 'I liked his appearance; I knew his appearance; he came from the right place; he was one of us.' (Cf. *LJ* ix, 43, 73, 93, 106, 224, 325, 331, 336, 416).

[17] This passage appeared in the Rosenbach typescript. Watt quotes and analyses this passage in *Conrad in the Nineteenth Century*, 316–17. Of course, it should be noted that Conrad is not discussing ethnic differences here. I merely use the passage by way of comparison.

people is one of the mechanisms that allows for the maintenance of identity.

Cultural identifications and anxieties in Conrad's 'Amy Foster' and other works correspond to the growth of ethnography, the study of ethnic identities in the late nineteenth century. Ethnography explored the cultural development of diverse peoples and attempted to group them in categories according to customs, beliefs, etc. Ethnography represented a cartography of human cultures; anthropology was an attempt to make the 'alien' more familiar. Marlow's journey in *Heart of Darkness* is peculiarly iconic of modernist wanderings—disjointed, uprooted and off-centre. Marlow's voyage is a process of negotiating the tenuous personal and cultural identities so often described in anthropological works, of defending and even reconstituting these identities in the face of the knowledge that such identities cannot be taken for granted. For example, Michael Levenson comments on

a condition that persists all through Conrad's work, a radical *disorientation* that obliterates any stable relation between the self and the world, and that raises the question of whether there *is* a world to which the self belongs. The fragility of identity, the barriers to knowledge, the groundlessness of value—these great Conradian (and modern) motifs appear most often in terms of sensory derangement that casts the individual into unarticulated space, a space with no markers and no boundaries, with nothing behind, nothing above, nothing below.[18]

Conrad often depicts this sense of alienation in spatial terms, as when Marlow imagines that 'There was nothing either above or below him—and I knew it. He had kicked himself loose of the earth' (*HD* 65). This image is the culmination of the fears that travelling to the far corners of the world would result in the loss of self; it is a modern psychological equivalent to the medieval fears of falling over the edge of the world. Indeed, anthropology itself rested upon an older exoticist tradition that derives from the medieval era, of the traveller—*homo viator*—who makes a dangerous pilgrimage

[18] Levenson, *Modernism and the Fate of Individuality*, 6. Levenson's comment suggests a similar problem to that posed in relation to anthropological fieldwork: 'the depression our student is feeling is at least partially rooted in the difficulties associated with maintaining a stable sense of self/identity while in the field. Most notably, in separating from his home world, the student-anthropologist has lost the innumerable identifications forged with that home world and the mirroring functions of his significant others (self-objects). In a word, he has lost two of the most potent means available for maintaining his sense of identity.' Wengle, 20.

to the limits of the known world, and returns with tales of his experience.[19] The concept of what that known world contained, and what lay beyond it probably derived from an even more ancient Greek concept of the 'ecumene' (*oikoumene*), the inhabited and circumscribed world beyond which lay only darkness and barbarism. Marlow can be seen, on one level, as the modern equivalent of the *homo viator*; but this view must be qualified by the acknowledgement that Africa at the time of Conrad's writing was not, by any means, unknown. Indeed, by this time Africa had already been explored and charted, its edges defined; in short, a paradox exists here that is clarified by reference to geography.

In choosing Africa as the site of his novella, Conrad followed numerous travellers and anthropologists who had already explored the 'dark continent'. The irony implicit here is that the 'heart of darkness' would not, in fact have been very dark at all; it was not a *terra nuova*. Many Gooralls had landed on these coasts and found themselves strangers. Geographically, the 'blank spaces' on the map, as Marlow puts it, had begun to be filled in. Yet, the darkness here, as I hope to show, is also a valid image for the anthropological ambiguities evident in Conrad's text. Travellers and anthropologists 'knew' Africa only in a very limited sense; and, perhaps more honestly than his contemporaries, Conrad's Marlow constantly admits to his lack of knowledge. In fact, the relationship to Africa is paradoxical—known and yet unknown; discovered and yet misunderstood; explored and yet unfathomable.[20]

Nearly thirty years before the publication of Conrad's novella, missionaries had spoken of Africa in these primitivist tropes as 'distinguished from every country under heaven by its misery and degradation', and lying, 'as of old, in the outer darkness'.[21] By

[19] I am indebted to Gíslí Pálsson for this analogy. See Pálsson, 6.

[20] Basil Davidson has noted that such histories of Africa were written from the outside: 'with a few outstanding exceptions the records are built uniquely to a single domination attitude: they are the journals of men who look at Africa resolutely from the outside (. . .) If they tried to understand the minds and actions of Africans they knew, it was by the way, and it was rare. Nearly all of them were convinced they were faced by "primeval man", by humanity as it has been before history began, by societies which lingered in the dawn of time'. Basil Davidson, *The African Past: Chronicles from Antiquity to Modern Times* (London: Longman, 1964), 36–7. Edward Said quotes this passage in *Culture and Imperialism* (New York: Knopf, 1993), 99–100.

[21] Quoted in Christine Bolt, *Victorian Attitudes to Race* (London: Routledge & Kegan Paul, 1971), 6.

1898, when Conrad began to write his novella, however, Africa had already become a superficially familiar, if misperceived, world through enormously popular works such as Brodie Cruickshank's *Eighteen Years on the Gold Coast of Africa* (1853);[22] the *Last Journals of David Livingstone, in Central Africa* (1874);[23] Henry M. Stanley's *Life and Finding of Dr. Livingstone* (1880)[24] and *The Congo and the Founding of Its Free State: A Story of Work and Exploration* (1885);[25] Henry Drummond's *Tropical Africa* (1888);[26] Richard Burton's *Zanzibar; City, Island and Coast* (1872)[27] and *Two Trips to Gorilla Land and the Cataracts of the Congo* (1876);[28] Paul Du Chaillu's *Explorations and Adventures in Equatorial Africa* (1861)[29] and *Adventures in the Great Forest of Equatorial Africa and the Country of the Dwarfs* (1890);[30] and

[22] Brodie Cruickshank, *Eighteen Years on the Gold Coast of Africa, Including an Account of the Native Tribes, and Their Intercourse with Europeans*, 2 vols. (London: Hurst & Blackett, 1853).

[23] David Livingstone, *Last Journals of David Livingstone, in Central Africa, from 1865 to his Death*, Horace Waller (ed.), 2 vols. (London: John Murray, 1874).

[24] H. M. Stanley, *Life and Finding of Dr. Livingstone* (London: Dean & Son, 1880). Marianna Torgovnick says that 'Stanley's book about Africa and Africans helped form Euro-American attitudes toward the continent and its inhabitants. It was a best-seller, a book "no boy should be without," and it inspired other bestsellers'. Marianna Torgovnick, *Gone Primitive: Savage Intellects, Modern Lives* (Chicago: University of Chicago Press, 1990), 26.

[25] H. M. Stanley, *The Congo and the Founding of Its Free State: a Story of Work and Exploration*, 2 vols. (London: Law, Marston, Searle, & Rivington, 1885). Of the abundance of works available on the Congo in Conrad's time, Watt writes: 'One has the impression that at this period very few people connected with the Congo, from Stanley and Thys down to the ordinary missionaries, soldiers, explorer's, ship's captains, journalists, and commercial agents, did not publish their reminiscences, keep diaries, or even write novels.' Watt, 138.

[26] Henry Drummond, *Tropical Africa* (1888) (Reprinted London: Hodder & Stoughton, 1891). Although there is no direct evidence that Conrad had read this work, it was recently available when he made his trip up the Congo, and covered the same general territory. Certainly, Drummond's work was popular, as evidenced by the fact that by the fourth edition, published three years later, there were 25,000 copies in print.

[27] Richard Burton, *Zanzibar; City, Island and Coast*, 2 vols. (London: Tinsley Brothers, 1872).

[28] Richard Burton, *Two Trips to Gorilla Land and the Cataracts of the Congo*, 2 vols. (London: Low, Marson, Low, & Searle, 1876).

[29] Paul Du Chaillu, *Explorations and Adventures in Equitorial Africa: with Accounts of the Manners and Customs of the People, and of the Chase of the Gorilla, Crocodile, Leopard, Elephant, Hippopotamus, and other Animals*, 2 vols. (London: Murray, 1861).

[30] Paul Du Chaillu, *Adventures in the Great Forest of Equatorial Africa and the Country of the Dwarfs*, 2 vols. (London: Murray, 1890).

Mary H. Kingsley's *Travels in West Africa* (1897).[31] This is only a short list of the many sources on African travel and anthropology available before the publication of *Heart of Darkness*.[32] Another enormous category of writing—'ethnographic novels'—provides a second matrix of the place of Africa in European writing.[33] Ostensibly, then, the voyage Conrad outlines in his novella would have already been familiar to Victorian readers. The hotel Conrad imagines was already filled with bewildered wanderers.

Long after many of these precursors to Conrad's portrait of Africa have been relegated to dusty shelves, Marlow's journey remains a familiar one, perhaps even a typological one, in fiction on 'primitive' cultures:

> We penetrated deeper and deeper into the heart of darkness (. . .) We were wanderers on a prehistoric earth, on an earth that wore the aspect of an unknown planet (. . .) The prehistoric man was cursing us, praying to us, welcoming us, who could tell? We were cut off from the comprehension of our surroundings; we glided past like phantoms, wondering and secretly appalled.   (*HD* 37)

The locus of 'primitivism' in Conrad's work is, almost inevitably it seems, centred in *Heart of Darkness*. It is therefore natural to look for the roots of what I have termed the anthropological dilemma in this pivotal text. Why has Conrad's novel come to assume such a large importance in the cultural myth of European intervention in Africa? Perhaps, in part, the answer lies in Conrad's ability to

[31] Mary H. Kingsley, *Travels in West Africa* (London: Macmillan, 1897). Conrad writes of Kingsley in a letter dated 7 January 1899; 'I will send you a note on miss Kingsley's book on Africa. *C'est un voyageur et un écrivain très remarquable.* Her opinions on questions dealing with the colonies are thought a great deal of.' *Collected Letters of Conrad*, ii (1898–1902), 156. Clearly, then, it is conceivable that Conrad read this work at the end of 1898 when he was working on *Heart of Darkness*.

[32] Andrea White has recently written on Conrad's place in this exoticist context. She writes convincingly of the importance of the tradition of travel literature on Africa. Cf. Andrea White, *Joseph Conrad and the Adventure Tradition: Constructing and deconstructing the imperial subject* (Cambridge: Cambridge University Press, 1993), 10–11. Several other works in a similar vein ought to be noted: Brantlinger, *Rule of Darkness*; Martin Green, *Dreams of Adventure, Deeds of Empire* (New York: Basic Books, 1979); and Peter Knox-Shaw, *The Explorer in English Fiction* (New York: St Martin's Press, 1986).

[33] In his bibliography of fiction on Africa in the period from 1874–1939, G. D. Kallam lists 1000 titles. See G. D. Kallam, *Africa in English Fiction 1874–1939* (Ibadan: Ibadan University Press, 1968).

capture the difficult nature of what has come to be called 'cultural hermeneutics', or the study of how we come to knowledge of another culture. Perhaps, also, it is because Conrad is representative of his age in beginning to pose questions regarding the limits of terms such as 'primitive' and 'civilized', terms which anthropology also questioned.

In the Victorian era, the categories of travel writing and ethnology did not represent distinct spheres. Victorian travel writers, with whom Conrad had many affinities, and upon whom he had drawn, were often profoundly influenced by anthropology. They began to see 'exotic' scenes with a vision preconditioned by this new science. As Andrew Lang, a prominent folklorist and armchair anthropologist, commented, 'modern educated travellers are apt to see savages in the light cast on them by Mr. Tylor or Sir John Lubbock (...) Traders and missionaries have begun to read anthropological books, and their evidence is therefore much more likely to be biased now by anthropological theories than it was of old'.[34] Lang suggests here the impact of anthropology on the Victorian culture; however, he does not suggest what will become clear in tracing a few of these travel works—that despite confident theory-making, the lines of primitive peoples were still blurred and indistinct to the European vision. Even anthropology did not clarify these sights. According to some critics, Conrad's Marlow, like contemporary travel and ethnological writers, reproduces a phantasmagoric rather than a literal Africa: 'All this is before Marlow and is the "objective substance" of his graphically told story, but what he sees (...) belongs not to history but to fantasy, to the sensational world of promiscuity, idolatry, satanic rites and human sacrifices unveiled in nineteenth-century travellers' tales as the essence of an Africa without law or social restraint, a representation that was embroidered into colonial romances and charted by an ethnography still innocent of a discipline's necessary rules of evidence.'[35] Certainly, Marlow's vision of Africa, like Conrad's, depended upon European misconceptions of African cultures. Anthropology remained a nascent science until the end of the nine-

<hr />

[34] Andrew Lang, *Myth, Ritual and Religion* (1887), 2 vols. (Reprinted London: Longman, 1899), ii. 352.
[35] Benita Parry, *Conrad and Imperialism: Ideological Boundaries and Visionary Frontiers* (London: Macmillan, 1983), 29.

teenth century; however, it does not necessarily follow that the motivation for such distortions was cultural imperialism. Travel literature, ethnographic fiction, and anthropological writing appealed to the Victorians not only for their lurid descriptions of 'savagery'; rather, anthropologists and even travel writers often attempted to reproduce what they believed to be the most crucial characteristics of the other culture. While they often failed in this attempt, the intent seems far less insidious than Said and others would have us believe.[36]

The Victorian period can be characterized as an age of travel writing and a period that witnessed a proliferation of works on 'primitive cultures'. Publishers acknowledged the demand for such works by publishing large lists of travel books and ethnographic novels. Contemporary reviewers often placed Conrad in this 'exoticist' context, along with authors whose works made little attempt to clarify or explain, but only to entertain and titillate Victorian tastes for the exotic.[37] The folklorist and amateur anthropologist Andrew Lang commented that

There has, indeed, arisen a taste for exotic literature: people have become alive to the strangeness and fascination of the world beyond the bounds of Europe and the United States. But that is only because men of imagination and literary skill have been the new conquerors—the Corteses and Balboas of India, Africa, Australia, Japan, and the isles of the southern seas. All these conquerors (. . .) have, at least, seen new worlds for themselves; have gone out of the streets of the, over-populated lands into the open air; have

[36] Said writes: 'Orientalists and other specialists about the non-European world—anthropologists, historians, philologists—had that power, and, as I have tried to show elsewhere, it often went hand in glove with a consciously undertaken imperial enterprise.' Said, *Culture and Imperialism*, 48.

[37] Of course, this taste for exoticism was not limited to Britain. A contemporary of Conrad's, Jan Perlowski, writes: 'I recalled those old times when Kipling and Pierre Loti opened to us distant exotic worlds, which made us strangely unsettled in our grey, European, Polish reality.' Perlowski goes on to relate a conversation with Kipling regarding Conrad's work. Jan Perlowski, 'On Conrad and Kipling' in Zdzislaw Najder (ed.), *Conrad: Under Familial Eyes*, trans. Halina Carroll-Najder (Cambridge: Cambridge University Press, 1983), 160–1. Conrad worried at times about the limitations placed on his work, and complained to Richard Curle, who was preparing a review of the Uniform Edition of his works in 1923, that 'the public mind fastens on externals'. He wanted to avoid the 'danger of precise classification, either in the realm of exoticism or of the sea'. Quoted in Gérard Jean-Aubry (ed.), *Joseph Conrad: Life and Letters*, 2 vols. (Garden City, New York: Doubleday, Page & Co., 1927), ii. 320.

sailed and ridden, walked and hunted; have escaped from the fog and smoke of towns.[38]

Here Lang suggests the immense popularity of exoticist literature in Conrad's time almost as an antidote to the harsh realism of metropolitan Europe. Clearly, in this passage Lang exhibits the tendency Edward Said sees in so many orientalist writers—the implied elision between literature and imperialism. The imagery of conquest and exploration perhaps masks a justification for imperialism. But there are other facets to this 'exoticism'. Although we may now view this as a narrow category in which to situate a writer like Conrad, such an exoticist context fulfilled expectations for a literature that opened upon foreign lands to view.[39] For example, a reviewer of *Almayer's Folly*, Conrad's Borneo novel, wrote: 'Material for such books can only be brought to the writing table by the track of personal experience. It [*Almayer's Folly*] is as unmistakeably the book of a wanderer who has lived far from the ways and the atmosphere of European capitals'.[40] This acceptance of Conrad's fiction as being in almost an adjunct position in relation to travel literature should not surprise us. The lines between literature and travel writing were perhaps less clearly demarcated in this period than ever before or since. Writers such as Robert Louis Stevenson could maintain dual identities as writers of both popular adventure stories and travel/ethnographic works, opening up new geographical and literary territory.[41] This new *genre* of literature even earned

[38] Andrew Lang, 'Mr. Kipling's Stories', in Andrew Lang, *Essays in Little* (New York: Charles Scribner's Sons, 1891), 200–1. Cf. White, 8. White writes: 'Of course, the "exotic literature" that Lang describes here did not simply "arise," and readers did not magically "become alive" to the attactions of foreign climates. Those interests had been created, in great part, by the travel narratives that were also immensely popular, a genre whose initial construction of the imperial subject greatly influenced adventure fiction.' White, 9.

[39] John E. Saveson writes, 'That Conrad in his early fiction romanticized Malayan life is an accepted critical judgement; and it cannot be denied that he dressed his subject to satisfy Victorian taste for the sentimental and picturesque. Yet Conrad was treating subject matter which had unsentimental associations for a late Victorian audience'. John E. Saveson, *Joseph Conrad: The Making of a Moralist* (Amsterdam: Rodopi NV, 1972), 17. Conrad himself complained that ' "An Outcast of the Islands" belongs to those novels of mine that were never laid aside; and though it brought me the qualification of "exotic writer" I don't think the charge was at all justified. For the life of me I don't see the slightest exotic spirit in conception or style in that novel' ('Author's Note', *OI* ix).

[40] Unsigned review, 'New Writers: Mr. Joseph Conrad', *Bookman*, 10/56 (May 1896), 41.

[41] One reviewer wrote of Stevenson: 'What a good sample of a Briton was he to send to foreign lands! An adventurer who would see all he could, and dare not a

its own name—ethnographic fiction.[42] As we will see, this category did not easily contain a writer such as Conrad. Popular ethnographic fiction required no subtle layering or deep exploration; readers demanded little but adventure and an eye for the exotic. Indeed, it might be argued that one of the cultural and psychological functions of such fiction for a Victorian audience was reassurance—reassurance of Victorian cultural progress.

Ethnographic fiction often made its appeal to the smug expectations of its readership. The frame narrator of *Heart of Darkness* parodies this kind of cultural insensitivity in the contrast he draws between Marlow and other sailors: 'He was a seaman, but he was a wanderer too, while most seamen lead, if one may express it so, a sedentary life. Their minds are of the stay-at-home order, and their home is always with them—the ship—and so is their country —the sea (. . .) In the immutability of their surroundings, the foreign shores, the foreign faces, the changing immensity of life glide past, veiled not by a sense of mystery but by a slightly disdainful ignorance' (*HD* 9).[43] The sailors remain oblivious to the varieties of cultures and peoples seen on their journeys. Marlow suggests that even he occasionally approaches the complexities of travel with only the most superficial regard; he 'used to clear out for any part of the world at twenty-four hours' notice, with less thought than most men give to the crossing of a street' (*HD* 16). Ironically, in the way that both Marlow and these sailors remain

little, yet one who voyaged in the strange people's souls as well, and found so much to love and admire and interest that he had not time left for ridicule or scorn.' Unsigned, 'Stevenson's Voyages', *Bookman*, 10/65 (February 1897), 144. On Stevenson and Conrad see David Thorburn, *Conrad's Romanticism* (New Haven: Yale University Press, 1974), 4, 24–5, 32–5, 54–60, and John Batchelor, *Lord Jim* (London: Unwin Hyman, 1988), 26–31.

[42] Brian V. Street writes, 'The growth of Empire at this time and experiences of so many travellers in distant, exotic lands provided a ready-made alternative, and from the 1870s onwards fiction took up this theme. The "ethnographic novel," estranged in time and space from the claustrophobic Victorian drawing-room, became popular'. Brian V. Street, *The Savage in Literature: Representations of 'Primitive' Society in English Fiction, 1858–1920* (London: Routledge & Kegan Paul, 1975), 4. Andrea White writes: 'Closely related to travel writing was the adventure fiction of the day. In fact the line between the two discourses was often a thin one.' White, 39.

[43] One of Conrad's early reviewers wrote that the taste for ethnographic fiction was an acquired one: 'As a general rule, the British novel-reader likes the scene of his story to be laid in British soil. He is insular in his tastes, not easily interested in places and people who are outside his experience. When a writer contrives to hold his attention with such topics it is proof that he has handled them exceptionally well.' Norman Sherry (ed.), *Conrad: the Critical Heritage* (London: Routledge & Kegan Paul, 1973), 66.

unaffected by travel they are the equivalent of the Victorian armchair readers who read travel and anthropological works without
being affected or challenged by the shock of these new vistas. Some
readers did not apparently desire or welcome the probing and
questioning that Conrad would bring to the *genre*. Yet, even the
most pedestrian ethnographic works often reflected an element of
ambivalence regarding European civilization.

As a young man, Conrad was decidedly not of the 'stay-at-home
order'. Clearly, the tradition of travel writing deeply impressed
him, a fact he later acknowledged in the essay, 'Geography and
Some Explorers'.[44] Here he admits that the fascination of travellers'
tales in his childhood had been part of the motivation for his
journey to Africa. In a familiar passage he writes: 'One day putting
my finger on a spot in the very middle of what was then the white
heart of Africa, I declared that some day I would go there' (*LE* 16).
Conrad reflects on this geographical curiosity: 'I have no doubt that
star-gazing is a fine occupation, for it leads you within the borders
of the unattainable. But map-gazing, to which I became addicted so
early, brings the problems of the great spaces of the earth into direct
contact with sane curiosity and gives an honest precision to one's
imaginative faculty' (*LE* 13). Marlow echoes this sentiment in
Heart of Darkness:

Now when I was a little chap I had a passion for maps. I would look for
hours at South America, or Africa, or Australia and lose myself in the
glories of exploration. At that time there were many blank spaces on the
earth and when I saw one that looked particularly inviting on the map (but
they all look that) I would put my finger on it and say: When I grow up I
will go there. (. . .) But there was one yet—the biggest—the most blank, so
to speak—that I had a hankering after.
    True, by this time it was not a blank space any more. It had got filled
since my boyhood with rivers and lakes and names. It had ceased to be a
space of delightful mystery—a white patch for a boy to dream gloriously
over. It had become a place of darkness.   (*HD* 11–12)

The irony implicit in this passage is that, as Marlow discovers,
maps conceal more than they reveal; the cartographic certainty of a
world which has become filled in with the names of lakes, rivers
and towns, collides with the uncertainty of a world that is separated

---

[44] Conrad writes that 'the only comment made about it by my private tutor was
that I seemed to have been wasting my time in reading books of travel instead of
attending to my studies' (*LE* 13).

by cultural and conceptual gaps. Transcription cannot be equated with understanding. Marlow suggests the absurdity of the attempt to define the parameters of his journey when he imagines for a moment that 'instead of going off to the centre of a continent, I were about to set off for the centre of the earth' (*HD* 16) where maps clearly have no significance. Marlow recognizes the gap between the expectation and reality of travel. No *Baedecker's* exists to guide him where he is going. The analogous passages in the essay and novella are tempered with the tone of disappointment and ambivalence. The childhood dream is shattered when Conrad confronts the reality of the Congo in 1890. As he suggests in a later version of this story: 'And of course I thought no more about it till after a quarter of a century or so an opportunity offered to go there—as if the sin of childish audacity was to be visited on my mature head' (*PR* 13). Again, the reality of the Congo experience cannot be etched with the pleasing exactness of a map. This early geographical desire on Conrad's part to experience the 'primitive' was by no means unique. Another traveller, Sidney L. Hinde, wrote similarly of this childish fascination: 'From my boyhood, everything connected with this mysterious continent interested me; and I determined to see something of it if ever circumstances gave me the opportunity.'[45] Conrad's first ambitions and inclinations were, in many ways, more geographical than literary. He desired to experience what these travel writers had experienced. In this same essay, Conrad also records the influences of 'first-generation' explorers of Africa—Burton, Speke, Livingstone, and Mungo Park. 'The latest geographical news that could have been whispered to me in my cradle', he recalls, 'was that of the expedition of Burton and Speke' (*LE* 13). Here Conrad suggests that from childhood on he was already absorbing an image of Africa that he would carry with him to the Congo, an image that would need drastic revision in the light of 'real experience'.

One of the works that may well have introduced Conrad to Africa, Richard Burton's *Two Trips to Gorilla Land and the Cataracts of the Congo* (1876), may also have coloured his vision of the 'dark continent' he was to visit.[46] Some critics assume that such

---

[45] Sidney Langford Hinde, *The Fall of the Congo Arabs* (London: Methuen, 1897), 27.
[46] George W. Stocking, Jr writes of Burton: 'The first of those adventurous Victorians to disguise himself as an Arab in order to travel to the Moslem holy city

travel works had a hidden imperialist agenda; and in some cases this charge would be valid. But this is also too easy a stereotype. Among the impressions that Conrad might have culled from Burton's work, for example, was the sense of the imperial project in Africa as doomed from the start, a theme that was to become such a feature of Conrad's own experience in the Congo, and of the fictional record of that experience in *Heart of Darkness*. Burton's work is hardly the stuff of imperialist propaganda. For example, at the beginning of the work Burton writes, 'it is evident to me that the English occupation of the West African Coast has but slightly forwarded the cause of humanity, and that upon the whole it has proved a remarkable failure'.[47] Conrad's first visions of the West African port city which he portrays in *Heart of Darkness* partake of this sense of hopelessness. As Marlow wanders around the coastal port, he sees the abandoned and decaying relics of the imperial venture. Decay and degeneration become almost synonymous with the imperial project. The Victorians feared the degeneracy which they perceived as one common element of imperialism. In examining other travel works of this period, it becomes clear that Conrad's sense of despair and dislocation in the Congo were rooted in this Victorian anxiety regarding primitive' cultures.

As travel writing and ethnographic fiction opened up new areas of knowledge, they also created profound dilemmas. One of these dilemmas, the anthropological dilemma, underlies the record of Conrad's experience in the Congo. The anthropological dilemma, as I have already defined it, involved the difficulty of cultural hermeneutics. While anthropology and ethnography in the nineteenth century purported to advance European knowledge of and contact with other cultures, this new science also raised profound anxieties regarding the ability of people of one culture (particularly 'civilized' societies) to penetrate the thought of another society ('the primitive'). Conrad's early writings are pervaded by the prevalent corresponding fear that such cross-cultural contacts would prove dangerous to the members of each society. *Heart of Darkness* is one of the most profoundly disjunctive works of its time; it is

---

of Mecca, Burton's life was a fugue on the theme of dualism.' Indeed, Burton attempted to 'go native' in an almost Kurtzian manner: 'at once fascinated and repelled by non-European cultures, he authored diatribes against the 'abnormal cruelty' of the Africans after having joined the King of Dahomey in a *pas de deux* at a ritual decapitation dance.' George W. Stockings Jr, *Victorian Anthropology* (London: Macmillan, 1987), 253.

[47] Burton, *Two Trips to Gorilla Land*, i, p. xi.

narratively disjunctive, chronologically disjunctive, psychologically disjunctive, and, most significantly, *culturally disjunctive*.[48] The novella partakes of a condition which Georg Lukács has called 'transcendental homelessness'—of the novelist as fragmented, searching, dislocated.[49] On one level, it is a story about the psychological tension caused by contact with 'primitive' cultures. In a world opening up to strange new vistas, a world peopled by so-called primitives, a world in part defined by the colonialism and imperialism of its day, such dislocations would have already become familiar to the educated and culturally literate.

In Conrad's era, the 'primitive' occupied an ambiguous place as both the domain of contemporary 'savages' as well as a reminder of the past of Europe itself. In other words, the 'primitive' represented for the Victorians the borderlands of human behaviour; not only the literal colonies which were so replete with 'savage peoples', but the boundaries and extensions of the Victorian culture itself, searching back into the most remote past for an image of itself. Thus, Levenson says, in a slightly different context, *Heart of Darkness* is concerned with 'the end, the limit, the threshold, the edge, the border. Alongside the figures of penetration and invasion, the tale offers these figures of *extension*, a reaching toward some distant point on the limit of experience'.[50] At the opening of the novella, the frame narrator refers to the Thames as 'leading to the uttermost ends of the earth' (*HD* 8). Victorian culture sought through fiction like Conrad's and through anthropology itself to be taken to the 'uttermost ends', not only geographically, but culturally and psychologically. The cartography is both inner and outer. Not surprisingly, Marlow explores the limits and limitations of the European culture itself, as well as the boundaries between self and culture; all of these limits and limitations proved also to be of interest to anthropologists.

Anthropologists at this time examined the same geographical and cultural territory as did Conrad in his novella. These scientists explored the same problems of the complex layering of 'savage' and 'civilized'; and when Kurtz steps 'over the edge' (*HD* 69), he performs a sort of grotesque parody of what anthropology itself

---

[48] On disjunctions and dislocations within the text, see J. Hillis Miller, *The Poets of Reality: Six Twentieth Century Writers* (Cambridge, Mass.: Belknap Press of Harvard University, 1965).
[49] Cf. Torgovnick, 185–90.
[50] Levenson, *Modernism and the Fate of Individuality*, 7.

constantly attempted in this period—to extend the knowledge of other cultures. Following James Clifford's argument, Michael Levenson also sees this movement in Conrad's fiction as implied in historical anthropology:

> It is possible to situate, if not to explain, this paradox, by connecting it to a particular moment in the history of the European mind. One of the unintended consequences of neocolonial expansion at the end of the nineteenth century was that accumulation of anthropological insights. The search for new commodities inadvertently uncovered new cultures. Marlow travels to Africa as part of the new economic imperium, but his own deportment, as James Clifford has pointed out, is closer to the imperialist's ideological cousin, the ethnographer.[51]

The result of this ethnological striving is that Marlow 'comes to a perception that contemporary ethnographers were painfully sharing: namely that, faced with those who are called primitive, "what thrilled you was just the thought of their humanity—like yourself—the thought of your remote kinship with this wild and passionate uproar" (. . .) In the age of anthropology the European mind can only discover truths about is origins by going outside the physical limits of its culture. It can only learn all that it contains by passing its own boundaries'.[52] James L. Peacock, an anthropologist, writes similarly: 'Insight into the self is best obtained through relation to another person (. . .) insight into one's own culture is best obtained through relation to another culture (as in anthropology, where representatives of the other culture, the natives, help representatives of our culture, the anthropologists, to see their own culture more plainly and objectively than if they stay at home).'[53] The history of anthropology thus involved a mirroring back, a journey outward in order to extend the knowledge of one's own culture. At the same time that this exercise may be seen as ethnocentric and even narcissistic (what interests us is what they can reveal about us), it is also expansive and empathic.

As in Conrad's portrait of Goorall, ethnocentricity was constantly being both challenged and reinforced during this period by anthropology and travel writing. This idea can be foregrounded by considering how a traveller of an earlier generation than Conrad's describes the Gold Coast:

As the stranger approaches it from the Atlantic, and obtains the first hazy and indistinct view of its distant outline, it appears covered with a misty pall, and presents such a dream-like picture to the imagination, that little effort is needed to people these solitudes with beings of his own creation.

A dark impenetrable mystery seems to hang beneath the shades of those gloomy forests (. . .).[54]

Here we find the surrealistic atmosphere familiar to any reader of *Heart of Darkness*. Yet this passage comes from a work written over forty years earlier, *Eighteen Years on the Gold Coast* (1853) by Brodie Cruickshank, a colonial administrator.[55] I am not suggesting a source here but a historical analogy. Compare the sense of confusion Cruickshank evokes with that of Marlow's description of his voyage down the coast:

Watching a coast as it slips by the ship is like thinking about an enigma. There it is before you—smiling, frowning, inviting, grand, mean, insipid, or savage, and always mute with an air of whispering—Come and find out. This one was almost featureless, as if still in the making, with an aspect of monotonous grimness. The edge of a colossal jungle, so dark-green as to be almost black, fringed with white surf, ran straight, like a ruled line, far away along a blue sea whose glitter was blurred by a creeping mist. The sun was fierce, the land seemed to glisten and drip with steam (. . .) Nowhere did we stop long enough to get a particularized impression, but the general sense of vague and oppressive wonder grew upon me.   (*HD* 16–17)

The coast is depicted here as featureless, ill-defined, and misty, in precisely the way that Cruickshank's landscape is described as hazy, indistinct, dream-like.[56] It is unlikely that Conrad had read this work, an account of Cruickshank's experiences as a colonist on the Gold Coast. Nevertheless, it is striking how closely the sense of fascination, mystery, and disorientation that feeds Cruickshank's imagination resembles Marlow's. Together these descriptions map out the literary theme I am discussing: that of cultural dislocation—

---

[54] Cruickshank, i. 2–3.

[55] Phillip Curtin discusses Cruickshank briefly. See Phillip Curtin, *The Image of Africa: British Ideas and Action, 1780–1850* (Madison: University of Wisconsin Press, 1964), 400–1.

[56] The 'surrealistic' quality of Marlow's narration of his experience in Africa corresponds to a theme that Street has discovered in that of much other writing on so-called primitive cultures. See Street, 21. Numerous of corresponding examples of this theme in *Heart of Darkness* might be mentioned, such as when Marlow remarks on 'a touch of fantastic vanity which fitted well with the dream-sensation that pervaded all my days at the time' (*HD* 43).

the anthropological dilemma. The images of hazy and dream-like vistas all seem to fit into the cultural imperialist mode at first glance. But is this simply what Edward Said would call an imposition of the 'mysterious' and 'exotic' onto an alien culture in order to ease the annexation, both literary and political, of this foreign territory? It seems that there is something far less insidious, but more complex, occurring here. Marlow and Cruickshank share the difficulty of grasping what is essentially foreign to them. As Marlow comments, the ship does not stop long enough for him to get a particularized impression. The perspective of each man, allowed only a passing glimpse of the foreign culture, is sharply limited. Such disorientation, as I will argue, is a crucial aspect of Conrad's views of 'primitive' cultures.

Disorientation was only one facet of the response to Africa. In another passage, Cruickshank writes with admiration of the vitality of the African fishing boats cutting through the white surf along the dark coastline:

He is struck by the picturesque appearance of a struggling fleet of fishing canoes steering for the shore, with their ragged sails and matting, and their naked fishermen, lolling listlessly in their frail barks, which appear but ill calculated to brave the perils of the deep. He hears the indistinct notes of their rude songs, or, more nearly, the wild jabber of an unintelligible tongue.[57]

The last phrase here, the 'wild jabber of an unintelligible tongue', recalls the theme of linguistic discontinuity in *Heart of Darkness*. Marlow speaks of the 'dying vibration of one immense jabber, silly, atrocious, sordid, savage, or simply mean without any kind of sense' (*HD* 48–9). Cruickshank's 'unintelligible tongue' and Marlow's 'immense jabber' point to the difficulty of translation, both literal and figurative. The question that recurs over and over again in both these two works and in many Victorian travel works is that of how to translate the experience of another culture. This trope of the unintelligibilty of the primitive seems to have been a common one in literature of the Victorian period. When Charles Darwin landed on the coast of Patagonia, he described the Fuegians as untranslatable 'savages': 'We here saw the native Fuegian (. . .) in the naked barbarian, with his body coated with paint, *whose very gestures, whether they may be peaceable or hostile, are unintelligi-*

ble, with difficulty we see a fellow creature.'[58] The Fuegians, like the Africans in Conrad and Cruickshank, appear to be 'unintelligible'.

These passages from Conrad and Cruickshank are not merely dismissive of Africa. For example, there is another parallel in the two images of African canoeists. Marlow remarks: 'paddled by black fellows (. . .) they shouted, sang; their bodies streamed with perspiration (. . .) They had bone, muscle, a wild vitality, an intense energy of movement, that was as natural and true as the surf along their coasts. They wanted no excuse for being there' (*HD* 17). The sense of admiration for the Africans' vitality and their rightness in the landscape as opposed to the unease of the foreign observer— these are underlying themes of both descriptions. The sense of disorientation is also common to both—the inability to understand the 'intelligible tongue'.

The sense of disorientation in Conrad's writing like that of travel writing and Victorian anthropology in the Victorian period has been linked to racism.[59] This writing on Africa may be too easily stereotyped as racist and culturally imperialist. While many works undoubtedly partook of racist beliefs, they also represented an attempt, however flawed, to *see*, and to impart these sights to others. For example, Cruickshank's description represents an attempt to arrive at some visual truth that suggests a comparison to Conrad's literal landscape (the mists, the dark coastline, the white surf, etc.), as well as an imagined continent that suggests a sense of psychological discontinuity parallel to that of *Heart of Darkness*.[60]

Whatever the limitations—and there were many—of ethnology and travel writing in this period, the motivation was to bring back vistas of foreign countries to Victorian readers, many of who otherwise remained blind to the geographical and cultural diversity of their world. 'Into the heart of this mysterious Africa I wish to take

[58] Quoted in J. A. V. Chapple, *Science and Literature in the Nineteenth Century* (London: Macmillan, 1986), 131, italics mine.

[59] For example, Achebe writes: 'I am talking about a book which parades in the most vulgar fashion prejudices and insults from which a section of mankind has suffered untold agonies and atrocities in the past and continues to do so in many ways and many places today. I am talking about a story in which the very humanity of black people is called into question' (*HD* 259).

[60] Albert Guerard has written similarly that 'elsewhere he [Conrad] wants (. . .) to make his complacent European reader see (. . .) *Heart of Darkness* is a record of things seen and done'. Albert Guerard, *Conrad the Novelist* (Cambridge, Mass.: Harvard University Press, 1958), 34.

you', writes Henry Drummond in *Tropical Africa*.[61] He continues: 'It is an education to see this sight'.[62] Conrad's Marlow, sprawled out on the deck of the 'Nellie', similarly attempts to 'educate' his coterie regarding a culture with which they have had no contact. Marlow re-negotiates this difficult journey and attempts to translate his experience to his listeners within the text, just as Conrad attempts to translate an altered version of his own experiences in Africa for his Victorian audience through the novella: 'I don't want to bother you much with what happened to me personally (. . .) yet to understand the effect of it on me you ought to know how I got there, *what I saw*, how I went up that river to the place where I first met the poor chap' (*HD* 11, italics mine). To an extent, the problem of anthropology is analogous:

It is not the particular factual 'findings' of a gifted ethnographer, abstracted from their forms of presentation and summarized as a set of facts or substantive generalizations, that are significant. (. . .) What is significant is the *vision* of someone's (the native's) existence as interpreted through the sensibilities of someone else (the ethnographer) in order to inform and enrich the understanding of a third party (the reader or listener). Ethnography, in this sense, is like literature: as source of psychological and philo-. sophical insight (and possibly of aesthetic pleasure) when read as an author's struggle to elucidate a perspective on life through his portrayal of a way of living—as he experienced and analyzed it.[63]

The sights which Marlow perceives are not easily imparted; thus the language in which experiences are related is notoriously inexact. Nevertheless, the sense of sight, of clarity of vision, is an important, if compromised value in the novella. Marlow's audience, like the readers of anthropology, travel literature, and ethnographic fiction, is being asked to see new sights. Sight and insight are constantly upheld as virtues in the novella. The Harlequin's

[61] Of course, this is not to attribute accuracy to these views of Africa, or to argue that different authors presented the same vision. In answering the criticism of H. M. Stanley, Drummond made clear that there were different 'versions' of Africa: 'Mr. Stanley has never seen my Africa'. Drummond, *Tropical Africa*, p. vi.

[62] Although his motives are probably much less altruistic than he admits, James Brooke writes similarly: 'Could I carry my vessel to places where the keel of a European ship never before ploughed the waters—could I plant my foot where white man's foot had never before been—could I gaze upon scenes which educated eyes had never looked on—see man in the rudest state of nature—I should be content without looking to further rewards.' Gertrude L. Jacob, *The Raja of Sarawak. An Account of Sir James Brooke, K. C. B., L. L. D., Given Chiefly Through Letters and Journals*, 2 vols. (London: Macmillan & Co., 1876), i. 70–1.

[63] Peacock, 99–100, italics mine.

highest praise for Kurtz, after all, is that 'he made me see things—things' (*HD* 55). At the beginning of the second part of the novella Marlow says, 'As for me, I seemed to see Kurtz for the first time' (*HD* 34). It is the sights of his African journey that Marlow wants to relate to his listeners, and, particularly, his insight into Kurtz's character. The mingling of senses—sight and hearing—suggests the difficulty of his goal. Of course, this visualization is often skewed in the tale. The anthropologist who works in the field and records his or her experiences similarly relies on the sense of imparting visual and audio images to his or her audience; the mask the anthropologist assumes is that of the detached recorder. Anthropological authority is predicated upon the assumption that the anthropologist has 'been there', and is relating views of another culture to his or her readers. What anthropology has recently recognized is that there may be a tremendous difficulty in relating these visual truths to others, as when Marlow cries out in frustration, 'Do you see him? Do you see the story? Do you see anything?' (*HD* 30).[64] The middle question here is particularly striking. Marlow's audience is being asked not merely to *listen* but to *see* the story set out before them. The are asked for clarity of sight and insight; however, the truth is that they may in fact see nothing at all.

Conrad's work relies on the invocation of visual truth, 'the highest kind of justice to the visible universe' (*NN* xi). This famous statement aligns with prevailing views of Conrad's literary impressionism which Ford Madox Ford and other critics have insisted upon.[65] Many of Conrad's original reviewers stressed his descriptive powers and ability to bring home foreign vistas to his readers. Hugh Clifford, for example, who was himself a travel writer and author of ethnographic fiction, wrote of *Youth* in 1902:

Description unquestioningly is his forte (. . .) He is a realist in that he writes of *a real world which he has seen with his own eyes* (. . .) those of us who

[64] In this context, Mary Kingsley's comment on her African travels is interesting: 'I cannot show you anything clearly and nearly. I have to show you a series of pictures of things, and hope you will get from these pictures the impression which is the truth. I dare not set myself up to tell you the truth. I only say, look at it; and to the best of my ability faithfully give you, not an artist's picture but a photograph'. Mary H. Kingsley, *West African Studies* (London: Macmillan, 1901), p. xi.

[65] 'It was Ford Madox Ford who gave wide currency to the view that he and Conrad (. . .) had been writers of impressionist fiction.' Watt, 172. Cf. Watt, 168–200; Robert S. Baker, 'Watt's Conrad', *Contemporary Literature* 22 (1981), 116–26; and Bruce Johnson, 'Conrad's Impressionism and Watt's "Delayed Decoding"'

know the lands of which he writes have been carried back to distant scenes with so much vividness that we have awakened with a shock to the fogs of London (. . .)[66]

The notion of a reconstruction of foreign sights allies Conrad with many of the travel writers and anthropologists of his day; nor is this goal of presenting 'a real world which he has seen with his own eyes' limited to older anthropology. The goal of fidelity to visual truths suggested in Clifford's review fits in with what Conrad famously remarked at the beginning of what has often been taken as his artistic credo, the preface to *The Nigger of the 'Narcissus'* (1897): 'My task which I am trying to achieve is, by the power of the written work, to make you hear, to make you feel—it is, before all, to make you *see*. That—and no more, and it is everything' (*NN* xiv). Of course, Conrad's use of the word 'see' here clearly evokes cognition as well as visualization; but it is the sense of physical sight that is important for my purposes. Like Marlow's, then, Conrad's ostensible aim is to see and impart his vision to others. He continues:

The task approached in tenderness and faith is to hold up unquestioningly, without choice and without fear, the rescued fragment before all eyes and in the light of a sincere mood. It is to show its vibration, its colour, its substance of its truth—disclose its inspiring secret: the stress and passion within the core of each convincing moment (. . .) one may perchance attain to such clearness of sincerity that at last the presented vision of regret or pity, of terror or mirth, shall awaken in the hearts of the beholders that feeling of unavoidable solidarity; of the solidarity in mysterious origin, in toil, in joy, in hope, in uncertain fate, which binds men to each other and all mankind to the visible world.   (*NN* xiv)

The aim of Conrad's impressionistic art, as outlined in this manifesto, is fidelity to the presentation of this 'visible world'. Throughout Conrad's fiction and non-fiction, he reiterates this theme: 'To see! To see!—this is the craving of the sailor, as of the rest of blind humanity. To have his path made clear for him is the aspiration of every human being in our beclouded and tempestuous

in *Conrad Revisited: Essays for the Eighties*, Ross C. Murfin (ed.) (Birmingham, Ala.: University of Alabama Press, 1985), 51–70.

[66] Hugh Clifford, untitled review in the *Spectator* (9 November 1902), 827–8; italics mine. Clifford had earlier criticized Conrad's Malaysian works for anthropological errors; but the 1902 review suggests a very different opinion: 'There is knowledge here, real first-hand knowledge and experience' (827).

existence' (*MS* 87). Such a fidelity to visible truths is difficult and often obscured by the sort of African mists in Marlow's and Cruickshank's visions: 'And thus, doubtful of strength to travel far, we talk a little about the aim—the aim of art, which, like life itself, is inspiring, difficult—obscured by mists' (*HD* 226). Again, Conrad draws on this image of mistiness in one of his letters to his friend R. B. Cunninghame Graham; and here, too, there are suggestions of the kind of disorientation, both moral and sensory, that is so characteristic of Conrad's cultural refugees: 'Faith is a myth and beliefs shift like mists on the shore; thoughts vanish; words, once pronounced, die; and the memory of yesterday is as shadowy as the hope of tomorrow . . .'[67] The sense of dislocation is a common theme in writings on 'primitive' peoples. Many of Conrad's letters from Africa resonate with this sense of confusion. The process of crossing cultural boundaries, in other words, is no easy task. As Conrad writes in the preface to *An Outcast of the Islands*, in a somewhat different context, 'The discovery of new values in life is a very chaotic experience; there is a tremendous amount of jostling and confusion and a momentary feeling of darkness' (*OI* vii).

Conrad's artistic aims are closely tied to images of journeying and travelling, as in the well-known preface to *The Nigger of the 'Narcissus'*. Tellingly, in a less familiar passage, he writes of the artist's goals in relation to foreign vistas. The artist

speaks to our capacity for delight and wonder, to the sense of *mystery* surrounding our lives: to our sense of pity, and beauty, and pain: to the latent feeling of fellowship with all creation—and to the subtle but invincible, conviction of solidarity that knits together the loneliness of innumerable hearts (. . .) It is only some such train of thought, or rather of feeling, that can in a measure explain the aim of the attempt, made in the tale which follows, to present an unrestful episode in the obscure lives of a few individuals out of all the disregarded multitude of the bewildered, the simple and the voiceless. For, if there is any part of truth in the belief confessed above, it becomes evident that *there is not a place of splendour or a dark corner of the earth that does not deserve, if only a passing glance of wonder and pity.* (*NN* xii, italics mine)

The sense of 'mystery' evoked here, and the phrase, 'a dark corner of the earth', precede not *Heart of Darkness*, a tale of African 'primitivism', but rather *The Nigger of the 'Narcissus'*. Conrad's

---

[67] Quoted in Meyer, 166.

vision of scanning each 'dark corner of the earth' for a 'passing glance of wonder and pity' sounds very close to the goals of Victorian anthropology. Of course, there is an implicit paradox in these passages cited above, a paradox that parallels those in the Cruikshank book and in *Heart of Darkness* itself; on the one hand, there is an expressed desire to see, on the other a sense of mystery when sight fails—of a lacuna.[68] The tension between clarity of vision and the penumbra is one aspect of the anthropological dilemma which confronted the Victorians; they were faced with cultures which they wanted to see but which remained essentially mysterious.

While in theory anthropology offered answers to these difficulties of how to see primitive cultures, in practice anthropological texts often merely compounded the sense of confusion and disorientation. The Victorian image of 'primitives' may be summed up by Marlow's sense of disorientation on the Congo. As he looks out from the steamboat, shrouded in mist, he remarks: 'What we could see was just the steamer we were on, outlines blurred as though she had been on the point of dissolving, and a misty strip of water, perhaps two feet broad, around her. The rest of the world was nowhere, as far as our eyes and ears were concerned. Just nowhere. Gone, disappeared; swept off without leaving a whisper or a shadow behind' (*HD* 41). In this passage, Marlow seems to fear dissolution of everything, even his person and cultural identity, in the African fog. The entire familiar world of the European mind has dissolved and left nothing but Cruickshank's mists. Here the mists are not merely literal but figurative as well—images of the failure of one's empirical groundings when confronted with the unknown and alien.[69] Similarly, for many Victorians the outlines of 'primi-

[68] John A. McClure writes convincingly: 'he [Conrad] calls attention to the fact that any outsider will find it difficult to see with clarity the significant customs and values of the group he encounters. We are all "dazzled" by strangeness, and we are likely to find the experience threatening'. McClure, 100.

[69] In 'The Shadow Line', another of Conrad's stories of a disorienting encounter with the exotic and unexpected, the narrator remarks: 'Such must have been the darkness before creation (. . .) I knew I was invisible to the man at the helm. Neither could I see anything (. . .) Every form was gone too, spar, sail, fittings, rails; everything was blotted out in the dreadful smoothness of that absolute night' (*SL* 113). *Nostromo* presents an analogous image of a lacuna in Decoud's experience in the Placid Gulf: 'He didn't even know at times whether he were asleep or awake. Like a man lost in slumber, he heard nothing, he saw nothing. Even his hand held before his face did not exist for his eyes' (*N* 262).

tive' cultures remained equally blurred and indistinct. These images of disorientation abound in the novella:

It was not sleep—it seemed unnatural, like a state of trance. Not the faintest sound of any kind could be heard. You looked on amazed and began to suspect yourself of being deaf—then the night came suddenly and struck you blind as well (. . .) When the sun rose there was a white fog, very white and clammy, and more blinding than the night. It did not shift or drive, it was just there standing all around you like something solid. At eight or nine perhaps, it lifted, as a shutter lifts. (HD 41)

Marlow's perception constantly fails him in a way that demonstrates his sense of disorientation in the alien environment. For example, in a scene that Ian Watt gives as one instance of 'delayed decoding', Marlow almost comically fails to recognize that he is under attack. He sees 'sticks, little sticks . . . flying about' (HD 45), then recognizes that these are arrows. These objects are unfamiliar to Marlow because they are not part of his cultural frame of reference. Marlow is not culturally conditioned to see the arrows; he recognizes them with a sense of shock.

The 'solidarity' that Conrad evokes in the 'Narcissus' preface is a recurring motif in his writings on primitive cultures. Another example occurs in the preface to Almayer's Folly (1895). Despite the somewhat ironic tone, Conrad's justification for his 'exotic' tale rests on a sense of universality which anthropology commonly invoked. He abjures the criticism he has received for writing on 'decivilized' cultures:

I am informed that in criticizing that literature which preys on strange people and prowls in far-off countries, under the shade of palms, in the unsheltered glare of sunbeaten beaches, amongst honest cannibals and the more sophisticated pioneers of our glorious virtues, a lady—distinguished in the world of letters—summed up her disapproval of it by saying that the tales it produced were 'decivilized' (. . .)
    And there is a bond between us and that humanity so far away (. . .) I am content to sympathize with common mortals, no matter where they live; in houses or in tents, in the streets under a fog, or in the forests behind the dark line of dismal mangroves that fringe the vast solitude of the sea. For their land—like ours—lies under the inscrutable eyes of the Most High. (AF vii–viii)

This passage recalls the justifications of much of the travel literature and anthropology of the Victorian era; it invokes a sense of soli-

darity and of communality (the 'bond between us and that humanity far away'), as well as the ability 'to sympathize with common
mortals no matter where they live.'

Sympathetic or empathic reconstruction of the 'native's point of
view' is often cited as one of the goals of anthropology. In defending his portrait of what many Victorians would have abjured as
'decivilized' cultures, Conrad is very close to the anthropological
writing of the period. We find hints here and elsewhere in Conrad
of a nascent cultural relativism that he attributed to his upbringing:

An impartial view of humanity in all its degrees of splendour and misery
together with a special regard for the rights of the unprivileged of this
earth, not on any mystic ground but on the ground of simple fellowship
and honourable reciprocity of services, was the dominant characteristic of
the mental and moral atmosphere of the houses which sheltered my haz-
ardous childhood—a matter of calm and deep conviction both lasting and
consistent.   (PR vii)

When Conrad calls for 'An impartial view of humanity', he defines
the kind of cultural relativism for which anthropology would later
strive. Although the extent to which Conrad's 'sympathy', and that
of the anthropologists, allowed them to bridge cultural gaps to so-
called primitive peoples will be debated, the intention is indisput-
able.[70] While stressing a 'universalism', Conrad also reminds us in
this preface that, though the picture drawn of a different way of life
may be similar to our own, it is nevertheless difficult to see clearly:
'the picture of life, there as here, is drawn with the same elaboration
of detail, coloured with the same tints . . . in the cruel serenity of the

[70] Theodor Waitz, a German anthropologist whose work will be discussed later,
wrote of this sympathy: 'This leads him [the anthropologist] to draw all mankind
into the circle of his investigations.' Theodor Waitz, *Introduction to Anthropology*,
trans. J. Frederick Collingwood, 2 vols. (London: Longman, 1863), i. 12. Bronislaw
Malinowksi, one of the founders of functionalist anthropology, who will be discussed at some length in the following chapter, wrote at the end of his seminal
Argonauts of the Western Pacific of this goal of sympathy or empathy: 'Nothing can
teach us a better lesson in this matter of ultimate importance than the habit of mind
which allows us to treat the beliefs and values of another man from his point of view.
Nor has civilised humanity ever needed such tolerance more than now, when
prejudice, ill will and vindictiveness are dividing each European nation from another
(. . .) The Science of Man, in its most refined and deepest version, should lead us to
such knowledge and to tolerance and generosity, based on the understanding of
other men's point of view.' Bronislaw Malinowski, *Argonauts of the Western
Pacific: An Account of Native Enterprise and Adventure in the Archipelagoes of
Melanesian New Guinea* (1922) (Reprinted New York: E. P. Dutton & Co., 1950),
518.

sky, under the merciless brilliance of the sun, the dazzled eye misses the delicate detail, sees only the strong outlines, while the colours, in the steady light seem crude and without shadow' (*AF* ix). In Conrad's metaphor, the writer paints portraits of other cultures; however, he stresses that the exactness that comes from cultural immersion, or what the anthropologist would call empathic reconstruction, is not available to him. He must necessarily blur some of the 'elaboration of detail'. In depicting another culture it is easier, he argues, to draw broad strokes, the 'strong outlines' rather than the 'delicate detail'. Conrad asserts here, in a view which is not consistent in his work, a universalist confidence: 'Nevertheless it is the same picture' (*AF* ix).

Victorian writing on primitive cultures often depended upon a central paradox. On one level, there existed a universalist confidence.[71] As E. B. Tylor wrote: 'Surveyed in a broad view, the character and habit of mankind at once display that similarity and consistency of phenomena which led the Italian proverb maker to a declare that all the world is one country, "tutto il mundo e paese".'[72] Conrad's doctrine of solidarity parallels this universalist comment by Tylor. Such a universalist sentiment may appear to us now to be condescending; and there is a great disparity between the professed goal and the underlying racism in much of the anthropology and travel writing on primitive cultures during this period. Yet anthropology also stressed the relativity of values, the diversity of cultures, and often proved a challenge and not an aid to Western hegemony. Of course, Conrad and many other writers, including Victorian anthropologists themselves, were less confident about their ability to penetrate primitive cultures. Conceptual and cultural gaps resisted closure. The interest in many of these travel books and anthropological works lies precisely in their cultural and conceptual disparities.

Attempts to equate the sense of mystery in *Heart of Darkness* with a covert racism, as Chinua Achebe has done, are usually reductive, not taking into account the historical or artistic context. It is easy to forget that Conrad's description contains his perception of visual truths recorded during his African journey—that it is, as he wrote, 'experience pushed a little (and only very little) beyond

---

[71] Again, Waitz writes: 'there is a universal and unchangeable human nature'. Waitz, i. 12.

[72] Tylor, *Primitive Culture*, i. 5.

the actual facts of the case' (*HD* 4). The apparent haziness of the text does not represent subterfuge, but merely the description of an indistinct coastline in an alien culture that both Conrad and his Marlow have to learn to see. The sense of 'mystery' that hangs over *Heart of Darkness* has often been seen to be at the centre of the novella, either as part of a compelling psychological portrait or as a detrimental fogginess and obscurantism.[73] As E. M. Forster famously wrote in *Abinger Harvest*:

What is so elusive about him is that he is always promising to make some general philosophical statement about the universe, and then refraining in a gruff disclaimer . . . there is a central obscurity, something noble, heroic, inspiring half a dozen great books, but obscure! Obscure! Misty in the middle as well as at the edges, the secret cask of his genius contains a vapour rather than a jewel.[74]

Ironically, Forster, a writer who in *A Passage to India* wrote so eloquently of the dislocations caused by colonialism, failed to recognize that Conrad's ambiguity resembled the anxiety of his own European characters in the face of cultural isolation. Just as Forster's characters are irrevocably shaken by the disorienting experience of the Marabar Caves, so Conrad's Marlow is profoundly affected by the African journey. The fogginess in Conrad's African landscape is not evoked in order to obscure, but rather to depict as realistically and poignantly as possible the dislocations of colonial experience. If we take Conrad at his word, he himself was puzzled and disturbed by the fogginess of the work. For example, he wrote to Garnett: 'My dear fellow, you quite overcome me. And your brave attempt to grapple with the fogginess of *Heart of Darkness*, to explain what I myself tried to shape blindfold, as it were, has touched me profoundly.'[75] This lack of clarity has also been viewed by Achebe and others as a way of mystifying the African culture in order more easily to dismiss it.[76] On the contrary, like Cruickshank, Drummond, and countless other travellers, Conrad merely ap-

[73] Ian Watt sees the novella's 'fogginess' as a facet of Conrad's impressionism: 'Mist or haze is a very persistant image in Conrad.' Watt, 169.

[74] E. M. Forster, *Abinger Harvest* (New York: Harcourt, Brace & Co., 1936), 138.

[75] *Collected Letters of Conrad*, i. 468–9.

[76] Strangely, Achebe uses Leavis as a touchstone, here, even though their in terpretations of Conrad could not be more different. 'The eagle-eyed English critic, F. R. Leavis drew attention to Conrad's "adjectival insistence upon inexpressible and incomprehensible mystery." That mystery must not be dismissed lightly, as

proached Africa with a sense of disjointedness, which is hardly surprising given the time period in which the novella was written. As Marlow expresses this confusion, 'We were cut off from the comprehension of our surroundings' (quoted above). In short, Marlow is journeying into a world in which the 'so-called facts' of European existence are challenged, just as the anthropologists of later years were forced to abandon their preconceptions in their desire to understand 'primitive' cultures.

many Conrad critics have tended to do, as a mere stylistic flaw; for it raises serious questions of artistic good faith. When a writer, while pretending to record scenes, incidents and their impact is in reality engaged in inducing hypnotic stupor in his readers through a bombardment of emotive words and other forms of trickery much more has to be at stake than stylistic felicity.' (*HD* 253). Torgovnick sums up these views: 'My objection is not Leavis's objection that Marlow makes a virtue out of not knowing what he means. Rather my objection is that his vagueness can be and has been so often linked to terms like "psychological complexity" or the "mystery and enigma of things." The work's language veils not only what Kurtz was doing in Africa, but also what Conrad is doing in *Heart of Darkness*.' Torgovnick, 146. See also Brantlinger, *Rule of Darkness*, 269–74.

2

Cultural Immersion and Culture Shock in Conrad's Fiction

> Suddenly I was overcome by the feeling that my last tie with Europe, the last link, was now severed. A new life lay before me. A strange, an unknown life. On that old liner there were still white people, the vessel was still Europe, that's where she came from and that's where she would be six weeks from now. She was a little piece of my country, of my home, of my race.
>
> Ladislao Szekely, *Tropical Fever*[1]

> In the light of these points an interesting problem arises: as the fieldworker experiences feelings of discontinuity and identity fragmentation, where will he find a suitable mirror to reflect back to him a secure sense of identity: The anthropologist is, by definition, adrift in a sea of foreigners; the eyes that mirror his soul are alien, unfamiliar.[2]

No Surrender: Denationalization in Conrad's Fiction

The response that Marlow displays in his relationship to Africa recalls the dualism implied in many anthropological models—the desire to hold the primitive at arm's length or to embrace it. In the manuscript version of *Heart of Darkness*, Marlow remarks, 'It could only be obtained by conquest—or by surrender, but we passed on indifferent, surprising, less than phantoms, wondering' (*HD* 37n.). The colonialist, in other words, can simply blunder into the 'primitive' landscape, remaining resistant through sheer ignorance and self-delusion, or he can attempt to understand. But understanding involves 'surrender'; and 'surrender' invokes Kurtzian dangers: 'Did he live his life again in every detail of desire, temptation, and surrender during that supreme moment of com-

---

[1] Ladislao Szekely, *Tropical Fever: The Adventures of a Planter in Sumatra* (New York: Harper and Brothers, 1937), 5.
[2] Wengle, 25–6.

plete knowledge?' (*HD* 68). Kurtz, after all, is the one who 'had stepped over the edge, while I [Marlow] had been permitted to draw back my hesitating foot' (*HD* 69). The danger of immersion, in Conrad's view seems to be that in going too far in embracing a culture, a process the Victorians call 'going native', there may be no possibility of return. While the anthropologist returns to his own world, Conrad's characters often do not; as the Harlequin says: 'I went a little farther, . . . then still a little farther—till I had gone so far I don't know how I'll ever get back' (*HD* 54). The Russian is a almost a pastiche of Kurtz, a more comic version of cultural isolation: 'The glamour of youth enveloped his parti-colored rags, his destitution, his loneliness, the essential desolation of his futile wanderings' (*HD* 55). Cultural isolation, the condition of so many of Conrad's characters who are stranded in other cultures, is a necessary comcomitant of anthropological fieldwork.[3]

The process of fieldwork takes almost as a prerequisite the anthropologist's isolation from his or her own culture. The anthropologist's credibility among his or her 'informants' is largely based on the fact that he or she is immersed in the community as an observer rather than as an authority figure. In order to achieve the status of an 'insider', the anthropologist must minimize his or her contacts with home. In his famous treatise, *Social Anthropology*, Evans-Pritchard writes: 'What is perhaps even more important for his work is the fact that he is all alone, cut off from the companionship of men of his own race and culture, and is dependent on the natives around him for company, friendship, and human understanding.'[4] The sense of being 'cut off', as Evans-Pritchard puts it, provides a summary of the experience of many of Conrad's characters; however, this isolation in Conrad's fiction does not bring transcultural understanding but rather despair to many of his colonialist exiles. Like the anthropological fieldworker, Conrad's characters make a jump into the unknown. As Marlow says: 'Neither Stein nor I had a clear conception of what might be on the other side when we, metaphorically speaking, took him up and

---

[3] A recent book by Christopher Herbert makes an interesting analysis of some of the dilemmas of fieldwork. See particularly his chapter on early South Pacific missionaries, 'Savagery, Culture and the Subjectivity of Fieldwork' in Christopher Herbert, *Culture and Anomie: Ethnographic Imagination in the Nineteenth Century* (Chicago: University of Chicago Press, 1991), 150–203.

[4] Edward E. Evans-Pritchard, *Social Anthropology* (London: Cohen and West, 1951), 79.

hove him over the wall with scant ceremony' (*LJ* 229). When Jim climbs over the wall into Patusan, he makes a leap into the unknown. Interestingly, as Conrad undoubtedly knew, the very etymology of the word exile suggests a jump (from the Latin *ex*, 'out of' and *salire*, 'to leap'); and it is precisely this kind of ethnic leap that both Conrad and his characters make. Unlike the anthropologist, though, Conrad's characters are often unable fully to penetrate the other culture. Marlow is aware of this sense of cultural isolation in *Heart of Darkness*. In relating his journey down the African coast, he remarks:

The idleness of a passenger, my isolation amongst all these men with whom I had no point of contact, the oily and languid sea, the uniform sombreness of the coast, seemed to keep me away from the truth of things, within the toil of a mournful and senseless delusion.   (*HD* 13)[5]

The possibility of bridging conceptual gaps in order to discover the 'truth of things' is predicated upon the ability to find some 'point of contact'. Through exploring the anthropological methods of fieldwork, we may come to a better understanding of this cultural anxiety.

The anthropological fieldworker occupies a borderland. The fieldworker is often caught paradoxically between worlds as 'friend and stranger, (. . .) as participant and observer, (. . .) anthropologist as there but not there, present but unobtrusive'.[6] Like the anthropologist who engages in fieldwork, Conrad's characters often isolate themselves from their own cultures; thus, Jim's time in Patusan is marked by loneliness:

I can't with mere words convey to you the impression of his total and utter isolation. I know, of course, that he was in every sense alone of his kind there, but the unsuspected qualities of his nature had brought him in such close touch with his surroundings that this isolation seemed only the effect of his power. His loneliness added to his stature.   (*LJ* 272)

Jim's exile is both chosen and enforced upon him: 'These proceedings had all the cold vengefulness of a death sentence, had all the

---

[5] The sense of isolation is also emphasized in *Lord Jim*: 'It is when we try to grapple with another man's intimate need that we perceive how incomprehensible, wavering, and misty are the beings that share with us the sight of the stars and the warmth of the sun. It is as if loneliness were a hard and absolute condition of existence . . .' (*LJ* 179–80).

[6] Robert Lawless, Vinson H. Sutlive, Mario D. Zamora (eds.) *Fieldwork: The Human Experience* (New York: Gordon and Breach Scientific Publishers, 1983), p. xiii.

cruelty of a sentence of exile' (*LJ* 158).[7] The 'exile' that both Kurtz and Jim undergo is a disassociation from one's own culture, a leap into another world. Jim's fate is ironic because his betrayal of his own culture (that of the merchant seamen) is based upon his failure to identify with people of another race; his failure, in other words, is a failure of empathy. His abandonment of the pilgrims appar- ently occurs because he does not view them as culturally connected to him. Yet, this abandonment of the pilgrims forces him into an identification with an equally alien people: 'Jim took the second desperate leap of his life—the leap that landed him into the life of Patusan, into the trust, the love, the confidence of the people' (*LJ* 380). Only through abandoning his identification with his own race is Jim able to establish his status in the community of Patusan. Similarly, Kurtz purposefully cuts himself off from his own culture in order to assimilate to the Congolese culture. At the station Marlow discovers that Kurtz actually attempted to return at one point: 'Kurtz had apparently intended to return himself, the Station being by that time bare of goods and stores, but after coming three hundred miles, had suddenly decided to go back' (*HD* 34). In other words, Kurtz is not one of Conrad's characters like Willems, who is isolated by accidental circumstances.

Kurtz makes a conscious decision to remove himself from his cultural moorings:

> They were at a loss for an adequate motive. As to me, I seemed to see Kurtz for the first time. It was a distinct glimpse: the dugout, four paddling savages, and the lone white man turning his back suddenly on the head- quarters, on relief, on thoughts of home—perhaps; setting his face towards the depths of the wilderness, towards his empty and desolate station.
>
> (*HD* 34)

The abandonment of one's culture in favour of another may be seen on several levels. On the stereotypical levels of Victorian 'denation- alization', or 'going native', Kurtz becomes a cultural renegade; on another level, he enacts the ostensible goal of much fieldwork anthropology—the goal of cultural immersion.[8] To what degree are these two phenomena, cultural immersion and 'going native' equivalent? John Wengle calls the process of 'going native' second-

---

[7] Marlow calls Jim 'a seaman in exile from the sea' (*LJ* 4).

[8] Numerous works on the motif of 'going native' exist in anthropological litera- ture. See I. C. Jarvie, *Thinking about Culture: Theory and Practice* (Drodecht: Reidel, 1986); Thomas Rhys Williams, *Field Methods in the Study of Culture* (New York: Holt, Rinehart and Winston, 1967).

ary identification. One of the possibilities, he argues, in maintaining one's sense of self in an alien culture is internationalization:

I am thinking here of what in popular jargon is known as 'going native,' or in my terminology, secondary identification with the native culture. Contrary to other defensive maneuvers mentioned above, in cases of secondary identification the student attempts to reconsolidate his sense of identity by internalizing various aspects and symbols of the native culture in which he is immersed. It is almost as if the student were operating on the principle that any sense of identity is better than none at all—at least temporarily. Secondary identification enables the student to feel that once again he has a place where he belongs, that he is again a member of a larger, more enduring whole. It enables him to experience the powerful and positive overtones associated with acceptance by members of the native culture.[9]

The fieldwork strategy that Wengle speaks of here, secondary identification, or 'going native' is, of course, a common feature of the colonial experience as well. The definition of secondary identification applies perfectly to many of Conrad's characters. Jim's sense of belonging in Patusan is a surrogate for his need of acceptance by his own culture.

The notion of the 'surrender' of one's ethnic identity in the process of transculturation is, of course, a dominant theme in Conrad's works, and not isolated in *Heart of Darkness*. The 'Eastern' works, *Almayer's Folly, An Outcast of the Islands, Lord Jim*, and *The Rescue* share this sense of cultural anxiety. Perhaps the most well-known statement regarding ethnic surrender is in Marlow's correspondence with 'the privileged man' to whom he addresses his account of the last stage of Jim's life in Patusan: 'You said that "that kind of thing" was only endurable and enduring when based on a firm conviction in the truth of ideas racially your own, in whose name are established the order, the morality of an ethical progress (. . .) You said also—I call to mind—that "giving your life up to them" (them meaning all of mankind with skins brown, yellow, or black in colour) "was like selling your soul to a brute" ' (*LJ* 339). Self-sacrifice, the privileged man tells Marlow, is predicated upon an unqualified belief in racial superiority, or what Kipling famously called the 'white man's burden'. Paradoxically, the imperialist must maintain an identification with his own people

---

[9] Wengle, 31.

while he serves the interests of another culture; thus, the imperialist must be a 'homo duplex'. Marlow's debate over 'giving your life up' to the ethical system of an alien culture is carried on, in heterodox forms, throughout Conrad's fiction. Lingard, for example, in *The Rescue* is caught between two worlds—the European and the Malaysian—while his companion, Jorgenson, has resolutely 'thrown his lot in' with the Malaysians. Jorgenson, who in Victorian terms has 'gone native', hopes for Lingard, too, 'to be absorbed, captured, made their own either in failure or in success (. . .) What he really wanted Lingard to do was to cease to take the slightest interest in those whites' (R 388).

In the manuscript of *The Rescue*, on which Conrad worked intermittently from 1896 to 1899, just before and during the composition of *Heart of Darkness*, Wyndham, an adventurer/colonist recites a litany of the dangers of assimilation that reads like a textbook case of the Victorian fear of 'going native':

'Don't go in too deep with them . . . I say to you *don't*. Take a warning from me; I can't get away now . . . I am ready to go—but I can't. I've given myself up to them. (. . .) We are no better, perhaps, but we are different. There is about them a fascination of primitive ideas—of primitive virtues, perhaps. Something enticing and bitter in the life—in the thought around you, if once you step into the world of their notions. Very bitter. We can never forget our origin. Don't give yourself up. Primitive virtues are poison to us—white men. We have gone on different lines. Look on, trade, make money . . . Above all, don't fight with them. That's how it begins. First you fight with them—then you fight for them—no closer tie than spilt blood— then you begin to think they are human beings . . . They are—very. That's the worst of it—for when you begin to see it your ideas change. You . . . see injustice and cruel folly of what, before, appeared just and wise. Then you begin to love them—that fascination you know.[10]

The idea that bridging the conceptual gap to another culture is an enticing prospect fraught with danger occurs again and again in Conrad's work. The 'fascination' of the primitive, the allure of ethnological understanding, is counterpoised to the surrender inherent in the act of tranculturation. When Wyndham warns of the danger 'if once you step into the world of their notions', one is immediately reminded of both the anthropological goal of fieldwork, and the dangers that the Victorians viewed as inherent in

---

[10] Quoted in Parry, 48.

such boundary crossing. 'The world of their notions' is analogous to what an anthropologist might call 'the natives' point of view'. In a common Victorian view, the colonial administrator, like the successful anthropologist, must be able to 'go in' with the other culture, without 'going too far'.

In *Heart of Darkness*, Marlow is also fascinated by the 'primitive'; yet, as if Wyndham's admonition were echoing in his mind, he refuses to 'give himself up' to a different cultural system. Marlow famously remarks of the 'surrender' of Kurtz in several passages: 'I think it had whispered to him things about himself which he did not know, things of which he had not conception till he took counsel with his great solitude—and the whisper had proved irresistibly fascinating'; 'I tried to break the spell—the heavy, mute spell of the wilderness—that seemed to draw him to its pitiless breast by the awakening of forgotten and brutal instincts, by the memory of gratified and monstrous passions' (*HD* 65). In these passages Conrad clearly seems to be echoing his own concerns in the early version of 'The Rescuer'. Another theme common in 'The Rescuer' passage and *Heart of Darkness* is the notion of 'primitive' cultures as repositories of instincts still extant but submerged in 'civilized' Europe: 'We can never forget our origin. Don't give yourself up. Primitive virtues are poison to us—white men. We have gone on different lines.'[11]

Culture Shock

While it would be absurd to reduce the complexity of Conrad's portrait of Marlow to such a simplistic level, what Marlow experiences in the Congo is not very different from a term coined by the anthropologist Kalervo Oberg and now popularized—'culture shock'.[12] While this term has become so amorphous as to lose a

[11] Interestingly, D. H. Lawrence, though certainly not aware of this manuscript passage, writes similarly: 'The truth of the matter is, one cannot go back. Some men can: renegade. But Melville couldn't go back: and I know that I could never go back. Back towards the past, savage life. One cannot go back. It is one's destiny inside one. There are these other peoples, these savages. One does not despise them. One does not feel superior. But there is a gulf in time and being.' *Studies in Classic American Literature*, 51–2.

[12] 'Culture shock is, in some ways, the defining characteristic of anthropologists. Although they know more than others what to expect about experiencing another

great deal of its significance, Oberg describes the phenomenon in the following way: 'Culture shock is precipitated by the anxiety that results from losing our familiar signs and symbols of social intercourse. These signs or clues include the thousand and one ways in which we orient ourselves to the situations of daily life (. . .) All of us depend for our peace of mind and our efficiency on hundreds of these cues, most of which we are not consciously aware'.[13] Signs of culture shock, according to Oberg, include: feelings of strain or loss; confusion and incomprehension; disgust and indignation; and feelings of impotence and the inability to cope in the foreign environment. Oberg's comments parallel Marlow's groping for ratification in banal familiar events: 'These little things make all the great difference. When they are gone you must fall back on your own innate strength, upon your own capacity for faithfulness' (*HD* 50). Marlow constantly searches for familiar signs in negotiating not only the physical but psychological journey in the Congo.

Marlow maintains his relative sanity only through looking to the ordinary 'signs' a seaman must rely on rather than the 'hidden' and alienating signs of this different culture:

I had to keep guessing at the channel; I had to discern, mostly by inspiration, the *signs* of hidden banks; I watched for sunken stones; I was learning to clap my teeth smartly before my heart flew out when I shaved by a fluke of some infernal sly old snag that would have ripped the life out of the tin-pot steamboat and drowned all the pilgrims; I had to keep a look-out for the *signs* of dead wood we could cut up in the night for the next day's steaming. When you have to attend to things of that sort, to the mere incidents of the surface, the reality—the reality I tell you—fades.

(*HD* 36, italics mine)

During the trip upriver, Marlow finds a book entitled ' "An Inquiry into Some Points of Seamanship" by a man Towser, Towson— some such name'; this book fills him with a strange sense of satisfaction. However, this satisfaction can be understood as part of

culture, that they voluntarily subject themselves to the process and experience of culture shock, uncomfortable as it often is, is a guarantee they are really confronting the reality of the other culture. There are a number of good descriptions of culture shock in the literature.' Nancy Howell, *Surviving Fieldwork: A Report of the Advisory Panel on Health and Safety in Fieldwork* (Washington, D. C.: American Anthropological Association, 1990), 154.

[13] Quoted in Adrian Furnham and Stephen Bochner, *Culture Shock: Psychological Reactions to Unfamiliar Environments* (London: Methuen, 1986), 48.

Oberg's search for 'familiar signs and symbols of social intercourse (. . .) the thousand and one ways in which we orient ourselves to the situations of daily life'. Marlow comments: 'The matter looked dreary enough with illustrative diagrams and repulsive tables of figures (. . .) The simple old sailor with his talk of chains and purchases made me forget the jungle and the pilgrims in a delicious sensation of having come upon something unmistakably real' (*HD* 39). In short, the book helps him to establish his proverbial groundings through allowing him contact with the reassuring and universal signs of seamanship. For Conrad himself, the 'Congo Diary' and 'Upriver Book' seem to have provided the same sense of psychological stability.[14] Although the passages of unelaborated longitudinal and latitudinal figures, nautical terms, and bland descriptions initially appear uninteresting, they seem to have kept him in contact with the 'signs and symbols' of his own familiar world, in contrast to his shifting understanding of Africa. Conrad's own letters from the Congo make clear that the problem of culture shock was shared by Conrad along with his characters. To take but one example, in a well-known letter Conrad writes to his aunt Marguerite Poradowska:

They (your letters) were as a ray of sunshine piercing through the grey clouds of a dreary winter day; for my days here are dreary. No use deluding oneself. Decidedly I regret having come here. I even regret it bitterly (. . .) Everything here is repellent to me. Men and things, but men above all. And I am repellent to them, also (. . .) I feel somewhat weak physically and not a little demoralized.[15]

Many of Conrad's letters reveal the same sense of despair in the foreign environment.

The sense of cultural or psychological dislocation is a common feature of the colonial situation. James Clifford has written convincingly of this phenomenon: 'The most acute observers of the colonial situation, Orwell and Conrad, for example, have portrayed it as a power-laden, ambiguous world of discontinuous, clashing realities. Like Orwell's young district officer who unwillingly shoots an elephant to avoid being laughed at by a crowd of

[14] Conrad writes in *A Personal Record*: 'It may be my sea training acting upon a natural disposition to keep good hold on the one thing really mine, but the fact is that I have a positive horror of losing even for one moment that full possession of myself which is the first condition of good service' (*PR* xvii).

[15] Letter of 26 November 1890, *Collected Letters of Conrad*, i. 62.

Burmese, and like all the characters in *Heart of Darkness*, displaced Europeans must labor to maintain their cultural identities, however artificial these may appear.'[16] The French symbolist, Rimbaud, wrote in 1888 from Abyssinia, almost simultaneously to Conrad's voyage to the Congo, of this sense of cultural dislocation:

I am lonely and bored. I have never known anyone as lonely and bored as I. Is it not wretched, this life I lead, without family, without friends, without any intellectual companionship or occupation, lost in the midst of these negroes, whose lot one would like to improve, and who try, for their part, to exploit you? (. . .). The worst thing is the fear of becoming doltish oneself, isolated as one is, and cut off from any intellectual companionship.[17]

We ought to note the parallels between this passage and Marlow's depiction of being 'cut off from the comprehension of our sur-roundings'.[18] Clearly, we must not simply gloss over the racial implications of both of these passages; however, we ought to make some effort to understand the mindset that led even that most culturally relativistic of early field anthropologists, Bronislaw Malinowski, to echo the most brutal racist cant of a Kurtz.[19] George W. Stocking, Jr writes:

Joseph Conrad's name crops up on several occasions in Malinoswki's diaries. Conrad knew only too well what happened to Europeans who ventured into *The Heart of Darkness*. Without his being fully aware of it, Malinowski felt in himself something of the psychology of a Mistah Kurtz. He spoke disparagingly of Europeans who 'have such fabulous oppor-tunities—the sea, the ships, the jungle, power over the natives—and don't do a thing!' He imagined the plot of a novel in which a European 'fights against the blacks, becomes absolute master' and then a benevolent despot. He enjoyed the 'delightful feeling that now I alone am the master of this

---

[16] Clifford, *Predicament of Culture*, 78–9. See George Orwell, 'Shooting an Elephant' in *Inside the Whale and Other Essays* (1936) (Reprinted London: Penguin, 1957).

[17] Quoted in Meyers, 105.

[18] This is not an uncommon description of fieldwork experience: 'I mean it's an odd experience to plop down into a foreign culture and deal with it, with all the strangeness of it, and I felt, because of my particular approach to the field, that *I had been cut off in a shocking sort of way*.' Quoted in Wengle, 88, italics mine.

[19] 'At moments I was furious at them, (. . .) On the whole my feelings toward the natives are definitely tending to, "*exterminate the brutes.*"' Bronislaw Malinowski, *A Diary in the Strict Sense of the Term* (New York: Harcourt, Brace & World, Inc., 1967), 69, italics mine. See Geertz, *Local Knowledge*, 55–8. See also 'Trauma in the Field: Reflections on Malinowski's Fieldwork', in Wengle, 107–29.

village with my "boys." ' And at one point he even spoke of his feeling toward the natives as 'decidedly tending to "Exterminate the brutes" '— which was of course exactly the end to which Kurtz' benevolent despotism led, and almost exactly a quotation of Kurtz' barbaric footnote.[20]

Stocking adds that 'Malinowski was far from being Kurtz',[21] but we are left with the discomfort of fieldwork anthropology's founder as implicated in a strange version of life imitating art. At the very least, the case of Malinowski teaches us that cultural empathy is often a hard-won goal, and that Malinowski's anthropology represented a sort of bridge between early and modern anthropology.

The publication of Malinowski's *Diary in the Strict Sense of the Term*, which amounted to a skeleton from the anthropological closet, shocked many students of anthropology. Malinowski's friend and protégé, Raymond Firth, writes in the introduction that 'Other passages again may even nowadays offend or shock the reader, and some readers may be impressed as much by the revelation of elements of brutality, even degradation, which the record shows on occasion'.[22] Aside from Malinowski's paraphrase of Kurtz's 'exterminate all the brutes', the *Diary* is filled with his bitterness toward the anthropological subjects of his fieldwork. In a passage full of discouragement about the potential of bridging cultural divides, Malinowski wrote: 'As for ethnology: I see the lives of the natives as utterly devoid of interest or importance, something as remote from me as the life of a dog.'[23] The dehumanization of the Trobriand Islanders here must be seen as part of the realistic history of cross-cultural disillusionment. Clifford Geertz comments that the publication of Malinowski's unexpurgated *Diary*, with all of its sporadic racism and bitterness exposed to view, 'rendered established accounts of how anthropologists work fairly well implausible. The myth of the chameleon fieldworker, perfectly self-tuned to his exotic surroundings, a walking miracle of empathy, tact, patience, and cosmopolitanism, was demolished by the man who had perhaps done most to create it'.[24] Stocking frames this failure in a Conradian manner. Of the publication of the *Diary*, he comments:

[20] George W. Stocking, Jr, 'Empathy and Antipathy in the Heart of Darkness', in Regna Darnell (ed.) *Readings in the History of Anthropology* (New York: Harper & Row, 1974), 282–3.
[21] Ibid. 283.
[22] Raymond R. Firth, 'Introduction', in Malinowski, *Diary*, p. xix.
[23] Malinowski, *Diary*, 167.   [24] Geertz, *Local Knowledge*, 56.

Suddenly there seemed to have been uncovered a long-repressed Conradian horror—what the culture-hero of the fieldwork myth had 'actually' been feeling during his long and presumably empathetic immersion in the Trobriand *gemeinschaft*. Longing for white civilization and white woman-hood, he had relieved his frustration with outpourings of aggression against the 'niggers' who surrounded him.[25]

Stocking adds: 'Although Malinowski had by the 1960s lost his status as a shaper of anthropological theory (...) his place as a mythic culture hero of anthropological method was at once con-firmed and irrevocably compromised by the publication of his field diaries (...) which revealed to a far-flung progeny of horrified Marlows that their Mistah Kurtz had secretly harbored passion-ately aggressive feelings towards the "niggers" among whom he lived and laboured—when he was not withdrawing from the heart of darkness to share the white-skinned brotherhood of local pearlfishers and traders'.[26]

The failure or the limits of cultural relativism are common themes in writings on 'primitive' cultures, as George W. Stocking, Jr, James Clifford, Clifford Geertz, and others have shown. In cleaning their own house, anthropologists have come to recognize the difficulties of transcultural identification:

the genuinely profound question his book [Malinowski's] raised was ig-nored; namely, if it is not, as we had been taught to believe, through some sort of extraordinary sensibility, an almost preternatural capacity to think, feel, and perceive like a native (a word, I should hurry to say, I use here 'in the strictest sense of the term'), how is anthropological knowledge of the way natives think, feel, and perceive possible? (...) The issue is epistemo-logical. If we are going to cling—as, in my opinion, we must—to the injunction to see things from the native's point of view, where are we when we can no longer claim some unique form of psychological closeness, a sort of transcultural identification with our subjects? What happens to *verstehen* when *einfuhlen* disappears?[27]

[25] George W. Stocking, Jr (ed.), 'History of Anthropology' in *Observers Ob-served: Essays on Ethnographic Fieldwork; History of Anthropology* (Madison: University of Wisconsin Press, 1983), i.8.

[26] George W. Stocking, Jr, 'The Ethnographer's Magic: Fieldwork in British Anthropology from Tylor to Malinowski', in *Observers Observed*, 71.

[27] Geertz, *Local Knowledge*, 56. Juxtaposed to this must be the counter-argument—that Geertz applies Malinowski's failure of empathy to anthropology generally: 'But then, in what can only be called an unjustified psychological leap, Geertz apparently assumes that Malinowski's characteristic attitudes and feelings, particularly his inability to empathize with the natives, are typical and apply to the

Geertz refers here to Malinowski's famous formulation in *Argonauts*, which provided the goal for later anthropological fieldwork:

These three lines of approach lead to the final goal, of which the Ethnographer should never lose sight is to grasp the native's point of view, his relation to life, to realize *his* vision of *his* world (. . .) Perhaps as we read the account of these remote customs there may emerge a feeling of solidarity with the endeavours and ambitions of these natives. Perhaps man's mentality will be revealed to us, and brought near, along some lines which we never have followed before. Perhaps through realizing human nature in a shape very distant and foreign to us, we shall shed some light on our own.[28]

The word 'solidarity' here resonates with particular significance in relation to Conrad's work; for Conrad, the goal of solidarity is constantly invoked by Conrad as a goal for the artist who would present visions of other cultures. He writes of the 'solidarity that knits together the loneliness of innumerable hearts: to the solidarity in dreams, in joy, in sorrow, in aspirations, in illusions, in hope, in fear, which binds together all humanity' (*NN* xiii). Anthropology can be viewed as a natural corollary to this expressed goal in Conrad's work; and the disparities between the hope of solidarity in Malinowski's anthropology and the reality of the difficulty of bridging conceptual gaps, clearly relates to Conrad's works. This discussion of Malinowski introduces another theme in Conrad's writing that will be clarified through reference to the genealogy of cultural anthropology.[29] Conrad's writing coincides with a transformation from Victorian to modern anthropology.

Participants and Observers

Marlow might be seen to represent the distinction between nineteenth-century anthropology and the later rise of the participant-

majority of anthropologists.' Wengle, 159. Wengle continues: 'Fieldworkers are not perfect empathizers or social chameleons; nobody is. (. . .) By the same token, (. . .) empathy or secondary identification is an important device to help the anthropologist experience, and therefore to know in a wider sense, the native's point of view.' Wengle, 160.

[28] Malinowski, *Argonauts*, 25.

[29] Street takes some note of the change from armchair to immersionist anthropology. See Street, 16–17.

observer school of A. C. Haddon,[30] Rivers,[31] Malinowski,[32] and
others.[33] It is difficult to overrate Malinowski's importance in this
process of developing fieldwork methodologies. Interestingly,
Malinowski's original fieldwork was initially distrusted because of
its 'man in the field' approach.[34] Before the pioneers of fieldwork
argued for the importance of the anthropologist as an observer of
primitive cultures, anthropologists did not soil their hands with
fieldwork. In his early works, culminating in *Argonauts of the
Western Pacific* (1922), Malinowski radically altered anthropological methodologies; he called for fieldwork as the basis of ethnographic understanding:

This expedient for an Ethnographer consists in collecting concrete data of
evidence, and drawing the general inferences for himself. This seems obvious on the face of it, but was not found out or at least practiced in
Ethnography till field work was taken up by men of science.[35]

Before considering the problems of anthropological fieldwork as
a corollary to Conrad's novella, it is necessary to define briefly what
is meant by fieldwork. Fieldworkers have been labelled 'marginal
natives' and 'professional strangers', two phrases that are particularly *apropos* to Conrad himself. In other words, fieldworkers are
caught between worlds. Many anthropological memoirs address
the issue of cultural boundaries. The rite of passage for the
fieldworker, the moment of cultural acceptance, is a common
theme; however, the feeling of being a permanent stranger is often
lamented:

I felt like a comfortable 'insider.' But of course I wasn't. I could never leave
my own cultural world despite my partial successes in entering theirs. In

[30] On Haddon's importance in the development of fieldwork, see Henrika
Kuklick, *The Savage Within: The Social History of British Anthropology, 1885–
1945* (Cambridge: Cambridge University Press, 1991), 15.
[31] Of fieldwork, Rivers wrote, 'A typical piece of intensive work is one in which
the worker lives for a year or more among a community of perhaps four or five
hundred people and studies every detail of their life and culture (. . .) It is only by
such work that it is possible to discover the incomplete and often misleading
character of much of the vast mass of survey work which forms the existing material
of anthropology'. Quoted in Kuper, 7.
[32] Of Malinowski, Kuper writes: 'There [in the Trobriand Islands] he passes the
war inventing intensive fieldwork by participant observation, working through the
vernacular, and living as one of the people, in total isolation from European
contacts.' Kuper, 10.
[33] See Stocking, 'Ethnographer's Magic'.
[34] Clifford, *Predicament of Culture*, 26–8. [35] Malinowski, *Argonauts*, 12.

fact, the lonely isolation, after ten months with scarcely a word of English (and mail service only once a month), was taking me near the edge of psychological balance. I choose two small episodes late in my fieldwork to illustrate both my precarious state and the unbridged and unbridgeable gulf between their world and mine.[36]

This recognition of the ambiguous quality of the fieldworker is not a new phenomenon. An eccentric German ethnographer in the early 1900s, Leo Frobenius, reflected on his divided self, or his status as what Conrad would have called a 'homo duplex': 'I myself (. . .) live a double life, one in the enjoyment of our culture, the other buried in the past, absorbed in the original elements of savage life.'[37] Frobenius's biography provides an extreme example of the tenuous balance between observation and participation. During his dozen trips to Africa, he claimed to have participated in numerous ceremonies, and even tried to restore defunct rituals.[38]

Fieldwork represents a self-imposed exile, a detachment from the norms of the anthropologist's own culture. John Van Maanen provides a useful description of the goals and methodologies of cultural immersion in fieldwork which reflects on Conrad's tenuous status as an exile:

Fieldwork usually means living with and living like those who are studied. In its broadest, most conventional sense, fieldwork demands the full-time involvement of a researcher over a lengthy period of time (typically unspecified) and consists mostly of ongoing interaction with the human targets of study on their home ground (. . .) To do fieldwork apparently requires some of the instincts of an exile, for the fieldworker typically arrives at the place of study without much of an introduction and knowing few people, if any (. . .) Whether or not the fieldworker ever really does 'Get away' in a conceptual sense is becoming increasingly problematic, but physical displacement is a requirement.[39]

[36] Roger M. Keesing, 'Not a Real Fish: The Ethnographer as Insider Outsider' in Philip R. DeVita (ed.), *The Naked Anthropologist: Tales from Around the World* (Belmont: Wadsworth, 1992), 75.

[37] Leo Frobenius, *The Childhood of Man: A Popular Account of the Lives, Customs and Thoughts of the Primitive Races*, trans. A. H. Keane (London: Seeky & Co., 1909), 21–2.

[38] See Leo Frobenius, *The Voice of Africa: Being an Account of the Travels of the German Inner African Exploration Expedition in the Years 1910–1912*, 2 vols., trans. Rudolph Blind (London: Hutchinson & Co., 1913), ii. 393–7.

[39] John Van Maanen, *Tales of the Field: On Writing Ethnography* (Chicago: University of Chicago Press, 1988), 2–3.

Van Maanen's characterization of the fieldworker's experience as consonant with that of the exile gives a sense of why this concept of anthropological participant-observation may be particularly relevant to the writings of Joseph Conrad, a notable European *déraciné*. The anthropological fieldworker must accomplish the task of suspending his or her own cultural perspective and prejudices in order to gain a better understanding of the society being studied. Success in fieldwork seems to require the kind of cultural leap that Lord Jim makes into Patusan:

That's how he ascended the Patusan river. Nothing at all could have been more prosaic and more unsafe, more extravagantly casual, more lonely. Strange, this fatality that would cast the complexion of a flight upon all his acts, of impulsive unreflecting desertion—*of a jump into the unknown.*

(*LJ* 229, italics mine)

Of course, Conrad similarly describes this sort of leap out of his culture upon leaving Poland: 'I verily believe mine was the only case of a boy of my nationality and antecedents taking a, so to speak, standing jump out of his racial surroundings and associations' (*PR* 120-1).[40] Fieldwork anthropology may be said to be predicated on such a 'standing jump' out of one's culture. If characters such as Jim, Kurtz, and Lingard remind us of the anthropologist who crosses cultural boundaries to become a participant, Marlow is the quintessential observer who resolutely remains at the border.

Ignorant of language ('one immense jabber') and customs, like many of the Victorian writers who travelled in foreign cultures, Marlow encounters many barriers that separate him from comprehension of the Congo.[41] Although he wants to understand, he is often denied this possibility. When the helmsman is dying, Marlow remarks: 'I declare it looked as though he would presently put to us some question in an understandable language, but he died without uttering a sound' (*HD* 47). Here he desires a link to the dying Congolese—some notion of understanding; but even this is denied. Language is only one aspect of the distancing that occurs for Marlow. Rather than the fieldworker, he is linked much more

---

[40] For an interesting account of Conrad's place in the literature of exile see Michael Seidel, *Exile and the Narrative Imagination* (New Haven: Yale University Press, 1986).

[41] On the place of the anthropologist in relation to his or her subject, see also Geertz, *Interpretation of Cultures*.

closely to the earlier anthropology or ethnology, which is now seen to be reactionary, but which could more accurately be viewed as a groping toward some knowledge of a world opening up slowly to cultural diversity. The difficulty is one of transcription and of interpretation, of observation and comprehension. A passage in Wittgenstein parallels the issues I have been discussing:

We . . . say of some people that they are transparent to us. It is, however, important as regards this observation that one human being can be a complete enigma to another. We learn this when we come into a strange country with entirely strange traditions; and, what is more, even given a mastery of the country's language. We do not understand the people. (And not because of not knowing what they are saying to themselves.) We cannot find our feet with them.[42]

Wittgenstein provides here a fine definition of Marlow's difficulty (a difficulty that is exaggerated by a lack of knowledge of language) of finding his feet in Africa. It is not that he simply lacks curiosity. Marlow says in trying to interpret a custom of the Congolese: 'I looked at them as you would on any human being with a curiosity of their impulses, motives, capacities, weaknesses' (*HD* 43). Marlow's ethnographic curiosity never develops into genuine understanding.

Marlow represents the initial stage of the anthropological urge— to understand and interpret. He is even capable of a nascent cultural relativism, such as when he attempts to understand the significance of the Congolese's drumming: 'Perhaps on some quiet night the tremor of far-off drums, sinking, swelling, a tremor, vast, faint; a sound weird, appealing, suggestive, and wild—and perhaps with as profound a meaning as the sounds of bells in a Christian country' (*HD* 23). Marlow does not discount the validity of the religion of the Congolese. On the other hand, he refuses to empathically reconstruct Kurtz's darker experiences, referring notoriously to 'unspeakable rites'. The distinction here is between an interest in the Congolese themselves and a distaste for Kurtz's ersatz primitivism. If we invoke the participant-observer analogy, Kurtz has gone far beyond merely participating in the Congolese culture to recreating it along his own lines. Such a problem may again be framed in an anthropological manner. In his discussion of the methods of fieldwork, Evans-Pritchard writes:

[42] Quoted in Geertz, *Interpretation of Cultures*, 13.

This is not merely a matter of physical proximity. There is also a psychological side to it. But living among the natives as far as he can like one of themselves the anthropologist puts himself on a level with them. Unlike the administrator and the missionary he has no authority and status to maintain, and unlike them he has a neutral position. *He is not there to change their way of life but as a humble learner of it.*[43]

Evans-Pritchard's remark may be read as an ironic gloss on Kurtz's actions, for he comes to the Congo with a missionary zeal, ready to 'reform' the Congolese. Ironically, he does apparently 'change their way of life', but only in a degenerative sense. Evans-Pritchard's advice to a young fieldworker is to 'live as far as possible in their villages and camps, where he is, again as far as possible, physically and morally part of the community'.[44] In the Malinowskian tradition, the anthropologist must be a participant; however, Evans-Pritchard stresses that limitations exist: 'He then not only sees and hears what goes on in the normal everyday life of the people as well as less common events, such as ceremonies and legal activities, but *by taking part in those activities in which he can appropriately engage*, he learns through action as well as by ear and eye what goes on around him.'[45] What he suggests here is the difference between a sensitive observer and a 'cultural convert'. In other words, even in anthropology there are limits on 'those activities in which he [the ethnographer] can appropriately engage'.

In Kurtz, we see the dangers of transgressing cultural boundaries and passing this off as cultural relativism. Even such human practices as cannibalism, headhunting, and human sacrifice are cultural constructs, circumscribed by the mores of a *particular* culture. While Europeans have often exaggerated the prevalence of such practices in human cultures, their existence is explained by very careful empathic reconstruction. Thus, anthropology has enacted Menander's dictum that nothing human is foreign to man. Marlow is even willing to adopt a culturally relativistic approach (with a somewhat patronizing European tone) to the cannibalism of his crew. This acceptance seems to derive from his view of cannibalism as a human necessity ('he and his chaps must be very hungry, they must have been growing increasingly hungry for at least this month past', *HD* 42). Marlow seems to explain their 'restraint' in a typically progressivist anthropological manner as the first glimmer

---

[43] Evans-Pritchard, 78–9, italics mine.   [44] Evans-Pritchard, 78.
[45] Ibid., italics mine.

of ethical growth. However, what is important here is that he does not simply condemn them and remains curious about their 'impulses, motives, capacities, weaknesses' (*HD* 43).

Culturally and intellectually curious, Marlow is, nevertheless, unwilling to 'abandon himself' in order to understand; he is no fieldworker who will conform to Evans-Pritchard's later maxim: 'To succeed in this feat a man must be able to abandon himself without reserve, and he must also have intuitive powers which not all possess.'[46] Marlow is unwilling or unable to break down the cultural boundaries that he often hints may be the only safeguards to sanity in the colonial experience; he is unwilling to surrender his cultural identity, a mistake that he views as Kurtz's downfall.[47] Although curious, Marlow has enacted only the second half of the phrase that summarizes the goal of Malinowskian anthropology— he is an observer but not a participant. Malinowski decried those who could not achieve empathy with another culture but who approached the 'primitive' as tourists:

Some people are unable to grasp the inner meaning and the psychological reality of all that is outwardly strange, at first sight incomprehensible, in a different culture. These people are not born to be ethnologists.[48]

In part, this statement must be taken as Malinowskian bravado: some people—ethnologists—are born with the capacity to understand other cultures, while others are deprived of this ability. However, Malinowski's own writings make clear that such an empathic reconstruction is not easily made.

Another comment on the knot that the fieldworker must untie is relevant to Marlow's borderland status: 'The new way of seeing the world is normally claimed to be similar to the native's point of view. But careful attention is given to insuring that the fieldworker does not appear to be fully altered, the proverbial cultural dupe or convert. The attitude conveyed is one of tacking back and forth between an insider's passionate perspective and an outsiders dispassionate one.'[49] Here, again, we have the opposition between a

---

[46] Evans-Pritchard, 82.

[47] One critic, with whom I strongly disagree, has argued that Marlow's failure is in not joining Kurtz. See Peter J. Glassman, *Language and Being: Joseph Conrad and the Literature of Personality* (New York: Columbia University Press, 1976), 228–30

[48] Malinowski, *Argonauts*, 517.

[49] Van Maanen, 77.

Frobenius and an Evans-Pritchard in anthropology, or a Kurtz and a Marlow in fiction. In the attempt to negotiate what he perceives to be a treacherous cultural divide, Marlow is not only asked to translate Africa but, at a further remove from the culture, to translate Kurtz's translation of Africa. In other words, Marlow is twice removed from cultural immersion. His dilemma is in trying to observe from a safe distance, in trying to maintain an empirical 'objectivity' regarding the foreign culture. This detachment is emphasized, in part, by the very barrier to understanding that the boat presents. With a few notable exceptions, Marlow remains on board the steamboat that seems a fragile piece of European culture. Imagine the anthropologist who never disembarks, who is content to watch from the ship. In this manner, Marlow is not unlike those Victorian anthropologists who were two steps removed from the process of what would later be called fieldwork. Much of the genuine fieldwork in anthropology prior to 1914 can be attributed to traders, missionaries, and colonial administrators rather than to anthropologists: 'Not until after World War I, when colonial authority seemed secure in most parts of the empire, did it become routine for anthropologists to go into the field to collect their own data for analysis (. . .) In the prewar era, scholarly anthropological analyses based on extensive field experience were written, but they were produced by men who were themselves colonial agents— missionaries and colonial administrators.'[50] In other words, some of the first anthropological observers were men not very different from Kurtz. What separates Kurtz, after all, from the other traders is his ability to assimilate into the primitive culture; and yet, it is a perverse version of assimilation that, from the Victorian perspective, causes his downfall.[51]

Reflecting on the revelations of the *Diary*, Geertz casts Malinowski's attraction–repulsion from participation in 'primitive' life in a very Conradian manner:

Whether accurately or not, Malinowski has come down to us, partly because of his own insistence on the fact, partly because of the extraordinary evocativeness of the work, as the prime apostle of what might be

---

[50] Kuper, 287.
[51] Anthropologists doing fieldwork 'are also expected not to withdraw from the passing cultural scene but to become as involved and fully engrossed in the daily affairs of the people studied as possible'. Van Maanen, 80.

called, transforming his own irony, join-the-brutes ethnography (. . .) One grasps the exotic not by drawing back from the immediacy of encounter into the symmetries of thought, as with Lévi-Strauss, not by transforming them into figures on an African urn, as with Evans-Pritchard. One grasps it by losing oneself, one's soul maybe, in those immediacies.[52]

The *Diary* beautifully illustrates the degrees of anxiety and tension associated with what Malinowksi often ostensibly refers to as a simple process of cultural immersion. As Geertz seems to imply here, Malinowski himself believed that there were Kurtzian dangers to anthropology: 'One grasps the exotic not by drawing back from the immediacy of encounter (. . .) One grasps it by *losing oneself, one's soul maybe*, in those immediacies' (italics mine).[53] For Malinowski, ethnography could involve an almost 'Faustian' bargain: knowledge came at the possible price of 'one's soul'. As Stocking writes of Malinowski: 'For long periods, he was in fact alone among the natives, almost without any contact with European culture, during a period when his personal life was undergoing an extended crisis. Like Kurtz, he was alone with his instincts in the heart of darkness.'[54]

The demystification of the process of anthropological fieldwork over the last few years has also revealed the failures of cultural relativity even among those professional cultural relativists, anthropologists. For example, Stocking writes of Malinowski that 'a long previous tradition of European primitivism was part of the cultural baggage that these ethnographers carried into the tropics, that they were aware of this tradition, and that Malinowski, at least, clearly saw aspects of his own career in relation to it—including some of its darker Kurtzian possibilities'.[55] Along similar lines, Clifford comments enticingly on two less well-known fieldworkers and contemporaries of Conrad's, Nikolai Miklouho-Maclay and Jan Stanislaus Kubary. The case of Maclay provides a classic example of the ethnographer who transgresses cultural and ethical boundaries. Abandoned alone among a group of uncontacted Papuans in the late nineteenth century, Maclay came

---

[52] Geertz, *Works and Lives*, 78–9.
[53] The fear of 'loss of self' is, of course, a common theme in Conrad's work. The despairing Razumov in *Under Western Eyes*, for example, thinks: 'Was it possible that he no longer belonged to himself?' (*UW* 301).
[54] Stocking, 'Empathy and Antipathy', 283.
[55] Stocking, 'Ethnographer's Magic', 215.

to a position of quasi-divinity among the people, a clear Kurtz figure:

he came to be regarded as a 'really extraordinary being' (. . .) At once god and man, Maclay seems to have created for himself a remarkable position of trust and power (. . .) To think of Maclay as Conrad's Kurtz, alone in the jungle, surrounded by adoring natives he had come to uplift, would be to mythicise in a different mode; Maclay's self-empowering impulses were never reduced to Kurtz's horrific exterminating scrawl. But not to hear the Kurtzian resonances in the life of this 'nineteenth century scientific humanity' would be tone-deafness to historical complexity.[56]

If anthropology can be used to throw light on the character of Kurtz, Stocking implies here that Conrad's novella can also illuminate historical anthropology.

Kubary provides another example of the fine line between ethnographic truth and fiction, a cultural exile in New Guinea who again attained a Kurtz-like position. Stocking quotes from his diaries:

My relations with the natives have remained unchanged. . . . The advantages which I once won from them I have maintained, an my personal safety is not endangered, even in if the ship should delay in arriving for a long time. My stay is not precisely comfortable, according to our ideas, for no one would want to live alone in the midst of these savages, whose good behavior was achieved only after long struggles. The bond that unites me to the natives is fear and the feeling of their own weakness (. . .) They had become insolent by virtue of the murder of Cheyne, and perhaps also because of their treatment by greedy white speculators.[57]

Again, using Kurtz as a model, Stocking writes, 'It is said that during his New Guinea years Kubary boasted he was the "Lord God of Astrolabe Bay" (. . .) Recalling his youthful period of moral breakdown and political duplicity—and the moral schizophrenia endemic in so many colonial situations—it is not surprising that he should eventually descend into a Kurtzian darkness unrelieved by utopian visions, or that, having witnessed there "the horror," he might in the end have taken his own life'.[58]

The anthropologist, though clearly in a different manner than Kurtz, negotiates the tenuous divide between genuine participation and observation, both of which must be maintained in a complex balance. The anthropologist who loses observational skill also loses

[56] Ibid. 223, 231–2.   [57] Quoted in 'Ethnographer's Magic', 236.
[58] Ibid. 239.

the ability to communicate in a meaningful way his or her experience to others. Conversely, the anthropologist who fails to be a participant lacks the insight necessary to empathically reconstruct the other culture. The anthropologist must avoid becoming a cultural dupe or a cultural convert. One of the principal goals of anthropology, the empathic reconstruction of what is referred to as the 'native's point of view', presupposes a temporary suspension of the anthropologist's own conceptual framework—the ability to 'get inside the mind' of a person from another culture. As Malinowski expresses this desire: 'What interests me really in the study of the native is his outlook on things, his *Weltanschauung*, the breath of life and reality which he breathes and by which he breathes.'[59]

The school of anthropology founded by Malinowski aims at 'seeing life and the world from various angles, peculiar to each culture, (. . .) real desire to penetrate other cultures, to understand other types of life'.[60] D. H. Lawrence, who struggled intensely with this problem in his own works, wrote of Crevecoeur in his *Studies in Classic American Literature*: 'He wanted, of course, to imagine the savage way of life, to get it all off pat in his head. He wanted to know as the Indians and savages know, darkly, and in terms of otherness (. . .) He wanted to know that other state, the dark savage mind. He wanted both.'[61] Lawrence here sums up some of the objections to the anthropological paradox: 'He wanted both.' Clearly, Lawrence's comment here can be read as semi-autobiographical, for he, too, wanted to reconstruct in his work the 'native point of view'. For example, Lawrence's friend Earl Brewster wrote of their travels in Mexico that 'Lawrence talked much of the difficulty of entering into the thoughts of another race'.[62] Although Conrad never indulged in the same desire for anthropological knowledge as did Lawrence, both writers shared some of the same concerns and difficulties regarding cross-cultural contacts. Clearly, Lawrence displayed more bravado in his belief in his capacity to bridge conceptual gaps. In the essay 'Au Revoir,

[59] Malinowski, *Argonauts*, 517.   [60] Ibid.

[61] Lawrence, *Studies in Classic American Literature*, 15–16.

[62] Earl Brewster, *D. H. Lawrence: Reminiscences* (London: Heinemann, 1934), 9. This problem of bridging apparent conceptual gaps has probably been a feature of anthropology since its inception. Henry Drummond wrote: 'I often wished I could get inside an African for an afternoon, and just see how he looked at things (. . .).' Drummond, *Tropical Africa*, 57.

U. S. A.' (1923), he disdains the old image of the armchair anthropologist such as Tylor or Frazer: 'The anthropologists may make
what they like of myths. But come here and you'll see the gods
bit.'[63] At the same time, Lawrence admits in this essay that he is not
an ethnologist, and often berates his inability to understand 'primitives' during his travels.

While other later writers such as Lawrence adopted appro-
priative views of primitive cultures, Conrad, like his Marlow,
maintained a respectful distance. This distance undoubtedly arose
in part from fear and misunderstanding, the fear of becoming
subsumed and lost in the experience of a savage culture. Not
only does Marlow refuse to go ashore for a 'howl and a
dance', he stoutly refuses to abandon the safe confines of the ship
for Kurtz's perverse version of cultural immersion, or what the
Victorians would call 'going native'. It is important to draw a
distinction between Kurtz and Marlow. Only Kurtz, the atavist,
has any claim to really 'knowing' the primitive culture. This
distinction between participation and observation is clearly evoked
when Marlow asks Kurtz if he comprehends the actions of the
Africans upon the steamboat's departure. 'Do you understand
this?', Marlow asks. Kurtz's reply, 'Do I not?' (HD 66), places
him in the role of ethnological participant, one initiated into the
tribe itself, while Marlow clearly stands on the outside.[64] The
language in which Marlow describes Kurtz's cultural assimilation is
the language of abandonment and surrender. Similarly, though I
would not press the analogy too far, Van Maanen writes: 'In much
confessional writing, a sort of tentative "surrender" is used by the

[63] D. H. Lawrence, 'Au Revoir, U. S. A.' in Edward McDonald (ed.), *Phoenix: The Posthumous Papers of D. H. Lawrence* (1931) (Reprinted London: Heinemann, 1961), 105.

[64] Clearly, Kurtz's atavism, in my view, his success in becoming a 'cultural insider', is not praiseworthy, as has been suggested by critics from K. K. Ruthven some time ago to Peter Glassman more recently. K. K. Ruthven reads the novella as a covert argument for 'primitivism'. See K. K. Ruthven, 'The Savage God: Conrad and Lawrence' in *Critical Quarterly* 10 (1968), 39–54. Peter Glassman argues that Kurtz's failing is in not going far enough in his role as a participant in the primitive culture. See Glassman, 229. In the face of these arguments, Juliet McLauchlan's answer seems persuasive: 'The fact is that Kurtz has gone quite outside the human. He has descended below the savage in specific ways yet to be discussed—which must be discussed, since Marlow has recently been rebuked for "opposing" Kurtz instead of "joining" him in his attempt to return to the wilderness. It is a recurring critical view that Kurtz is not degraded at all.' Juliet McLauchlan, 'The Value and Signifi-cance of *Heart of Darkness*' (1983) (Reprinted HD 385).

fieldworker as a temporary resolution to the daily problems of fieldwork.'[65]

In sharp contrast to Kurtz, Marlow maintains a distance from Africa. After hearing Kurtz's disturbing answer, Marlow asks for no further explanation from him. Marlow's response to this incident is literally to grasp onto the reality of the steamboat: 'I pulled the string of the whistle (. . .)' (*HD* 66). Nevertheless, Marlow is not merely the callous foreigner, blundering through the African landscape. If not culturally relativistic, he at least approaches this state: Benita Parry writes, perhaps not entirely seriously, of the 'much-travelled and worldly Marlow, who shows himself to be a convinced cultural-relativist'.[66] She speaks of 'Marlow's academic tolerance of savagery'.[67] Certainly, he is characterized by a desire for interpretive knowledge which parallels anthropological queries: 'Was it a badge—an ornament—a charm—a propitiatory act?' (*HD* 20). This desire is limited, though. At other times he simply abjures these ethnological interpretations: 'I do not want to know anything of the ceremonies used when approaching Mr. Kurtz' (*HD* 58).

Of course, it is not to be inferred from this anthropological analogy that Kurtz is the prototype of a nascent anthropological fieldworker. However, Kurtz's brutality is one of the anxieties that surrounded the whole notion of fieldwork from the start. Many Victorians worried that such close contact with primitive peoples would have degenerative effects on the European in such close contact with the native. The fear of 'going native' arose from these cultural anxieties.[68] Moreover, Kurtz's actions represent a sardonic pastiche of cultural and ethical relativism, an abandonment of any pretensions to morality. The American philosopher Richard J. Bernstein highlights the anthropological dilemma I have been sketching:

One task of the anthropologist who engages in field work is to try to understand alien, or what are sometimes called 'primitive,' societies, and in doing this he or she must both do justice to the phenomenon being studied and make claims that are intelligible and illuminating to those who have not had direct experience with the societies that are studied. The history of

---

[65] Van Maanen, 77.   [66] Parry, 30.
[67] Ibid.
[68] Examples from anthropology abound. See Wengle, 33, 42. Peacock writes: 'The lore is full of anthropologists who went native (. . .) Perhaps every fieldworker who has become absorbed in the life of a foreign group has felt the tug to go native.' Peacock, 57.

anthropology provides plenty of evidence for the two temptations that we mentioned as problems in understanding alien phenomena: the temptation to impose, read into, or project categories and moral standards that are well entrenched in our own society onto what is being studied, and the dialectical antithesis of this—the temptation to go native, to suppose that we only understand the Azande, Nuer or Balinese when we think, feel, and act like them.[69]

The first temptation (the attempt to impose a pattern on and bring our own moral judgements to bear on the indigenous culture) characterizes much of Victorian anthropology; the second reveals the problem of anthropological field work as well as illustrating the Victorian fear of 'going native'. The first temptation, to draw a rather bald analogy, is the danger faced by Marlow, the second that by Kurtz.[70]

[69] Richard J. Bernstein, *Beyond Objectivism and Relativism: Science, Hermeneutics and Praxis* (Oxford: Blackwell, 1983), 93–4.

[70] Parry rightly says that 'what the fiction validates is Marlow's conviction that the choice before a stranger exposed to an alien world lies between a rigorous adherence to ethnic identity, which carries the freight of remaining ignorant of the foreign, or embracing the unknown'. Parry, 34. I would add that this is almost the prototypical problem of Victorian and even modern anthropology. Peacock writes of this apparent paradox: 'Objectivity is impossible, subjectivity is undesirable, if one's end is understanding humanity in general rather than simply oneself. (. . .) The trick is to grasp the other while seeing oneself (or one's culture) sharply in terms of the other. The danger is that one will see too much or too little of oneself in the other—excesses of subjectivity or objectivity.' Peacock, 87.

3

'Pioneers of Trade and Progress':
Conrad's Civilization and
its Discontents

'In a hundred years, there will be perhaps a town here. Quays, and warehouses, and barracks, and—and—billiard rooms. Civilization, my boy, and virtue—and all.'

(OP 95)

To the man from outside, whatever his political or religious faith, Africa can often seem to be in a state of becoming.[1]

Degeneration: Europe and the People without History

In a frequent cultural stereotype of the Victorian era, Africa is often perceived as a static and, perhaps above all, degenerate culture, utterly lacking in civilization. Degeneration is the word on which I would like to focus, for it is the notion of debasement that was refracted in later literature. The ideas of 'going native', of colonists becoming 'decivilized', were predicated on stereotypes of African cultures themselves as inherently debased. The foundation for degeneration applied to African cultures was laid in the late eighteenth and early nineteenth century by nascent ethnology and anthropology.[2] For example, George Cuviers (1769–1832), a prominent Swiss physical anthropologist who largely founded palaeontology and geology in France, referred to Africans as 'the most degraded of human races, whose form approaches that of the beast and whose intelligence is nowhere great enough to arrive at

---

[1] V. S. Naipaul, *Finding the Center: Two Narratives* (New York: Knopf, 1984), 78.

[2] Throughout this section I am indebted to Daniel Pick's study of the history of degenerationism. See Pick.

regular government'.[3] The degenerate nature of Africa and Africans could be both overtly and covertly connected with colonialism in a complex tautology. The degeneration of the 'primitive' provided, after all, a perfect excuse for the rehabilitating influence of Europe. Thus, the perceived incapacity for self-government, following out this circular argument, necessitated foreign domination, a justification upon which King Leopold II depended. By the same token, the ability of Europeans to rule was founded upon their resistance to degeneration.

This theme of imperialism predicated upon degeneration surfaces even in ostensibly aesthetic writing of the Victorian period. As Ruskin remarked at the beginning of his Slade Lectures at Oxford in 1870: 'There is a destiny now possible to us—the highest ever set before a nation to be accepted or refused. We are still *undegenerate in race*; a race mingled of the best northern blood. We are not yet dissolute in temper, but still have the firmness to govern, and the grace to obey.'[4] The sword of culture and imperialism which Ruskin invokes here is decidedly two-edged, for if the ability to rule is based on the freedom from degeneracy, then any sign of degeneration must be seen as necessarily disqualifying Britain from rule. Ruskin's imperial imperative is based on purity, the idea of an England 'polluted by no unholy clouds', which can be counted on to 'guide the human arts, and gather the divine knowledge, of distant nations, transformed from savageness to manhood, and redeemed from despairing into peace'.[5] According to this notion of English regeneration, the degenerate 'primitives' can be saved. As we will see, though, not all of Ruskin's Victorian contemporaries accepted the notion that the English were 'undegenerate'. Indeed, the opposite is true: England was often portrayed as already infected by degeneracy. However racist theories such as Ruskin's were, though, they were not *always* tied to an explicit political platform. Cuvier's opinions on African degeneration pre-dated imperialism in Africa by many decades, though these theories may have helped to lay the groundwork for imperialism.

[3] Quoted in Stephen Jay Gould, *The Mismeasure of Man* (London: Pelican, 1984), 36.
[4] John Ruskin, 'Inaugural Lecture' (1870) in *The Works of John Ruskin*, XX, T. Cook and Alexander Weddenburn (eds.) (London: George Allen, 1905), 41–3. Quoted in Said, *Culture and Imperialism*, 103–4.
[5] Quoted in Said, *Culture and Imperialism*, 104.

One of the principle reasons for this misconception that labelled Africa as degenerate lay in the belief that the lack of any written manuscripts on African history implied a history-less past. Leo Frobenius wrote in 1913, fourteen years after the publication of *Heart of Darkness*:

Light in Africa? In that portion of the globe to which the stalwart Anglo-Saxon, Stanley, gave the name of 'dark' and 'darkest.' Light upon the peoples of that Continent whose children we are accustomed to regard as types of natural servility, with *no recorded history; mere products of the moment*? (. . .) where all power is said to degenerate into the reign of brute-force alone (. . .) I have spent many an hour in gloom there. But I failed to find it governed by the 'insensible fetish.' I failed to find power expressed in degenerate bestiality alone.[6]

Here, Frobenius elides the two principal issues I am discussing; degeneracy and the lack of history are somehow equivalent. Degeneracy, in fact, is predicated on a historical blankness.[7] Africans were perceived, as the anthropologist Theodor Waitz put it, as 'those who have no history'.[8] Historians of anthropology such as Johannes Fabian and Talal Assad have recently re-examined this theme of the 'historylessness' of the African past as a European imposition of blankness onto Africa in order to ease conquest.[9] Indeed, Said criticizes Conrad for acknowledging the darker ironies of imperialism without being able to attribute to other cultures a sense of hegemony: 'It is no paradox, therefore, that Conrad was both imperialist and anti-imperialist, progressive when it came to rendering fearlessly and pessimistically the self-confirming,

---

[6] Frobenius, *Voice of Africa*, i, pp. xii–iv, italics mine.
[7] See Christopher Miller, *Blank Darkness: Africanist Discourse in French* (Chicago: University of Chicago Press, 1985).
[8] Waitz, i. 9. Chinua Achebe introduced this topic at the beginning of his well-known essay on Conrad: 'For did not that erudite British historian and Regius Professor at Oxford also pronounce that African history did not exist?'. Achebe, 251.
[9] See Johannes Fabian, *Time and the Other: How Anthropology Makes Its Object* (New York: Columbia University Press, 1983) and Talal Assad (ed.), *Anthropology and the Colonial Encounter* (London: Ithaca Press, 1975). Said criticizes the 'tendency in anthropology, history, and cultural studies in Europe and the United States (. . .) to treat the whole of world history as viewable by a kind of Western super-subject, whose historicizing and disciplinary rigor either takes away or, in the post-colonial period, restores history to peoples and cultures "without history"'. Said, *Culture and Imperialism*, 35. See also Eric Wolf, to whom Said seems to be implicitly referring, *Europe and the People without History* (Berkeley: University of California Press, 1982). The title of this section is borrowed from Wolf.

self-deluding corruption of overseas domination, deeply reactionary when it came to conceding that Africa or South America
could ever have an independent history or culture, which the imperialists violently disturbed but by which they were ultimately
defeated.'[10]

Conrad largely accepted the Victorian notion that primitive
peoples lacked a 'history' in the sense of a record of substantive
cultural changes over time. Marlow remarks of Dain Warris in
Lord Jim: 'Such beings open up to the Western Eye, so often
compared with mere surfaces, the hidden possibilities of races and
lands over which hangs the mystery of unrecorded ages' (*LJ* 262).
The word 'unrecorded' here almost appears synonymous with non-
existent. The primitive culture is one of the 'lost, forgotten, unknown places of the earth' (*LJ* 323). The culture is lost because it
is outside the mainstream of Western history; the culture is unknown because it is unimportant to the West. Marlow describes
Patusan in similar terms:

'I don't suppose any of you had ever heard of Patusan?' Marlow resumed
(. . .) 'It does not matter; there's many a heavenly body in the lot crowding
upon us that of a night that mankind had never heard of, it being of now
earthly importance to anybody but to the astronomers who are paid to talk
learnedly about its conduct, the aberrations of its light—a sort of scientific
scandal-mongering. Thus with Patusan'.   (*LJ* 218)

Primitive places such as Patusan, Marlow suggests with a degree of
irony, are of interest only to scientists, colonial administrators, or
business-people. Such images abounded in the Victorian era. For
example, Conrad's contemporary, Hugh Clifford, wrote of the
degeneracy and lack of history of the Malaysians: 'A race (. . .)
who, never since time began, have had their day or played a part
in human history.'[11] The marginalization of so-called primitive
peoples here is representative of a common current in Victorian
thought. Primitives are out of time. In other words, the past which
is not written down disappears; and, for this reason, so-called
primitive cultures can be seen paradoxically as both the 'old mankind' (*LJ* 226)—trapped in the remote past—and child-like and
young. The depiction of Africa as static recalls Hegel's argument in
Lectures on the Philosophy of World History:

[10] Said, *Culture and Imperialism*, p. xviii.
[11] Hugh Clifford, *In Court and Kampong* (London: Grant Richards, 1897), 176.

It (Africa) has no historical interest of its own, for we find its inhabitants living in barbarism and savagery in a land which has not furnished them with any integral ingredient of culture. From the earliest recorded times, Africa has remained cut off from all contacts with the rest of the world; it is the land of gold, for ever pressing in upon itself, and the land of childhood, removed from the light of self-conscious history and wrapped in the dark mantle of night.[12]

Hegel's depiction of Africa as childlike and lacking in 'culture' provide the paradigm for much of the writing on Africa that was to follow.

Only gradually would Europeans begin to break down this conflation of 'written history' and 'culture', and to recognize that the absence of the former did not mean the absence of the latter. In the case of Africa and many other so-called primitive cultures, it would take the rediscovery of monuments, art works, and artifacts in Benin and other places before Europeans would begin to credit so-called primitive peoples with long and complex histories of their own. It is in this context that we must read the well-known passage in Conrad's *Heart of Darkness*: 'We could not understand because we were too far and could not remember because we were travelling in the night of the first ages, of those ages that are gone, *leaving hardly a sign—and no memories*' (quoted above, italics mine). This passage works on two levels. The signs and memories that are absent represent the pre-history of man, which remained for the Victorians a subject of much speculation. There are no signs or memories of these cultures because, in essence, there is no written history of them. On another level, however, Conrad and his contemporaries did not view this remote primitive past as utterly lost; in a common anthropological formulation this primitive past remained uncomfortably close to the surface even in 'civilized' cultures, its vestigial forms extant in Europe.

Law of Evolution and Laws of Progress

By 1898, the year in which Conrad began *Heart of Darkness*, ideas of decline and atavism in both individuals and civilization at large had become an irrevocable part of Victorian culture, taking their

[12] Georg William Friedrich Hegel, *Lectures on the Philosophy of World History* (1822–30) (Reprinted Cambridge: Cambridge University Press, 1980), 174.

place beside images of progress. Contrary to the impression of the Victorian era as confident and melioristic, the exploration of other cultures such as Africa mirrored back to the Victorians disturbing images of recidivism that sometimes shook their faith in the very idea of progress. One of the battlegrounds for those who confidently argued for cultural progress and those who feared regress was anthropology. The anthropological battle was waged between degenerationists (or degradationists), who argued that 'primitive' people such as Africans represented a regression from a previous state of civilization, and the progressionists (or developmentalists), who argued for the steady advancement from primitive to civilized. The progressionists, E. B. Tylor, John Lubbock, J. F. McLennan, and Henry Maine in Britain, and Lewis Morgan in the United States, may be seen as representative of a linear model of cultural evolution that developed in the 1860s. In the view of the progressionists, all cultures could move along the line of development which eventually led to civilization. Degenerationists argued, on the contrary, that 'savages' were originally blessed with civilization, but somehow fell into a state of barbarism.

The leading advocate of the degenerationist model of culture was Richard Whatley (1785–1863), archbishop of Dublin, whose pamphlet on 'The Origin of Civilisation' (1854) was widely circulated.[13] In this pamphlet, Whatley restated views presented in *Introductory Lectures on Political Economy* (1831) that 'civilized Man has not emerged from the savage state;—that the progress of any community in civilization, by its own internal means, must have always begun from a condition removed from that of complete barbarism; out of which it does not appear that men ever did or can raise themselves'.[14] In other words, Whatley allowed little or no hope for 'primitive' cultures to develop. Using evidence from anthropology that seemed to suggest that primitive people had remained in a relatively static condition, and had perhaps even degenerated, Whatley concluded that civilization was the natural condition of humanity, and barbarism secondary. W. Cooke Taylor, a disciple of Whatley's, advanced the theory that Whatley had rehearsed,

[13] Richard Whatley, 'The Origin of Civilisation' (1854) in *Lectures Delivered Before the Young Men's Christian Association from November 1854 to February 1855* (Reprinted London: Nisbet, 1879). Cf. Herbert, 61–2.
[14] Whatley, *Introductory Lectures on Political Economy* (London: B. Fellowes, 1831), 119.

applying it to society in an explicitly anthropological manner. Taylor argued that civilization represented the natural state of man—the state which God intended for him, and the condition in which could realize his potential. He argued that 'civilization is natural to man'.[15] Taylor harnessed his theories to a teleological view of human advancement, arguing that Europe represented the realization of God's plan for man's advance. Primitive peoples, on the other hand, represented a degenerate culture which could only be revived through the aid of Europe. Unlike Whatley, though, Taylor argued for the potential even of primitive peoples to attain a higher level of civilization: 'the idea of progress, development, amelioration, or extension' could be applied to primitives as well as to more 'advanced' societies.[16] Nevertheless, despite Taylor's nod to primitive peoples' ameliorative capacity, degenerationist theory often squared with imperialist agendas. In typically Victorian rhetoric, Taylor argued that 'civilization is progress', while 'barbarism is stationary'.[17] This degenerationist theory was refuted by anthropologists such as E. B. Tylor, who posited almost a universal and innate improvability in man.

The degenerationists, though largely deplored by mainstream anthropology, nevertheless represented a strong undertow in European culture, which threatened the firm footing of progressionist theory. John Lubbock, an anthropological ally of Tylor's as well as a prominent Victorian archaeologist, summarized the views of both schools in his *Origin of Civilisation* (1876):

Many writers have considered that man was at first a mere savage, and the course of history has on the whole been a progress towards civilisation, though at times—and at times for centuries—some races have been stationary, or even retrograded. Other authors, of no less eminence, have taken a diametrically opposite view. According to them, man was, from the commencement, pretty much as he is at present (. . .) Savages they consider to be the degenerate descendants of far superior ancestors.[18]

Even Lubbock here, though fundamentally a developmentalist, was forced to make a bow to the 'eminence' of his adversaries. In an earlier work, *Pre-Historic Times*, Lubbock had also suggested the

---

[15] W. Cooke Taylor, *The Natural History of Society in the Barbarous and Civilized State: An Essay Towards Discovering the Origin and Course of Human Improvement*, 2 vols. (London: Longman, 1840), i. 19.
[16] Taylor, i. 5.   [17] Ibid.
[18] John Lubbock, *Origin of Civilisation* (London: Longman, 1876), 369.

prominence of the degenerationist position, though he argued against it. He wrote:

It is a common opinion that savages are, as a general rule, only the miserable remnants of natives once more civilised; but, although there are some well-established cases of national decay, there is no scientific evidence which would justify us in asserting that this is generally the case. No doubt there are many instances in which nations, once progressive, have not only ceased to advance in civilization, but have even fallen back. Still (. . .) we shall find no evidence of any general degradation (. . .) In some savage tribes we even find traces of improvement.[19]

While this debate over degeneration and progression of cultures may seem to be far removed from Conrad's work, his early novels trace a similar pattern of advance and decline, both in individuals and cultures.[20] To the Victorians, such patterns of advance and decline seemed natural; they recognized progression and regression but rarely stasis as possibilities.

Although in *Primitive Culture* (1871) Tylor allows some scope for the possibility of degeneration, he asserts with confidence that 'notwithstanding the continual interference of degeneration, the main tendency of culture from primeval up to modern times has been from savagery to civilization'.[21] Tylor allowed that 'Progress, degradation, survival, revival, modification, are all modes of the connexion that bind together the complex work of civilization'.[22] Progressionist anthropologists like Tylor believed that human cultural development followed a general law. Primitive peoples, representing the lowest rung on the cultural ladder, merely enjoyed a slower, and sometimes imperceptible, development in relation to the European civilization that occupied the highest rung. This teleological paradigm comprised three stages, savagery, barbarism, and civilization that formed a 'natural as well as a necessary sequence of progress'.[23] As John McLennan stated this idea: 'The

[19] John Lubbock, *Pre-Historic Times* (London: Williams and Norgate, 1865), 337.
[20] This theme is noted several times in O'Hanlon's study of Conrad and Darwinism. Redmond O'Harlon, *Joseph Conrad and Charles Darwin: The Influence of Scientific thought on Conrad's Fiction* (Edinburgh, Salamander Press, 1984), *passim*. See also R. B. Kershner, 'Degeneration: The Explanatory Nightmare', *Georgia Review* 40 (1986), 416–44, and Brian W. Shaffer, *The Blinding Torch: Modern British Fiction and the Discourse of Civilization* (Amherst, Mass: University of Massachusetts Press, 1993), 22–4.
[21] Tylor, *Primitive Culture*, i. 19.   [22] Tylor, *Primitive Culture*, i. 16.
[23] Lewis Henry Morgan, *Ancient Society* (London: Macmillan, 1877), 11.

history of human society is that of a development following very closely one general law, and that the variety of forms of life—of domestic and civil institutions—is ascribable to the unequal development of the different sections of mankind.'[24] *Primitive Culture, The Origin of Civilisation, Ancient Society*, and other contemporary anthropological works, set out to define this natural law. Although often the evidence subverted the idea of such universal rules, anthropologists largely kept faith simply by the confident assertion that such laws were in operation, even if they could not always be proven.

Tylor's friend, Sir John Lubbock, posed the quintessential progressionist question in *The Origin of Civilisation*: 'Is there a definite assured law of progress in human affairs—a slow gradual ascent from the lower to the higher (. . .) or was primeval man a superior being who has retrograded and degenerated into the savage state?'[25] This question proved to be a crucial one which many anthropologists in the Victorian era felt obliged to answer. Recognizing the importance of this debate over social evolution—man's slow gradual ascent—not only from a scientific but a social perspective as well, Lubbock argued that 'to know the fundamental law of movement in humanity is the prerequisite of all wise and successful measures of social amelioration'.[26] The knowledge of the progressive or regressive tendency of mankind would be necessary, he implied, for any sort of social planning, or prediction of future progress. Such knowledge could also be useful for colonial administration. Lubbock addresses the colonial theme explicitly in another passage. The justification for the science of anthropology lies, in part, in the service it can provide to colonial administration. He hopes that his study may 'contribute something towards the progress of a science which is in itself of the deepest interest, and which has a peculiar importance to an Empire such as ours, comprising races in every stage of civilisation yet obtained by man'.[27]

Conrad might have been familiar with the debate over degeneration through his reading. For example, Gertrude L. Jacob's book on James Brooke, *The Raja of Sarawak* (1876), makes clear reference to Malaysia as a degenerate culture. Degeneracy furnished the ostensible motive for Brooke's expedition to Borneo. In a passage

---

[24] J. F. McLennan, *Studies in Ancient History* (1876) (Reprinted London; Macmillan, 1886), 14–15.
[25] Lubbock, *Origin of Civilisation*, p. iv.   [26] Ibid.   [27] Ibid., p. viii.

very reminiscent of Leopold's justifications for conquest of the Congo, Brooke writes:

It is not my object to enter into any details of the history of the Malayan nations, but I may refer to the undoubted fact that they have been in a state of deterioration since we first became acquainted with them; and the records of our early voyagers, together with the remains of antiquities still visible in Java and Sumatra, prove that once flourishing nations have now ceased to exist, and countries once teeming with human life are now tenantless and deserted. The causes of such lamentable changes need only be alluded to, but it is fit to remark that whilst the clamour about education is loud, and extravagant dreams are entertained of the progressive advance-ment of the human race—a large tract of the globe has been gradually relapsing, and allowed to relapse, into barbarism.[28]

Along with many of his contemporaries, Conrad seems to have been seduced by Brooke's vision of a more beneficent colonialism that aimed to reverse the 'deterioration' of indigenous peoples. Indeed, on one level, Brooke's ostensible aim was ethnographic; he wished to 'retrace the customs which once obtained . . . long ban-ished from this country . . . the best of which I wish to restore'.[29] As Conrad writes in *The Rescue* of Lingard's precursor (Brooke): 'Almost in our own day we have seen one of them—a true adven-turer in his devotion to his impulse—a man of high mind and of pure heart, lay the foundations of a flourishing state on the ideas of pity and justice' (*R* 3–4). However, the reality of imperialist ven-tures, particularly in Africa, undermined such apparently altruistic sentiments.

One of the principal criteria that anthropologists could fall back on in measuring the likelihood and speed of development of various cultures was a decisively Victorian one—Carlylian notions of re-straint, work, and discipline.[30] All cultures, many Victorian anthro-pologists argued, possessed the potential for development, but the failure to develop could often be explained by a lack of effort or a lack of restraint. Societal development did not follow a Darwinian evolutionary course—that is, one that was inherently accidental and fortuitous—but, on the contrary, a Lamarckian model of con-scious will.[31] As Arthur Mitchell wrote: 'It is universally admitted

---

[28] Jacob, i. 70–1.   [29] Cf. White, 27.

[30] For example, Arthur Mitchell writes that 'Progress implies action or work on the part of all who really share in it'. Mitchell, 56.

[31] See Kuper, 2–3.

that a nation may pass out of a state of savagery—in other words out of a lower culture and civilisation, into a high state of civilisation. We ourselves furnish an illustration. Less than two thousand years ago we were barbarians, and now we boast that nowhere in the world is there a civilisation more advanced than ours. Is it possible that we should ever lose it. Is civilisation a thing which is maintained by an effort, as it was acquired by an effort?'[32]

This discussion of Carlyle brings us to an important point in our examination of the relationship between anthropological ideas and *Heart of Darkness*. Although Carlyle has been pointed to as a model for Conrad's ethical system, this parallel to Carlyle has not been related to the intellectual concerns of anthropology regarding cultural development. Consider an encapsulated version of Conrad's view of the development of primitive cultures: 'We were wanderers on a prehistoric earth, on an earth that wore the aspect of an unknown planet. We could have fancied ourselves the first of men taking possession of an accursed inheritance, to be subdued at the cost of profound anguish and of excessive toil' (*HD* 37). The 'accursed inheritance', of course, has Biblical models in the punishment Adam must endure by working the land. The acquisition of civilization and the rise from a 'prehistoric' state is a difficult task, requiring 'profound anguish' and 'excessive toil'. Elsewhere, in an analogous passage, Conrad quotes Leonardo da Vinci: 'Work is the law. Like iron that lying idle degenerates into a mass of useless rust (. . .) so without action the sprit of man turns to a dead thing, loses its force, ceases prompting us to leave some trace of ourselves on this earth' (*NL*, 194–5).

Thomas Huxley added another element to the Victorian developmental pattern: not only restraint, work, and discipline, but cooperation and altruism were necessary concomitants to the development of society. Using the analogy of a colony, Huxley wrote that if the 'work of the colonists be carried out energetically' the result would be a gradual ascent in civilization. On the other hand, 'if they are slothful, stupid or careless; or if waste their energies in contest with one another, the chances are that the state of nature will have the best of it'.[33] These themes of work, discipline and restraint as natural corollaries to progress must be familiar to

[32] Mitchell, 214.
[33] T. H. Huxley, *Evolution and Ethics*, ix of *The Collected Essays*, 9 vols. (London: Macmillan, 1894), 43.

any reader of Conrad. For the Victorians, this common theme could be a justification for the imperial project, as Conrad was probably aware. An article on Kipling, for example, in *Blackwood's* quoted him on this issue: 'Law, Order, Duty, and Restraint, Obedience, Discipline!—these are the foundations of a prosperous state.'[34] Kipling epitomizes a common theme in the Victorian era, which is also present in Stanley's *The Congo and the Founding of Its Free State*, a work Conrad might have known: 'There is a law of Nature which has decreed that a man must work.'[35] Indeed, the subtitle of Stanley's book has a Carlylian ring: 'A Story of Work and Exploration'. Of course, such a theme could be used to justify the imperial project. Leopold enjoined his agents that 'They must accustom the population to general laws, of which the most salutary is assuredly that of work'.[36] Even Conrad's comment, which has been seized upon by critics who try to portray him as a proto-imperialist, partakes of this theme: 'The criminality of inefficiency and pure selfishness when tackling the civilizing work in Africa is a justifiable idea.'[37]

The 'Dust-Bin of Progress'

These two apparently irreconcilable models of human development—indeed, of human nature—progressive and degenerative, are worked out in *Heart of Darkness*, though in the novel these themes are situated within an internal debate. Conrad was never as optimistic about the progression of culture as many developmentalist anthropologists such as Tylor and Lubbock; thus, his narrative in *Heart of Darkness* is dialogic.[38] Rather than ideologically evasive, as Terry Eagleton has called the text, Conrad's novella responds to and subverts many of the common assumptions of his time regarding the ascendancy of European civilization.[39] In *Heart of Dark-*

[34] 'The Works of Mr. Kipling', *Blackwood's*, vol. 164/897 (October 1898), 285.
[35] Stanley, *Congo and Free State*, p. xiv.
[36] Appendix I, 'Letter from the King of the Belgians' in Guy Burrows, *The Land of the Pigmies* (London: Arthur Pearson, 1898), 482.
[37] *Collected Letters of Conrad*, ii. 139–40.
[38] See Michael M. Bakhtin, *The Dialogic Imagination* (Austin: University of Texas Press, 1981). Cf. White, 177.
[39] See Terry Eagleton, *Criticism and Ideology* (London: NLB, Humanities Press, 1976), 136.

ness, Marlow openly ridicules the way in which the word progress, so crucial to anthropologists such as Tylor and Lubbock, has become subsumed in imperialist rhetoric. He speaks of the 'dust-bin of progress, amongst all the sweepings and, figuratively speaking, all the dead cats of civilization' (*HD* 51).[40]

A popular work of the time, Henry Drummond's optimistic study of cultural and ethical evolution was entitled *The Ascent of Man* (1891). Drummond probably gives his title this melioristic tone in direct contrast to Darwin's *Descent of Man*. Both of these works were well-known in the Victorian period. Underlying both these texts, I would argue, is a deeply felt anxiety regarding 're-barbarization'. Although many Victorians preferred the implied optimism of Drummond's title, others undoubtedly associated Darwin's *Descent* with degeneration. When Marlow speaks of Kurtz's 'ascendency' with great irony, then, it is perhaps not exaggerated to imagine that Conrad may have had these works in mind: 'His ascendancy was extraordinary. The camps of these people surrounded the place and the chiefs came every day to see him. They would crawl . . .' (*HD* 58). Paradoxically, ascent is here associated with a moral descent; Kurtz's 'progress' among the natives marks a regression. The ascendancy of humanity had become by this point in Victorian culture a catch-phrase, a cliché that had lost much of its integrity with the onslaught of scientific theories suggesting humanity's humble origins in some ape-like progenitor. Ascendancy, the rise toward a higher moral or material culture, was clearly a tenuous movement. Consider a comment of H. G. Wells, Conrad's friend and correspondent, in his essay 'On Extinction' (1893): 'Even now, for all we can tell, the terror may be crouching for its spring and the fall of humanity at hand. In the case of every other predominant animal the world has ever seen, we repeat, the hour of its complete ascendancy has been the beginning of its decline.'[41] Conrad may well have discussed this theme with Wells. In any case, the idea was widely disseminated in the sort of popular scientific and literary journals for which Wells wrote. The cultural irony in Wells's formulation is that, as many Victorians would have believed, the apparent pinnacle of a species' advance often ironi-

[40] On the ironic connotations of 'civilization' in Conrad's early works see Jeffrey Meyers, *Fiction & the Colonial Experience* (Ipswich: The Boydell Press, 1973).
[41] H. G. Wells, 'The Extinction of Man', *Pall Mall Gazette*, 59 (25 September 1894), 3.

cally marked its descent. Thus, at a time when dinosaurs dominated the earth, argues Wells, they were already moving towards extinction.

Another parallel issue which must be considered here briefly is the way in which biological doctrines subverted notions of human progress.[42] As several critics have noted, Darwin's theory of evolution gave rise to a counter-argument of degeneration: 'in the less meticulous hands of Darwin's "brethren" his work eventually gave a very fine edge to the broader concept of degeneration. Inevitably so; for any layman of imagination could perceive that devolution was but the dark obverse reverse of a theory whose bright obverse was biologically endorsed progress'.[43] Indeed, the Victorians recognized progression or regression as corollaries; degeneration appeared to be one natural pattern for human development:

This specter of extinction or, as it is more appropriately termed, *degeneration*, despite Darwin's and other's progressivist assurances, loomed ever larger in the imagination of the late nineteenth century, blending with and lending scientific support to a historicist trope of decline and fall . . .[44]

H. G. Wells's argument in 'On Extinction' thus presented a grim rejoinder to some of the anthropological arguments regarding the progress of civilization. The anthropocentric fallacy was already under heavy attack in the decade in which Conrad wrote *Heart of Darkness*. As Wells wrote in 1891, subverting what he perceived to be the fallacious confidence of many of his contemporaries, 'There is, therefore, no guarantee in scientific knowledge of man's permanence or permanent ascendancy'.[45] Again, ascendancy here is a loaded word. The notion of the possible brevity of humanity's existence is also a secondary theme in the novella. Marlow imagines, for example, that the jungle observes the actions of man with complete objectivity: 'And outside, the silent wilderness surrounding this cleared speck on the earth struck me as something

[42] This issue of literature and theories of biological degeneration has been admirably examined in Peter Morton's *The Vital Science: Biology and the Literary Imagination* (London: George Allen & Unwin, 1984). See also Peter Allen Dale's informative study, *In Pursuit of a Scientific Culture: Science, Art, and Society in the Victorian Era* (Madison: University of Wisconsin Press, 1989), Tess Coslett's *The 'Scientific Movement' and Victorian Literature* (Sussex: The Harvester Press, 1982), and Chapple.
[43] Morton, 91.   [44] Dale, 225.
[45] Wells, H. G., 'On Extinction', *Chambers's Journal*, 10 (30 September 1893), 623, 623–4.

great and invincible, like evil or truth, waiting patiently for the passing away of this fantastic invasion' (*HD* 35). Marlow implies here the imminent and inevitable extinction of humanity in contrast to the relative permanence of this primeval forest.

If extinction is a pervasive theme in Wells's work, it is also a subtle subtext of *Heart of Darkness*. The ichthyosaurs that Marlow imagines splashing around in the river may be iconic of the extinction of species, a grim reminder that the ascendancy of species is, at best, only temporary. Again, Marlow holds up the pathetic quality of humanity's existence to ridicule: 'The great wall of vegetation, an exuberant and entangled mass of trunks, branches, leaves, boughs, festoons motionless in the moonlight, was like a rioting invasion of soundless life, a rolling wave of plants piled up, crested, ready to topple over the creek to sweep every little man of us out of his little existence. And it moved not. A deadened burst of mighty splashes and snorts reached us from afar as though an ichthyosaurs had been taking a bath of glitter in the river' (*HD* 32). Conrad subtly juxtaposes here Marlow's fear of nature's implacable disregard for human life ('to sweep every little man of us out of his little existence') with the ichthyosaurs, a species similarly disregarded by the forces of nature. As Wells bleakly remarked in 'On Extinction', 'The future is full of men to our preconceptions, whatever it may be in scientific truth'.[46] 'A Vision of the Past', one of Wells's earliest short stories, although almost certainly unknown to Conrad, similarly sets out a fable of extinction for the late Victorian period. A man dreams of walking in the countryside and encountering a dinosaur. The man informs the dinosaur of its own imminent demise; however, the central irony of the story, as in so much of Wells's writing, is the anthropocentric fallacy of which the man is iconic. If the fate of extinction, the young Wells implies, awaited these creatures, then the same fate could easily await man.[47]

The progress–regress, ascent–descent debates which underlay accounts of humanity's evolution worked themselves out in Conrad's novella in transmuted form. For example, Ian Watt calls Kurtz 'the supreme exhibit of the dialectic between progress and atavism', and adds that 'Kurtz is obviously intended as the climactic

[46] Wells, H.G., 623.
[47] 'A Vision of the Past', in Robert M. Philmus and David Y. Hughes (eds.), *H. G. Wells: Early Writings in Science and Science Fiction* (Berkeley: University of California Press, 1975), 153–7.

example of the inner void which Marlow has found in all the representations of Western progress'.[48] It is not always recognized that the word progress, like evolution could be a neutral term, implying merely movement, not teleology. The prominent zoologist E. Ray Lankester wrote in *Degeneration: A Chapter in Darwinism* (1880):

With regard to ourselves, the white races of Europe, the possibility of degeneration seems to be worth some consideration. In accordance with a tacit assumption of universal progress—an unreasoning optimism—we are accustomed to regard ourselves as necessarily progressing, as necessarily having arrived at a higher and more elaborated condition than that which our ancestors reached, and as destined to progress still further. On the other hand, it is well to remember that we are subject to the general laws of evolution, and *are as likely to degenerate as to progress* [italics mine].[49]

This observation regarding degeneration could not have been very reassuring to Conrad's contemporaries. Again, Henry Maudsley, a Victorian psychiatrist, whom I will discuss at some length in the eighth chapter, wrote: 'A decline from a higher to a lower level of being, a process, that is to say of degeneration, is an integral and active part of the economy of nature (. . .) A law of degeneration is manifest in human events; that each individual, each family, each nation may take either an upward course of evolution or a downward course of degeneracy.'[50]

Progress and Regress

Just as the word progress in science did not necessarily imply improvement, so in Conrad's works the concept of progress is deconstructed. In 'An Outpost of Progress', perhaps more than any other of Conrad's works, the word is tinged with heavy irony. At the end of the story, having murdered his companion over a teaspoonful of sugar, Kayerts hears the steamer's whistle:

[48] Watt, 233.
[49] E. Ray Lankester, *Degeneration: A Chapter in Darwinism* (London: Methuen, 1880), 59–60.
[50] Henry Maudsley, *Body and Will: Being an Essay Concerning Will in its Metaphysical, Physiological and Pathological Aspects* (London: Kegan, Paul, Trench, 1883), 237–8.

Progress was calling to Kayerts from the river, progress and civilization and all the virtues. Society was calling to its accomplished child to come, to be taken care of, to be instructed, to be judged, to be condemned; it called him to return to that rubbish heap from which he had wandered away, so that justice could be done.   (OP 116)

'Progress', 'civilization', and 'society' are all words that are tinged with irony in this passage. The story illustrates the internal disintegration of a culture that claims to be spreading progress abroad. Faced not with guilt over his savagery, but only with shame over its imminent discovery, Kayerts hangs himself. All of these examples point to Conrad's subversion of the notions of progress and civilization which were so prevalent in his period.

The very word 'progress' has a curious locus in Conrad's work; it is so often satirized that it quickly becomes devalued as a concept. For example, Marlow sees a map and remarks that 'There was a vast amount of red—good to see at any time, because one knows that some real work is done in there, a deuce of a lot of blue, a little green, smears of orange, and, on the East Coast a purple patch to show where the jolly pioneers of progress drink their jolly lager-beer' (HD 13). The phrase 'jolly pioneers of progress', and, in particular, the repetition in the next word, 'jolly', is dripping with irony. Just as in the title of 'An Outpost of Progress', the notion of cultural advancement is implicitly challenged. The only advancement which has occurred is in Europe's improved rhetoric. As Conrad was undoubtedly aware, 'progress' had become a mere cynical mask for plunder. When speaking of the death of his predecessor, Fresleven, Marlow says, 'What became of the hens I don't know either. I should think the cause of progress got them, anyhow' (HD 13). Marlow is aware of the cynical rhetoric through which the exploitation of the Congo was legitimized. His aunt has accepted the rhetoric in the press ('There had been a lot of such rot let loose in the press' HD 15): 'She talked about "weaning those ignorant millions from their horrid ways," till, upon my word, she made me quite uncomfortable. I ventured to hint that the Company was run for profit' (HD 16). The end of 'Outpost' makes the elision of progress and trade even more explicit. After Kayerts hangs himself the ironic symbol of civilization and progress appears: 'the Managing Director of the Great Civilizing Company (since we know that civilization follows trade)' (OP 116). The progress from primitivism to a presumed civilization thus conveniently corresponded to the progress of capitalism in the Congo. Conrad again suggests this irony through Marlow's references to the avaricious traders of the Eldorado company as 'pilgrims'.

The notion of 'progress' was constantly invoked to support both the material and moral 'mission' of the colonization of the Congo. When Leopold II initiated the 'International Association for the Suppression of Slavery', a name which undoubtedly inspired Kurtz's 'Society for the Suppression of Savage Customs', Leopold wrote, in the dominant imperialist rhetoric of the period: 'To open to civilization the only area which it has not yet penetrated, to pierce the gloom which hangs over entire races, constitutes, if I may dare to put it this way, a Crusade worthy of this century of progress.'[51] The conflation here of the notions of progress, religious fervour, and imperialism provides a highly ironic comment on Kurtz's mission in Africa. It is particularly ironic that Leopold should have suggested as an analogy the Crusades, a notoriously hypocritical and cynical historical venture. Another passage from one of Leopold's speeches highlights the progressionist/degenerationist debate even more clearly in relation to the Congo:

Our only programme (. . .) is the work of moral and material regeneration, and we must do this among a population whose degeneration in its inherited conditions it is difficult to measure.[52]

He hopes that the Belgians 'will soon introduce into the vast region of the Congo all the blessings of Christian civilization'.[53] Leopold alludes here very clearly to the theme of the 'degeneration' of so-called primitive peoples as a justification for a regenerative project in Africa. In a Lamarckian sense, the Africans were deemed to be the products of acquired degenerative characteristics, passed on from generation to generation. Only by raising them to a higher level could it be hoped that they would pass on civilization to their children. This is the biological rhetoric hiding behind Leopold's hortatory words. In a manner common in his time, he opposes this degeneration to the 'regeneration' which 'Christian civilization' might bestow upon a degraded people. Conrad might well have known this 'Letter' from Leopold, which forms an appendix to Guy Burrows's *The Land of the Pigmies* (1898). When Marlow speaks of the 'jolly pioneers of progress' (*HD* 13), Conrad might well be

[51] Quoted in Watt, 139.   [52] Burrows, 286-7.
[53] Ibid. 288. See Watt, 255.

parodying Leopold's comment on 'those upholders of manly traditions and pioneers of progress' in the Congo.[54] Mary Kingsley, a
writer whom Conrad had read, deplored this hypocritical justification for the imperialist venture. She objects to 'this idea that those
African are, as one party would say, steeped in sin, or, as another
party would say, a lower or degraded race'. She continues: 'The
religious European cannot avoid regarding them (the Africans) as
(. . .) more deeply steeped in sin (. . .) as "degraded" or "retarded"
either by environment, or microbes, or both.'[55]

'Africa Redivivus' remained a popular sentiment throughout the
period; and the reclaimable nature of 'primitive' peoples a common, if often hypocritical, goal. Thus, Kingsley wrote that 'The
white race seems to me to blame in saying that its interference in
Africa is the improvement of the native African, and then proceeding to alter African institutions without in the least understanding
them'.[56] Kingsley deplored the 'humbug (. . .) that we are only in
Africa for peaceful reasons of commerce, and religion, and education, and not with any desire for the African's land or property'.[57]
Interestingly, Kingsley quotes Conrad's friend, Hugh Clifford: 'In
these days the boot of the ubiquitous white man (. . .) crushes down
the forest, beats out roads, strides across the rivers, kicks down
native institutions, and generally tramples on the growths of natives
and the works of primitive man, reducing all things to that dead
level of conventionality which we call civilisation.'[58] Like Kingsley,
Conrad seems to have understood the rhetoric and found this
avarice masked in philanthropy to be highly suspect. Marlow
speaks ironically of the disparity between the regenerative goal and
the reality of the Congo in the figure of the African guard: 'They
passed me within six inches, without a glance, with that complete,
deathlike indifference of unhappy savages. Behind this raw matter
one of the reclaimed, the product of the new forces at work, strolled
despondently, carrying a rifle by its middle' (HD 19).

The improvability of 'primitive' cultures, and the allied question
of whether they had advanced or declined, is an important issue in
Heart of Darkness. During Conrad's time the 'civilizing mission'
in Africa was often portrayed as a failure. Thus in an article in
Blackwood's in 1898, which Conrad might well have read, one
observer wrote:

[54] Burrows, 285.   [55] West African Studies, 327, 328–9.
[56] Ibid., p. xvii.   [57] Ibid. 315.   [58] Ibid. 323–4.

There are places (. . .) where steamers call weekly and white officers break down their constitutions struggling to bring a better state of things about, and within ten miles the tribesmen still offer up human sacrifices in favour of their Ju-Ju gods,—so at least the bush traders say—and inaugurate devilish feasts.[59]

This passage partakes of many of the racist stereotypes so common in the writing on Africa; however, what is interesting is the pessimistic sense of the failure of the 'civilizing' project. Kurtz ostensibly comes to Africa as a sort of cultural emissary with the idea that 'Each station should be like a beacon on the road towards better things, a centre for trade of course, but also for humanizing, improving, instructing' (HD 34). Here, I would suggest, Conrad might well have had in mind Stanley's description of these stations in The Congo and the Founding of Its Free State (1885). After all, it was Stanley who had coined the term 'dark continent' and popularized images of light and dark to express the Congo mission:[60]

To such as seek protection, comfort, and care of the stations, a kindly refuge will be granted, and whatever may be done to improve their condition, such will be given the utmost of our power, with the utmost goodwill, with a view not only consolidating the influence of the stations, but of improving our means of civilising such peoples as may come in immediate contact or relationship with us.[61]

Clearly echoing the rhetoric of Stanley and the apologists for the Congo Free State, Kurtz is viewed ironically as an 'emissary of pity, and science, and progress, and devil knows what else' (HD 28). Like those missionaries whom Conrad parodies, Kurtz came to Africa with the goal of reclaiming the 'savages'. Implicit in this statement was the idea that primitive people must be aided in their development; that the acquisition of 'civilization' for primitive people depended upon the diffusion of already advanced culture rather than independent invention. The whole notion of cultural diffusionism, though, is subverted in the text. Kurtz does not reclaim the 'primitive' culture but destroys it. Gradually in the course of the novella, Kurtz turns to the more vehemently racist notion of

---

[59] Anon., 'Life and Death in the Niger Delta', Blackwood's Edinburgh Magazine, 162/1990 (April 1898), 451–62, 459.

[60] Stanley quotes a French statesman: 'You have thrown the light of knowledge on what you have well described as the Dark Continent.' Congo and Free State, p. vi.

[61] Ibid. 54.

the irreclaimable nature of 'savages', an idea that was still prominent in Conrad's time. Indeed, Kurtz not only rejects ideas of
progress in savage culture, but argues for the eradication of that
culture when he decides to 'exterminate all the brutes' (*HD* 51).
Here, Kurtz reflects the most rabid version of imperialism. Curiously, these two divergent views of 'primitive' cultures, as reclaimable and irreclaimable, could be sustained by a mental sleight of
hand. As one witness said before the parliamentary committee on
aborigines in 1857, with no hint of irony, 'The main point which I
would have in view would be trade, commerce, peace, and civilization. The other alternative is extermination; for you can stop nowhere'.[62] The issue of the progressive or degenerative tendency
could thus be used, in the extreme, as a justification for genocide.[63]

Try to Be Civil

At the heart of any cultural interpretation of Conrad's early novels
must be the question of how to define civilization and savagery.
Civilization, as Raymond Williams has noted, often expressed 'two
senses which were historically linked: an achieved state, which
could be contrasted with "barbarism" . . . and an achieved state of
development, which implied historical process or progress'.[64] At
one point in Marlow's narrative, one of the listeners on the 'Nellie'
interrupts him. 'Try to be civil, Marlow' (*HD* 36), says the man. A
tremendous irony is implied by this phrase. *Heart of Darkness*,
perhaps more than any of Conrad's works, poses this question of
what it is to be 'civil'. Those men who listen to Marlow's tale on the
'Nellie' are repeatedly informed of the fragility of the concept of
'civilization'. Civil, civility, civilization: all of these words are profoundly subverted by the text of the novella. The very nature of
these terms, and their usage, in effect, implodes in *Heart of Dark-*

---

[62] Quoted Watt, 159.

[63] Allan Hunter quotes Edward von Hartmann's *Philosophy of the Unconscious*
(1884), which similarly argues for the eradication of 'primitive' peoples already 'on
the verge of extinction'. As a natural outcome of evolution and even a humanitarian
act, 'the true philanthropist, if he has comprehended the natural law of anthropological evolution, cannot avoid desiring an acceleration of the last convulsion and
labouring for that end'. Quoted in Allan Hunter, *Joseph Conrad and the Ethics of
Darwinism* (London: Croom Helm, 1983), 23.

[64] Raymond Williams, *Marxism and Literature* (Oxford: Oxford University Press,
1977), 13–14. Quoted in Shaffer, 15–16.

ness. Marlow remarks of the manager that he was 'Neither civil nor uncivil' (*HD* 25). Beneath the surface meaning of such passages, Conrad implies ironically that his colonialist characters stand on the border between the civil and uncivil, civilization and primitivism. In other words, all of these distinctions, which seem so clear in other Victorian works, erode. Throughout 'An Outpost of Progress' and *Heart of Darkness*, Conrad subverts the meaning of words such as 'civilization' and 'progress'.[65] Similarly, the term 'culture', and the attempt to define it, to circumscribe its limits is, as Conrad is aware, riddled with difficulties. As the anthropologist James Clifford has written, even now 'Culture is a deeply compromised idea I cannot yet do without'.[66] Conrad was more aware than many of his contemporaries of the profound difficulty in defining culture or civilization. Clifford sees Conrad as one of the precursors of the self as a cultural construct, and of the multiplicity of cultures, a movement which undermined Victorian assumptions regarding Europe as the sole repository of *Kultur*. Clifford writes:

To say that the individual is culturally constituted has become a truism. (. . .) We assume, almost without question, that a self belongs to a specific cultural world much as it speaks a native language: one self, one culture, one language. I do not wish to dispute the considerable truth contained in even so bald a formula; the idea that individuality is articulated within worlds of signification that are collective and limited is not in question. I want however to historicize the statement that the self is culturally constituted by examining a moment around 1900 when this idea began to make sense as it does today.[67]

This 'moment around 1900' of which Clifford speaks corresponds to the publication of Conrad's *Heart of Darkness*; it is a moment which Clifford sees as imbued with great significance for the study of culture. Comparing Conrad with Malinowski, Clifford remarks that

[65] Variations on these words are frequently repeated, most often ironically: Marlow says of the Roman soldier that he can find 'precious little to eat fit for a civilized man' (*HD* 10). After returning from the East, Marlow says he was 'loafing about, hindering you fellows in your work and invading your homes, just as though I had got a Heavenly mission to civilize you' (*HD* 11). The first class agent stands by 'civilly' (*HD* 28). In 'An Outpost of Progress' the ironic accretions of these words are even more notable: 'civilized crowds'; 'civilized nerves'; 'rights and duties of civilization, the sacredness of the civilizing work'; 'the first civilized men to live in this very spot'; and 'The Great Civilizing Company (since we know that civilization follows trade' (OP 89, 89, 94, 95, 117). This is only a truncated list.
[66] *Predicament of Culture*, 10.   [67] Ibid. 92.

Self-identity emerges as a complex cultural problem in my treatment of two refugees, Joseph Conrad and Bronislaw Malinowski, Poles shipwrecked in England and English. Both men produced seminal meditations on the local fictions of collective life, and, with differing degrees of irony, both constructed identities based on the acceptance of limited realities and forms of expression. Embracing the serious fiction of 'culture' they wrote at a moment when the ethnographic (relativist and plural) began to attain its modern currency.[68]

In the late nineteenth and early twentieth centuries these views of culture as multiform and relativistic were not common, and Clifford sees Malinowski and Conrad as participants at two different stages of this ethnographic watershed. Clifford recognizes here the essential point regarding such terms as culture and civilization in Conrad's work—that Conrad viewed such concepts as necessary fictions.

If culture is defined as inclusive, it is also exclusive, as Said argues: 'As the twentieth century draws to a close, there has been a gathering awareness nearly everywhere of the lines *between* cultures, the divisions and difference that not only allow us to discriminate one culture from another, but also enable us to see the extent to which cultures are humanly made structures of both authority and participation, benevolent in what they include, incorporate and validate, less benevolent in what they exclude and demote.'[69] The ending of the novel and Marlow's infamous lie to the Intended, who is metonymic of 'civilization', is a typically Conradian attempt to shore up the fragile edifice that is the false concept of civilization or culture. Marlow depicts this meeting in intertwined images of death and worship: Having witnessed the horrible truth of an 'uncivilized' Kurtz—in the root sense of a man isolated from society, Marlow returns to the *civis*, the 'sepulchral city', to cast flowers at the foot of the tomb of civilized lies: 'bowing my head before the faith that was in her, before that great and saving illusion that shone with an unearthly glow in the darkness, in the triumphant darkness from which I could not have defended her—from which I could not even have defended myself' (*HD* 74). In an obviously sexist formulation, women are the upholders of the beautiful lies of civilization because so few of them have been acquainted with the worlds where such lies are exposed—the world of colonialism: 'Did I mention a girl? Oh, she is out of it—com-

[68] *Predicament of Culture*, 10.   [69] *Culture and Imperialism*, 15.

pletely. They—the women I mean—are out of it—should be out of it. We must help them to stay in that beautiful world of their own, lest ours gets worse' (*HD* 49). However, it is not merely women who are 'out of it' for Marlow. Marlow sees the inhabitants of the city disdainfully as being unaware of the collective lie they are unwittingly maintaining: 'They were intruders whose knowledge of life was to me an irritating pretence, because I felt so sure they could not possibly know the things I knew. Their bearing, which was simply the bearing of commonplace individuals going about their business in the assurance of perfect safety, was offensive to me like the outrageous flauntings of folly in the face of a danger it is unable to comprehend' (*HD* 70). Civilization, culture, and community are conventions that bound and insulate the bourgeois world from the threat of degeneration of which its citizens are ignorant. The individual like Kurtz, or like Kayerts and Carlier, degenerates when these artificial constraints or boundaries of civilization break down; therefore, even the lie with its taint of death seems preferable to the alternative—that all the boundaries of culture will erode. Marlow hints at this meaning when he says that the wilderness had 'beguiled his unlawful soul beyond the bounds of permitted aspirations' (*HD* 65). These 'bounds' mark out the collective lie of community; they are the walls that guard against the incursion of the 'horror'.

Around the turn of the century, notions of culture, heretofore widely disbursed, began to be challenged at every turn. James Clifford writes:

In the mid-nineteenth century to say that the individual was bound up in culture meant something quite different from what it does now. The European bourgeois ideal of autonomous individuality was widely believed to be the outcome of a long development, a progress that, although threatened by various disruptions, was assumed to be the basic, progressive movement of humanity. By the turn of the century, however, evolutionist confidence began to falter, and a new ethnographic conception of culture became possible. The word began to be used in the plural, suggesting a world of separate, distinctive, and equally meaningful ways of life.[70]

Conrad's perspicacity here in noting the change may have resulted from the skepticism he brought to bear on the use of language, the theme of truth and lies which pervades *Heart of Darkness*. Perhaps too, his conception of culture derived, as Clifford argues, from the

[70] *Predicament of Culture*, 92–3.

fact that Poland was an artificially constructed 'culture', a fiction, says Clifford, 'but an intensely believed, serious fiction—of collective identity'.[71] In any case, *Heart of Darkness* shows Conrad to have been extremely concerned with the construction of culture. How does this idea of the fragility of civilization and the concept of individuality relate to the theme of degeneration? If the self is an artificial and culturally constructed entity, then degeneration was a particularly acute worry. Pick recognizes this when he writes that degeneration 'was a process which could usurp all boundaries of discernible identity, threatening the overthrow of civilisation and progress'.[72] Degeneration involved the fear that the boundaries of self, and of the opposition between self and other, or subject and object, were not clearly defined.

Roughly thirty years earlier, E. B. Tylor seems to have had little difficulty in defining such abstract terms as civilization or culture. In the beginning of *Primitive Culture*, he wrote confidently that

Culture or civilization, taken in its wide ethnographic sense, is that whole complex which includes knowledge, belief, art, morals, law, custom, and any other capabilities and habits acquired by man as a member of society (. . .) (he then proceeds to) the investigation of these two great principles in several departments of ethnography, with special consideration of the lower tribes as related to the civilization of the higher nations.[73]

Tylor's definition and usage of the terms 'culture' and 'civilization' are problematic from the start. The first problem involves the equation of culture and civilization, words which anthropology would come to view as distinct. At first, it appears that Tylor will give a relatively value-free definition of culture which resembles that of modern anthropology—that culture merely comprises the accretions of customs, habits, rituals, etc. which form the basis of any human society or sub-culture. Thus, 'culture' is often made plural—there are any number of cultures or sub-cultures. The very title of Tylor's work implies this sort of relativism: it is his aim to study primitive culture, or, more properly, primitive cultures. The title of the work, however, strains against Tylor's ethnocentrism; and it quickly becomes clear that Tylor's usage is not relativistic, and does not allow for the multiple conception of cultures. By the end of the passage, note how Tylor has extracted the term civiliz-

[71] *Predicament of Culture*, 98.   [72] *Pick*, 9.
[73] *Tylor, Primitive Culture, i.* 1.

ation, originally equated with the bland and non-judgemental 'culture', and applied the term to European civilization specifically. There may be many cultures but they are not all possessed of European culture or civilization (that of 'the higher nations'). 'Civilization', in the end, belongs to the 'higher nations', as opposed to the lower tribes. In other words, Tylor implies that civilization is a sliding scale, with European culture at the top and 'primitive' cultures at the bottom. The dilemma here is not unique to Tylor's work, but is rather a reflection of the conception of 'culture' in nineteenth-century Europe generally.

Coinciding with this confusion over the definition of culture and civilization in this period, of course, is Matthew Arnold's *Culture and Anarchy* (1869), a work which argues for the defence of civilization against the incursions of anarchy. In Arnold's definition, which is widely accepted even in the modernist period, culture is viewed as the best part of a civilized society—all the best that is thought and written. Culture, for Arnold, becomes a method of organizing and protecting society against a slide into barbarism. In other words, in Arnold's work culture is that fragile concept that stands against the tide of recidivism. As Brian W. Shaffer writes, the word ' "culture," during this time, undergoes a nearly complete transformation from its Arnoldean sense as an achieved state of sensibility to its anthropological one as the collective social forms and expressions of a given group'.[74] Prior to this anthropological usage, culture equals civilization and is thus, almost by definition, that which primitive societies lack. Edward Said employs this definition of culture as the primary one in his recent work, *Culture and Imperialism*: 'culture is a concept that includes a refining and elevating element'.[75] Said continues: 'Now the trouble with this idea of culture is that it entails not only venerating one's own culture but also thinking of it as somehow divorced from, because transcending, the everyday world. Most professional humanists as a result (. . .) relegated these writers' ideas about colonial expansion, inferior races, and "niggers" to a very different department from that of culture, culture being the elevated area of activity in which they truly "belong" and in which they do their best work.'[76] As Said recognizes, such a version of 'culture' is obviously not value-free.

[74] Shaffer, 17.   [75] *Culture and Imperialism*, p. xiv.
[76] Ibid., pp. xv–xvi

What anthropology has developed as a definition of culture since Tylor's time is entirely different: it is multiform, manifold, inclusive rather than exclusive. James Peacock writes: 'Culture, then, is a name anthropologists give to the taken-for-granted but powerfully influential understandings and codes that are learned and shared by members of a group.'[77] Culture may be equated with language; it involves signs and symbols necessary successfully to negotiate a given society. Culture has been termed 'designs for living', a guidance system that Geertz compares to a computer program: 'Culture is best seen not as complexes of concrete behavior patterns—customs, usages, traditions, habit cluster—as has, by and large, been the case up to now, but as a set of control mechanisms—plans, recipes, rules, instructions (what computer engineers call programs) for governing behavior.'[78] Individuals are, to a profound extent, according to this definition, creatures of culture; they conform to particular sets of 'standards'.

In the modern and relativistic view, cultures vary with standards; they represent a sliding scale; in the Victorian era, such an idea was only gradually unfolding. As a life-long cultural outsider, Conrad seems to have been aware of this relativistic definition; however, he also stressed that within particular sub-groups or sub-cultures certain standards bound people together—what Marlow calls in *Lord Jim* a 'fixed standard of conduct' (*LJ* 52). Such standards might be fictions, but they proved to be necessary fictions for the maintenance of society as Conrad and his contemporaries imagined it. For Tylor, there was little relativism: Culture moved ever upward, from savagery to barbarism to civilization. Some contemporary writers recognized, along with Conrad, that civilization was being used as a cynical mask:

it is called 'elevating the African in the plane of civilisation.' It is hard on civilisation (. . .) to be used as a cloak for things (. . .) but I believe if people will look into it, I think this civilisation cloak will be stripped off. First, think what this word civilisation means. In its higher sense it means a compound thing, not a mixture of a certain state of perfection in arts and crafts, and it means a thing we have no word for in English, we have to go to Germany for it; there it is called *Bildung*, and the whole thing we call

[77] Peacock, 7.
[78] Clifford Geertz, 'The Impact of Culture on the Concept of Man', in J. R. Platt (ed.), *New Views on the Nature of Man* (Chicago: University of Chicago Press, 1965), 57.

civilisation is called *Kultur*, and a far better word it is too. (. . .) Well, we *may* by our present system of dealing with the African under the guise of elevating him in the plane of civilisation, advance him in the arts and crafts department, but in the *Bildung*, the improvement of the man's mind and soul, we are retarding him in his development, not aiding it.[79]

Perhaps in part due to the growing ambiguity of the term 'culture', not all of Conrad's contemporaries equated culture with civilization. Nor did many Victorians view cultural evolution as a given; rather, for each individual society progress or regress, advance or atavism remained equal possibilities.

[79] Kingsley, *West African Studies*, 444–5.

4

The Rise and Fall of Empires: Heart of Darkness *and Historical Cycles in the Victorian Era*

Civilization is a disease produced by the practice of building societies with rotten material.[1]

The Decline and Fall of Empires

Conrad's concern over development, both in the Congo and elsewhere, was by no means unique. The fundamental question of whether individuals and civilizations were improving or declining in civilization had been, of course, a common intellectual concern from the time of the Enlightenment and even earlier, back even to Hesiod's myth of the ages of mankind. Indeed, the idea of decay or retrogression can be viewed as one of the perennial myths of culture; however, this idea of degeneracy seems to have reached its apex in the Victorian period.[2] In the eighteenth century, the Scottish Enlightenment philosopher, Adam Ferguson, had suggested in *An Essay on the History of Civil Society* (1767) that this decay in culture figured as a prominent myth:

The poet, the historian, and the moralist frequently allude to this ancient time; and under the emblems of gold, or of iron, represent a condition, and a manner of life, from which mankind have either degenerated, or on which they have greatly improved.[3]

---

[1] George Bernard Shaw, *Man and Superman: A Comedy and a Philosophy* (1903) (Reprinted London: Penguin, 1957), 262.
[2] See Pick, *passim*. Patrick Brantlinger's *Bread and Circuses: Theories of Mass Culture as Social Decay* (Ithaca: Cornell University Press, 1983) also deserves attention.
[3] Adam Ferguson, *An Essay on the History of Civil Society* (Dublin, 1767; publisher unspecified), p. 2.

Indeed, the Scottish Enlightenment philosophers appear to have contributed greatly to the British conception of cultural progress.[4]

The question of whether mankind has either degenerated or improved upon its primitive state fascinated the Victorians, who, like Ferguson and other Enlightenment philosophers, were so obsessed with origins. The German idealist philosopher, Hegel, presented a similar argument. In his *Lectures on the Philosophy of World History*, Hegel identified the progress of culture in a tripartite manner, as a process of development, over-refinement and degeneration:

A nation makes internal advance; it develops further and is ultimately destroyed. The appropriate categories here are those of cultural development, over-refinement, and degeneration; the latter can be either the product or the cause of the nation's downfall.[5]

The post mortem on a nation's decline often revealed ambiguous causes of death; thus, Hegel fails to find any characteristic pattern for decline: 'The phenomenon of national degeneration in fact takes on many forms.'[6] The term degeneration did not have a precise meaning; indeed, it remained vague in its usage throughout the period I am examining. Bichat, a French *philosophe* and scientist of the eighteenth century, found recidivism to be a disease endemic to certain civilizations, leading to their decline. Following Gibbon, this conception of cultures remained a popular idea in the late eighteenth and early nineteenth centuries; as another philosopher wrote: 'It is admitted that the germ of destruction is inherent in the constitution of communities; that as long as it remains latent, exterior dangers are little to be dreaded; but when it has once attained full growth and maturity, the nation must die, even though its is surrounded by the most favourable circumstances.' 'Degeneracy', he concluded, 'was the name given to this cause of dissolution.'[7]

Degeneration remained an ambiguous term. Arthur de Gobineau, whose works on *The Inequality of the Human Races* and The *Moral and Intellectual Diversity of Race* became hallmarks of race theory and eugenics, complained in 1853 that the term 'degeneration' was not clearly defined:

---

[4] See Pick.   [5] Hegel, p. 56.   [6] Ibid., p. 60.
[7] Arthur de Gobineau, *Moral and Intellectual Diversity of Race*, H. Hotz (ed.) (Philadelphia: Lippincott & Co., 1856), 146.

'Degeneration,' was the answer; 'nations die when they are composed of elements that have degenerated.' The answer was excellent, etymologically and otherwise. It only remained to define the meaning of (a) 'nation that has degenerated.' This was the rock on which they foundered; a *degenerate people* meant, they said, 'a people which through bad government, misuse of wealth, fanaticism, or irreligion has lost the characteristic virtues of its ancestors.' What a fall is there! Thus a people dies of its endemic diseases because it is degenerate, and it is degenerate because it dies. This circular argument merely proves the science of social anatomy is in its infancy.[8]

He asked the question, 'How and why is a nation's vigour lost? How does it degenerate?'[9] The question remained relevant throughout the nineteenth century up until the time of Conrad's early works. De Gobineau's answer informed a later strain of degeneration theory. The solution for him seemed to lie in racial factors. 'The word degenerate, when applied to a people means (as it ought to mean) that the people no longer has the intrinsic value as it had before, because it has no longer the same blood in its veins, continual adulterations having gradually affected the quality of the blood.'[10] Thus degeneration is linked with miscegenation; it is caused by the mixing of blood. De Gobineau sees this miscegenation as the root of cultural degeneration:

But if, like the Greeks and the Romans of the later Empire, the people has been absolutely drained of its original blood, and the qualities conferred by the blood, then the day of its defeat will be the day of its death. It has used up the time that heaven granted at its birth, for it has completely changed its race, and with its race its nature. It is therefore degenerate.[11]

This image of racial degeneracy links up to the themes of cultural decline and fall prominent in an article that appeared with Conrad's *Heart of Darkness* in *Blackwood's*.

Gibbon's Ghosts

A strange millennial irony exists in the fact the first installment of 'The Heart of Darkness' appeared in the thousandth issue of *Blackwood's Edinburgh Magazine* in the last year of the nineteenth

---

[8] Arthur de Gobineau, *The Inequality of Human Races* (1853), trans. Adrian Collins (Reprinted London: Heinemann, 1915), 24–5.
[9] Ibid. 25.   [10] Ibid.   [11] Ibid. 34–5.

century. As if to herald the advent of a great modernist writer, *Blackwood's* fittingly published a special double issue. 'The Heart of Darkness' appeared as the first major item, and probably would have caught the readers' attention on this basis alone. Approaching 'The Heart of Darkness', readers would probably have drawn upon a whole series of cultural assumptions and associations that may seem remote from us today. On one level, they might have seen the story as part of the contemporary debate regarding the ascent or descent of man, the progression or re-barbarization of culture, as a journey back to the old ways of time, when their own ancestors were still 'savages'.

The three issues of *Blackwood's* that contained installments of 'The Heart of Darkness', February, March, and April, might have been on the bookshelf of a literate Victorian beside other works: E. B. Tylor's *Researches into the Early History of Mankind* (1865), *Primitive Culture* (1871) and *Anthropology* (1881); John Lubbock's *Pre-Historic Times* (1865) and *Origin of Civilisation* (1876); J. F. McLennan's *Ancient History* (1881) and *Patriarchal Theory* (1886); Henry Maine's *Ancient Law* (1881); and, almost certainly, Darwin's *The Descent of Man* (1871). All of these works dealt with the theme of progression or evolution of culture. Although this is purely speculative, if a typical reader of the 'Maga' might be posited, he would probably have been an educated Englishman with an interest in the Empire and thus, by extension, in so-called primitive cultures. This imagined reader might have been one of the many members of the 'Anthropological Society of London' which published translations of Friedrich Blumenbach's *Treatises on Anthropology* (1863) and Theodor Waitz's *Introduction to Anthropology*. This reader might have subscribed to a magazine such as *Popular Anthropology*. Such a *Blackwood's* reader might have known at least one of the works cited above, in which the progressionist theory of anthropology was expounded in some form. In reading 'The Heart of Darkness' in the magazine, many Victorians may have called to mind such works. This reader could have discerned Conrad's evolutionary pattern in the novella that paralleled the degenerationist and progressionist debate in anthropology.

We might think of such a reader as a smug imperialist, secure in his belief in the superiority of his civilization; however, it is just as likely that he would have been aware of a significant counter-

current to Victorian progressivism. Turning the pages of the February issue of *Blackwood's*, a Victorian reader would have found
an article that provided an accidental parallel to Conrad's story.
This imagined reader would have been immediately struck by the
title of the anonymous piece, 'From the New Gibbon'.[12] Nearly
every educated reader of *Blackwood's* would immediately note
the disturbing allusion to a key text on the destruction of empires.
This recollection of Edward Gibbon's great work must have been
particularly striking in the thousandth issue of a magazine appealing to imperial interests, in an empire perched on the edge of a
new century.[13] As a historian and archaeologist, Arthur Mitchell,
warned his countrymen in 1880: 'Where (. . .) is that Roman Empire now, which two thousand years ago planted the seeds of a high
civilisation among the barbarians of Great Britain? It will scarcely,
I think, be saying too much, if I say that the British Empire stands
now very much where the Roman Empire stood then, and occupies
a like dangerous place of breadth and prominence.'[14] Such historical analogies could not easily be overlooked. Gibbon's *Decline and
Fall of the Roman Empire*, after all, was almost *de rigueur* reading
for Victorian intellectuals. Moreover, Gibbon's work enjoyed a
resurgence of interest during this period because of the centenary of
his death in 1897.[15]

The Victorian reader might have reflected that the spectre of
Roman imperialism had been raised only a few pages earlier in a
very different work: 'I was thinking of very old times when the
Romans first came here, nineteen hundred years ago' (*HD* 9). Even
the most staid of Victorian readers might been struck by the co-
incidence that the Roman empire of nineteen hundred years earlier
was being evoked in a work at the end of the nineteenth century. As
a contemporary writer commented in the *Fortnightly Review*, 'the
community is, perhaps, a little over-presumptuous, if it imagines
that because it is England, or France, or the United States, it is

[12] Anon., 'From the New Gibbon', *Blackwood's Edinburgh Magazine* (February,
1899), 241–9. Cf. Andrea White, 40.
[13] Conrad was certainly familiar with Edward Gibbon's work. He recalled a
conversation regarding Gibbon at the time he was working on *Almayer's Folly*.
Recalling Gibbon, Conrad writes of 'Almayer's decline and fall' (*PR* 14–15).
[14] Mitchell, 214.
[15] There were many contemporary articles on the occasion. For example, an
anonymous reviewer wrote that Gibbon was the 'greatest historian who ever lived,
except, perhaps, Thucydides'. 'Edward Gibbon', *The Academy*, 51/1285 (27
February 1897), 249.

destined to immortality, though Greece, and Rome, and Spain, and the Mussulman powers are extinct forces'.[16] Were such historical cycles merely coincidences, or did the fall of one empire presage the fall of another? Although Conrad focused on the Belgian rather than the British version of imperialism, the note struck in Conrad's story is strangely similar to that in the Gibbon article. The frame narrator speaks of 'The dreams of men, the seeds of commonwealths, the germs of empire' (*HD* 8). The characters in Conrad's novel are familiar types, men involved in the 'trade', as the frame narrator remarks, for they had all 'followed the sea' (*HD* 8). On some level, all of Marlow's listeners appear to be implicated in the imperialist project. In short, the listener's of Marlow's tale were virtually mirror images of the readers of Conrad's story in *Blackwood's*.[17]

In order to understand the implicit parallels between Conrad's story and contemporary works, we should take a closer look at the 'New Gibbon' article. This essay begins with an ironic evocation of the late nineteenth century: 'The close of the nineteenth century beheld the British Empire at the highest pitch of its prosperity (. . .) Two centuries of empire had seemed insufficient to oppress or enervate the virile and adventurous spirit of the British race.'[18] After this apparently complacent depiction of the British empire, a different note is struck. The writer refers to Kipling's 'Recessional' and remarks: 'It was scarcely possible that the eyes of contemporaries

---

[16] Charles H. Pearson, 'An Answer to Some Critics', *Fortnightly Review*, 60/320 (August 1893), 151.

[17] Of the typically pro-imperialist readership of *Blackwood's* Conrad wrote in 1911: 'I regret Maga. One was in decent company there and a good sort of public. There isn't a single club and messroom and man-of-war in the British Seas and Dominions which hasn't its copy of Maga. . . .' Quoted in Lawrence Graver, *Conrad's Short Fiction* (Berkeley and Los Angeles: University of California Press, 1969), 22. Of course, only three years later J. A. Hobson was to argue that imperialism was the central fact which bound all of the British together at all levels of society. See J. A. Hobson, *Imperialism: A Study of Social Pathology* (1902) (Reprinted London: Allen & Unwin, 1938). Related studies abound. See, for example, Jonah Raskin, *Mythology of Imperialism* (New York: Random House, 1972); Gordon K. Lewis, *Slavery, Imperialism, and Freedom: Studies in English Radical Thought* (New York: Monthly Review, 1978); Ronald Robinson and John Gallagher, with Alice Denny, *Africa and the Victorians: The Official Mind of Imperialism* (1962) (Revised London, Macmillan, 1981); V. G. Kiernan, *The Lords of Human Kind: Black Man, Yellow Man, and White Man in an Age of Empire* (1969) (Reprinted New York: Columbia University Press, 1986); and Hugh Ridley, *Images of Imperial Rule* (London: Croom Helm, 1983).

[18] 'New Gibbon', 241.

should discern in the public felicity the latent causes of *decay and corruption* (. . .)'.[19] Discomfort must have begun to register in the mind of the *Blackwood's* reader at this point. A short story about the decay of a European in the service of empire appeared just before an article deriding the Victorian pretensions to progress. The writer adopts the satiric tone of an historian looking back on a decadent era, a new Gibbon surveying the decline and fall of a new Rome. He observes: 'The student of the age will find melancholy evidence of degeneration in the printed records, and especially in the newspapers of the time.'[20] This new Gibbon finds degeneration everywhere in British culture at the end of the nineteenth century. The 'noble' goal of empire has been displaced by petty trade of the sort that would appear in *Heart of Darkness* in the mercantile Belgians: 'The empire, that magnificent fabric founded upon the generous impulse to conquer and to rule, was now regarded as a mere machine for the acquisition of pounds sterling.'[21] The ideal of empire here conflicts with the sordid reality of mercantile colonialism. One thinks here of the degeneration of the Roman soldiers and traders who are depicted at the beginning of Conrad's novella. Marlow, after all, points to a similar discrepancy between the 'idea; and the unselfish belief behind the idea' and the actual Congo trade. As he remarks, 'They were going to run an oversea empire and make no end of coin by trade' (*HD* 10, 13). Although the original readers of the novella may have distinguished between British and Belgian colonial methods, the text largely glosses over such differences. It would have been difficult for a Victorian reader to take consolation in the fact that 'our' empire was more humane than 'theirs' (the Belgians').

The scene the new Gibbon observes is a familiar one. The last year of the century seemed to mark both the zenith of imperialism and its inevitable decline.[22] The 'degeneracy of the people' in urban centres, the depopulation or flight from the countryside, the debasement of morals and values, the decadence of an army recruited from the colonies, the decline of standards in art, and the failure in physique and sporting prowess of the populace, are all clear signs that the seeds of destruction have been sown.[23] All of these implicit parallels to the work of the first Gibbon must have elicited anxiety

---

[19] 'New Gibbon', italics mine.   [20] Ibid. 242.   [21] Ibid.
[22] See Said, *Culture and Imperialism*, 64.   [23] 'New Gibbon', 243–5.

in the minds of Victorian readers.[24] The conclusion of this bleak *fin de siècle* essay utterly subverts any melioristic optimism about the state of the empire:

the British Empire entered upon the twentieth century under the gloomiest of auspices (. . .) They prided themselves on the greatness of their dominion and hugged the specious perfection of their civilisation. Yet decline was already accomplished and irremediable, and fall was but too surely pending (. . .) Civilisation had completed its works in the suppression of the individual, and the British, the most virile of barbarians, the most forward and energetic of mankind, were dissipated (. . .) The diminutive stature of mankind was daily sinking below the old standard; Britain was indeed peopled by a race of pigmies, and the puny breed awaited only the onset of the first crisis to become the woeful patient of defeat and ruin.[25]

This anonymous essay illustrates the point that will be stressed again and again—that Conrad's novella emerges out of an age of cultural crisis when 'degeneration' had become a catchword. Far from being the confident progressivist period that it has often been labelled, the Victorian imperial ethos is constantly re-examined and subverted by writers, and challenged by the discoveries of anthropology. The words 'civilization' and 'progress' are often riddled with ironies, just as these terms are ironically charged in Conrad's novella. As the anonymous essayist put it: 'They prided themselves on the greatness of their dominion and hugged the specious perfection of their civilisation.'

The sense of hollowness or rottenness at the centre of the new Gibbon's empire raises interesting questions of how representative Conrad's novel was of contemporary anxiety over the decline of Western civilization. The representatives of 'civilization' in Conrad's novel, as in the new Gibbon's essay, are straw men, hollow at the core. Moreover, there is a sense of inevitability about cultural dissolution that recurs in many historical or anthropologi-

[24] A few years later G. B. Shaw wrote similarly: 'At this moment the Roman decadent phase of *panem et circenses* is being inaugurated before our eyes. Our newspapers and melodramas are blustering about our imperial destiny; but our eyes and hearts turn eagerly to the American millionaire.' Again, he observes that 'the whole political business goes to smash; and soon we have the Ruin of Empires, New Zealanders sitting on a broken arch on London Bridge and so forth'. *Man and Superman*, 25, 229.

[25] 'New Gibbon', 249. Brantlinger briefly mentions the theme of imperialist rhetoric and fears of atavism. See *Rule of Darkness*, 32–6 and *passim*.

cal works written at the end of the nineteenth century. As Arthur de Gobineau, a writer who later gained a following among eugenicists, had remarked at mid-century, in analysing the problem of cultural decline: 'The downfall of civilizations is the most striking, and at the same time, the most obscure of all the phenomena of history.'[26] Conrad's own affinities with the ideas introduced in the Gibbon essay can perhaps be inferred from his comment to William Blackwood regarding the February issue: 'I was delighted with the number. Gibbon especially fetched me quite.'[27]

One of the Dark Places of the Earth

At the beginning of *Heart of Darkness*, Marlow implies an important analogy between contemporary African 'savagery' and that of early Britain, an analogy which suggests a similarity to the 'comparative method' that dominated Victorian anthropology. The comparative method allowed anthropologists and ethnologists to view contemporary 'savages' as equivalent to ancient European peoples. The method, practised by E. B. Tylor and other Victorian anthropologists, consisted of taking primitive cultures as models and using observations regarding them to characterize truly 'primitive' people. Predicated on an evolutionary or developmentalist approach to anthropology, the comparative method presumed that any cultures in an equivalent stage of development could be usefully compared. Tylor sums up this ahistorical approach:

To general likeness in human nature on the one hand, and to general likeness in the circumstances of life on the other, this similarity and consistency may no doubt be traced, and they may be studied with especial fitness in comparing races near the same grade of civilization. Little respect need be had in such comparisons for date in history or place on the map (. . .) If we choose out in this way things which have altered little in a long course of centuries, we may draw a picture where there shall be scarce a hand's breadth difference between an English ploughman and a negro of Central Africa.[28]

[26] De Gobineau, *Moral and Intellectual Diversity*, 105.
[27] Letter to William Blackwood, 8 February 1899, *Collected Letters of Conrad*, ii. 162.
[28] *Primitive Culture*, i. 6.

As one later writer put it, 'the comparative method is the unbiased co-ordination of all comparable data irrespective of context or age'.[29]

The comparative method clearly presupposed what Tylor and other Victorian anthropologists constantly asserted, that 'continuity in culture (. . .) is no barren philosophical principle'.[30] Tylor's anthropological ally, Sir John Lubbock, wrote similarly that 'My argument, however, is that there is a definite sequence of habits and ideas; that some customs (some brutal, others not so), which we find lingering on in civilized communities, are a page of past history, and tell a tale of former barbarism'.[31] In other words, Europeans could see their remote prehistoric past 'writ large' in primitive 'survivals' in their own culture, as well as in so-called primitive societies which represented a kind of living museum of prehistoric cultures. Ironically, the comparative method claimed its significance as part of what Tylor called the reformer's science, anthropology. The recognition that elements in so-called civilized societies corresponded to those same elements in primitive cultures could be the basis for a cultural housecleaning: 'But the comparative study of the beliefs and institutions of mankind is fitted to (. . .) become a powerful instrument to expedite progress as it lays bare certain weak posts on which modern society is built—if it shows us that much of what we want to regard as solid rests on the sands of superstition rather than on the rock of nature.'[32]

The analogies in the comparative method rested upon what Brook Thomas, in a different context, calls the 'synchronicity of the nonsynchronic'. Thomas writes:

Europeans like Conrad, then, possessed not only a progressive, Eurocentric vision of world history but also a temporal sense of the synchronicity of the nonsynchronic. It seemed to them, in other words, that by studying other, primitive-seeming cultures existing simultaneously (or synchronically) with their own, they could study something chronologically disparate, namely their own deep, prehistoric past. Each culture, it seemed, had its own temporal logic. Whereas the West followed a fairly steady line of progress (despite a backward slide in the 'Dark Ages'), other cultures plotted differ-

---

[29] Stanley A. Cook, 'Religion' in James Hastings (ed.) *Encyclopaedia of Religion and Ethics* (Edinburgh: Clark, 1918), x. 664.

[30] Tylor, *Primitive Culture*, i. 17.   [31] Lubbock, *Origin of Civilisation*, 387.

[32] James G. Frazer, *The Golden Bough: A Study in Magic and Religion* (1890), 12 vols. (Reprinted London: Macmillan, 1917), i, pp. xv–xvi.

ent curves. Thus, at any moment, the world's cultures were at different stages of development. (. . .) Drawing on this notion of the synchronicity of the nonsynchronic, Conrad is able to turn a story about a present journey to Africa into a journey into Europe's past, as well as one into each human being's primitive psyche.[33]

Apparently without realizing it, Thomas here is resurrecting the common notion in Victorian anthropology of the comparative method. While Thomas attributes this sense of the 'synchronicity of the nonsynchronic' to developments in historiography, it would be more accurate to attribute the theory to its origin in progressive anthropology. Thus, the notion of journeying into the past of another culture (Africa) in order better to understand European culture did not only derive from anthropology, but pervaded the anthropological method in the late nineteenth century. The entire theory of development in civilization is predicated upon a Tylorean hierarchy, a sort of sliding rule of cultures. By applying the standards of material and even ethical development to various cultures, one could determine their place on the progressive scale. Progressivist anthropology rested upon this foundation.

Advocates of the developmentalist theory posited an intimate connection between 'barbaric' groups such as the ancient Teutons and extant 'primitives'. For example, the early English anthropologist James Prichard wrote that 'the ancient Britons were very much on a level with the New Zealanders or Tahitians of the present day, or perhaps not very superior to the Australians'.[34] In other words, ignoring historical disparities, Prichard is able to find synchronicity in the nonsynchronic—ancient Britons equal contemporary indigenous peoples in New Zealand. Later in the same work, in regard to the barbarism of the early Britons, he remarked that 'Of all Pagan nations the Gauls and Britons appear to have had the most sanguinary rites. They may well be compared in this respect with the Ashanti, the Dahomehs, and other nations of Western Africa'.[35] Interestingly, Prichard here implies an intimate connection between the ancient peoples of northern Europe and contemporary Africans. It probably came as no surprise to Victorian readers, then, when Marlow asserted that 'The mind of man is

---

[33] Murfin, *Case Study*, 247.
[34] James Prichard, *Researches into the Physical History of Mankind*, 5 vols. (London: Longman, 1831–7), iii. 182.
[35] Ibid. iii. 187.

capable of anything—because everything is in it, all the past as well as all the future' (*HD* 38). The 'remote kinship' (*HD* 38) that Marlow invoked corresponded to the anthropological idea that 'they' (the Africans) were really like 'us' (Europeans) a comparatively short time before. In other words, Marlow, like contemporary ethnographers, noted a distinct family resemblance in his African cousins. This sort of comparison was not unusual. In searching for the equivalent to the ancient Teutons in his *Decline and Fall of the Roman Empire*, Gibbon compared them to contemporary American Indian tribes.[36]

This brief introduction to the comparative method in anthropology, which sought out historical analogies among ancient and contemporary cultures, the synchronicity of the nonsynchronic, brings us to the beginning of Marlow's narrative. After the frame narrator has evoked the historical past of the Thames, Marlow's first words are, 'And this also (. . .) has been one of the dark places of the earth'. In other words, at the opening of his narrative he situates his discussion of Africa in the form of an analogy between apparently disparate and nonsynchronic cultures. After a pause, he continues, drawing out a comparison between various stages of colonialism and images of primitive cultures:

I was thinking of the very old times, when the Romans first came here, nineteen hundred years ago—the other day (. . .) But darkness was here yesterday. (. . .) Imagine him there—the very end of the world (. . .) Sandbanks, marshes, forests, savages—precious little to eat fit for a civilized man (. . .) Here and there a military camp lost in a wilderness, like a needle in a bundle of hay—cold, fog, tempests, disease, exile, and death,—death skulking in the air, in the water, in the bush. They must have been dying like flies here (. . .) Land in a swamp, march through the woods, and in some inland post feel the savagery, the utter savagery, had closed round him,—all that mysterious life in the wilderness that stirs in the forest, in the jungles, in the hearts of wild men.   (*HD* 9–10)

The cultural relativism implicit in this passage is fascinating. All the stereotypes of primitivist fear on the part of imperialist are inverted here: the savagery, the lack of 'civilized' food, the disease, and the sense of mystery are applied to European peoples themselves, albeit ancient ones. The implicit comparison between the 'decivilization' of the Roman legionnaire and the European colonists in Africa is all

---

[36] See Charles Kingsley, *The Roman and the Teuton* (1864) (Reprinted London: Macmillan, 1887), 8.

the more striking because it subverts the pretensions of European civilization to being a high culture. When Marlow remarks, 'precious little to eat fit for a civilized man' he seems to be parodying the sort of remarks his contemporaries would make regarding their travels to 'primitive' cultures. After all, Rome was viewed as one of the cradles of culture when ancient Britain was barbaric. Indeed, Victorians often invoked comparisons between the British and Roman empires such as the one outlined above in 'From the New Gibbon'.[37] The analogy is clear: if such a 'civilized' people as the Romans could degenerate in contact with 'savages', then the possibility of such recrudescence in European culture was just as great. The parallelism between this passage and the later African sections must be emphasized, for it is, I would argue, at the heart of Conrad's internal debate regarding progression and decline. To the Romans, the early British of only two thousand years before, Conrad implies, must have seemed a barbarous people, just as to contemporary British colonists the Africans appear to be in a primitive state.[38] Yet, if Europe makes a claim to being a high culture, how can it deny a place in the developmental series to Africa?

Allan Hunter suggests that Conrad may well have had in mind the *Prolegomena* to T. H. Huxley's lectures on *Evolution and Ethics* (1894).[39] Although this work was certainly widely known, the genealogy of the comparison between Africa and ancient Britain is much older than Hunter realizes. Indeed, any competent classical scholar in Conrad's time might have been familiar with Cicero's description of the ancient Britons in a letter to Atticus as barbarous and savage.[40] Huxley's analogy was certainly by no means unique. On the contrary, by the 1890s it seems to have already been

[37] The idea of Roman Britain fascinated the Victorians. In reviewing *Tales of Unrest*, Edward Garnett wrote: 'When we think of Romanized Britain our imagination becomes a blank wall with a few historical facts staring at us from it. But in Rome under the Caesars human life is as fresh and actual to us as in London to-day.' Quoted in Sherry, *Critical Heritage*, 105.

[38] See Norman Sherry, *Conrad's Western World* (Cambridge: Cambridge University Press, 1971), 121.

[39] Huxley writes: 'It may be assumed that, two thousand years ago, before Caesar set foot in Southern Britain, the whole country-side visible from the room in which I write, was in what is called the state of nature (. . .) man's hands had made no mark upon it.' Quoted in Hunter, 18.

[40] See W. Armistead, *A Tribute to the Negro: Being a Vindication of the Moral, Intellectual, and Religious Capabilities of the Coloured Portion of Mankind* (Manchester, William Irwin, 1848), 31.

something of a cliché.[41] This same sentiment was expressed in 1848 in an unattributed poem in an important abolitionist tract by William Armistead, *A Tribute to the Negro*: 'Let us not the Negro slave despise,/Just so our sires appeared in Caesar's eyes.'[42] Armistead draws out this comparison at some length:

The Romans might have found an image of their own ancestors in the representation they have given of ours. And we may form not an imperfect idea what our ancestors were, at the time Julius Caesar invaded Britain, by the present condition of the African tribes. In them we may perceive, as in a mirror, the features of our own progenitors, and, by our own history, we may learn the extent to which such tribes may be elevated by means favourable to their improvement.[43]

Armistead perfectly illustrates the way in which the comparative method could be used to reverse expectations regarding such concepts as progress and civilization. He concludes:

Were it not so indubitably recorded on the page of history, we should hardly be willing to believe that here was a time when our ancestors, the ancient Britons, went nearly without clothing, painted their bodies in fantastic fashion, offered up human victims to uncouth idols, and lived in hollow trees, or rude habitations, which we would now consider unfit for cattle. Making all due allowances for the different state of the world, it is much to be questioned whether they made more rapid advances than have been effected by many African nations, and that they were really sunk in the lowest degree of barbarism is unquestionable.[44]

Again, Armistead's didactic purpose in this passage seems clear: to hold up to the British a portrait of their savage past in order to argue for the progressivism of Africa (a progressivism which Armistead and others believed could only begin with the abolition of the slave trade that had prevented Africa from 'cultural advancement').

Conrad's evocation of the barbarous past of Britain also echoed the sentiments of other fiction writers. For example, Andrea White quotes a conversation from one of Marryat's popular novels:

[41] Cedric Watts quotes Conrad's friend, Cunninghame Graham, as a convincing source: ' "History informs us that the Romans once ruled the greater part of Scotland (. . .) What an abode of terror it must have been to the unfortunate centurion, say from Naples, stranded in a marsh far from the world, in a climate of the roughest, and blocked on every side by painted savages!" ' Quoted in Cedric Watts (ed.) *Heart of Darkness and Other Tales* (Oxford: Oxford University Press, 1990), 264–5, n. 139.

[42] Quoted in Armistead, 32.   [43] Ibid. 30–1.   [44] Ibid. 31–2.

'And so does every Englishman who loves his country. Recollect that when the Roman empire was in the height of its power, Great Britain was peopled by mere barbarians and savages. Now Rome has disappeared, and is known only in history, and by the relics of its former greatness, while England ranks among the highest of nations. How is the major portion of the continent of Africa peopled? by barbarians and savages; and who knows what they may become some future day?'
    'What! the negroes become a great nation?'
    'That is exactly what the Romans might have said in former days. What! the British barbarians become a great nation? and yet they have become so.'[45]

This passage encapsulates the arguments of developmentalist anthropologists such as Tylor, who argued that the comparative method clearly demonstrated the fallacy of attributing only to certain countries the capacity for improvement.

    Although such sentiments could be allied with a patroniz-ing imperialism aimed at 'reclaiming' and elevating contemporary Africans, just as the Romans had elevated the ancient Britons, it had become profoundly clear by the time of Conrad's novella that the opposite was occurring in Africa—under the false pretenses of the 'civilizing mission', Europeans were really contributing to the degradation, ruin, and extermination of the Congolese. It was as if, extending the historical analogy, the Romans had succeeding not in elevating but in decimating the ancient British. Of course, there is another side to this Roman analogy; and, as so often in the con-fused discourse of imperialism, it is dangerous to come to too reductive a conclusion. The Roman analogy could be used to justify the imperial project by arguing for the benefits which had accrued in England from the contact with the Romans: 'In India, in Egypt, in Central Africa (. . .) she (England) has shown herself the greatest educator of the human race since the days of imperial Rome.'[46] Indeed, Macaulay argued that the ideal of empire did not consist in military conquest but in cultural diffusion. Writing of nascent British imperialism in India and elsewhere, he remarks,

To have found a great people sunk in the lowest depths of slavery and superstition, to have so ruled them as to have made them desirous and capable of all the privileges of citizens, would indeed be a title to glory all

[45] Quoted in White, 66–7.
[46] Anon., 'The Ethics of Conquest', *Blackwood's Edinburgh Magazine*, 164/908 (December 1898), 849.

our own. The sceptre may pass away from us (...) Victory may be inconstant to our arms. But there are triumphs which are followed by no reverse. There is an empire exempt from all natural causes of decay. Those triumphs as the pacific triumphs of reason over barbarism; that empire is the imperishable empire of our art and our morals, our literature and our laws.[47]

Interestingly, Roman decline seems to be a feature of even this apparently confident and melioristic sentiment. The analogy seems to be submerged: even though the British empire might decline as did the Roman ('The sceptre may pass away from us'), the diffusion of culture of the sort that sowed the seeds of civilization in 'barbaric' England will ensure that the decline is not without its compensations.

Yet another example of a comparison between Roman and ancient British, and modern British and African cultures is found in the work of George Lawrence Gomme, a well-known folklorist and ethnologist in the Victorian era. Like Conrad, Gomme seems to have believed that looking at contemporary 'savages' from the British perspective resembled a journey back into British barbarism. In *Folk-Lore Relics of Early Village Life* (1883), Gomme wrote that 'Instead of taking with me the folk-lore of all Europe and going into the lands and homes of savages, I propose taking only the folk-lore of England (...) and showing how this journey of mine has been *equal to a journey backward through all the stages of English civilization at a time when inhabitants of this island belonged to the class of primitive man who would have supplied Greek or Roman inquirers with the self-same knowledge that the modern inquirer obtains from modern savages*'.[48] In other words, Gomme speculates that the Romans would have perceived the primitive English in the same manner that the contemporary Englishman would view African primitives. The implicit warning here seems obvious: cultures that had apparently advanced so far in such a short time could ill-afford to be confident of their inevitable ascendency; nor could they rationally deny to other cultures the capacity for progress. Arthur Mitchell had observed in 1880: 'We ourselves were already in our iron age, and had been so for we do not know how long,

[47] Thomas Babington Macaulay, 'Speech on the Government of India' (1833). Quoted in Brantlinger, *Rule of Darkness*, 30.
[48] George Lawrence Gomme, *Folk-Lore Relics of Early Village Life* (London: Macmillan, 1883), 849, italics mine.

when the Romans paid us the first of those visits which exercised such an important influence over the destinies of our islands; but we were also in a state of savagery if we do not disbelieve what has been written of our condition at that time. At this very day the negroes of Central Africa are in their iron age; yet, in the opinion of some, they are scarcely men.'[49]

Two thousand years, as Conrad had come to realize, perhaps largely due to the development of geology, archaeology, anthropology, and Darwinism, represented a very short period, a 'mere flicker' (*HD* 9). Time had been foreshortened to such an extent that such a brief period in the development of a civilization seemed a tiny fragment when compared with the prehistory of mankind, and the much vaster geological time-scale: 'Yet nothing is more certain than that, measured by the liberal scale of time-keeping of the universe, the present state of nature, however it may seem to have gone on forever, is but a fleeting phase of her infinite variety.'[50] Recognizing this enormous attenuation of time, Marlow refers to the gap between today and 'yesterday' (*HD* 9).[51] The corollary to this belief in the rapid progression from 'barbarism' to civilization was that of the rapidity of decline. If the cultural evolution of European cultures, as it was thought, had occurred in such a radically foreshortened period of time, then reversion, if it occurred, could be just as rapid and just as irrevocable. In fact, Conrad was representative of his time in believing that the accretions of civilization were far from secure.

Conrad explores the theme of the disjunctiveness of the colonial experience in largely non-racial terms; and it is in this context that the Roman theme at the beginning of the novella becomes so crucial. The implicit analogy that he draws between Roman and modern European colonialism suggests the anthropological detachment, so characterized by the comparative method, that Conrad brings to his portrait of Africa. Marlow presents a picture of a Roman's terrifyingly disorienting experience in Britain:

[49] Mitchell, 144. He also writes: 'We ourselves furnish an illustration. Less than two thousand years ago we were barbarians, and now we boast that nowhere in the world is there a civilisation more advanced than ours.' Mitchell, 214.

[50] Huxley, *Evolution and Ethics*, 2–3.

[51] Again, Huxley writes: 'Compared with the long past of this humble planet, all the history of civilized man is but an episode.' Ibid., p. 2.

There's no initiation either into such mysteries. He has to live in the midst
of the incomprehensible, which is also detestable. And it has a fascination,
too, that goes to work upon him. The fascination of the abomination—you
know, imagine the growing regrets, the longing to escape, the powerless
disgust, the surrender, the hate.   (*HD* 10)

In other words, decivilization affects colonial cultures other
than modern ones. To those who spoke so confidently of Africans
as 'savages', Conrad's novella suggests the savagery of their
own English ancestors, in Victorian terms not very distant on
the evolutionary scale. Although it would be false to misread too
much cultural relativism into Conrad's work, there are certainly
hints of the cultural ambiguity that was represented in anthropology by the comparative method. Indeed, it mattered little that
the Victorians often saw themselves as above their 'primitive'
counterparts, for once relativity in culture became a possibility, the
move toward modern anthropological doctrines became almost
inevitable.

The profound challenge of the contact of cultures, the disjunction
of personality resulting from the incomprehensibility of one's surroundings—all that has been summed up in the anthropological
dilemma—all of these difficulties are as relevant to an outsider's
view of British culture as they are to Britain's view of the 'other'.
Later, in *The Mirror of the Sea* (1905), Conrad writes similarly of
this disorientation:

The commander of the first Roman galley must have looked with an
intense absorption upon the estuary of the Thames (. . .) with a strange air
of mysteriousness which lingers about it to this very day (. . .) He would
have heard (. . .) instructive tales about native chiefs dyed more or less blue,
whose character for greediness, ferocity, or amiability must have been
expounded to him with that capacity for vivid language which seems joined
naturally to the shadiness of moral character and recklessness of disposition (. . .) watchful for strange men, strange beasts (. . .) Was the tribe
inhabiting the Isle of Thanet of ferocious disposition, I wonder, and ready
to fall with stone-studded clubs and wooden lances hardened in the fire,
upon the backs of unwary mariners.   (*MS* 101–2)

This passage again reflects the error in attributing to Conrad's
'mystification' of Africa racist overtones. Here again Conrad's analogy draws on comparative anthropology. He is only half-ironically
suggesting that the ancient Roman's stereotyped view of British
barbarism was analogous to modern visions of primitive peoples.

Indeed this whole passage is almost a pastiche of Marlow's journey in *Heart of Darkness*. The ancient Roman is little different from his modern counterpart setting off for 'savage' ports: he gathers information in the form of gossip and rumours, just as Marlow, too, collects rumours and gossip on his journey down the African coast; he believes stories of native savagery, just as Marlow believes the fate of his predecessor killed by Africans; most of all, he sees the whole country as invested with a dark mystery that grows out of primitivist fears. Conrad is fond of this sort of analogy between one culture and another; and one wonders what his readers must have thought of the implications—that they were only a few generations removed from primitivism themselves.

Marlow does distinguish between the Roman conquerors and the colonial experience in Africa. He remarks that 'What saves us is efficiency—the devotion to efficiency (. . .) They (the Romans) were no colonists. They were conquerors, and for that you want only brute force—nothing to boast of, when you have it, since your strength is just an accident arising from the weakness of others' (*HD* 10). In this well-known passage, Marlow draws a distinction between the conqueror and the colonist whose actions are redeemed only by an 'idea' (*HD* 9). In light of the 'unspeakable rites' later in the text, it is difficult to accept this language as free of black humour. Moreover, this sentiment fits in with the Carlylian theme discussed previously: that work, restraint, and discipline were believed to be necessary in the advance of society; and that the absence of these qualities led to regression.

The January 1899 issue of *Blackwood's* featured a story by John Buchan, 'No-Man's-Land', that throws light on the notion of extant primitivism in Britain. Drawing on the discoveries that archaeology, paleontology, and ethnology had made regarding the barbaric nature of the early inhabitants of Britain, Buchan's narrator is an academic interested in 'the ancient life of the North, of the Celts and the Northmen, and unknown Pictish tribes'.[52] Although in many ways very different from *Heart of Darkness*, 'No-Man's Land' depicts a parallel journey back into the remote anthropological past. Extending the images of British barbarism at the beginning of Conrad's novella, Buchan's narrator finds himself in a similar primeval landscape:

[52] John Buchan, 'No-Man's Land', *Blackwood's Edinburgh Magazine*, 165/994 (January 1899), 2.

But in spite of myself the landscape began to take me in thrall and crush me. The silent vanished peoples of the hills seemed to be stirring; dark primeval faces seemed to stare at me from behind boulders and jags of rocks.[53]

The theme of cultural degeneration of one people in relation to a more savage group is then introduced:

I thought of the Gaels who had held those fastnesses; I thought of the Britons before them, who yielded to their advent. They were all strong peoples in their day, and now they had gone the way of the earth (. . .) I reflected on that older and stranger race who were said to have held the hilltops. The Picts, the Picti (. . .) Heaven alone knew what dark abyss of savagery had once yawned in the midst of the desert.[54]

Although there is not space here to do more than take note of this theme in Buchan's story, it is an interesting example of the Victorian fascination with their own culture's past savagery, and, by implication, with the latent savagery still existing in some dark corner of their own mind. Too often, the Victorians' fascination with 'primitive' cultures is viewed as a smug opposition between low and high civilizations. On the contrary, though, Conrad's contemporaries were deeply concerned with vestigial forms of 'savagery' in their own culture. Moreover, the Victorians were, as Buchan implies, painfully aware that their 'cultural ascendency' rested upon a fragile foundation: 'They were all strong peoples, in their day, and now they had gone the way of the earth.' Conrad's *Heart of Darkness* shares similar concerns regarding cultural rise and fall, particularly in relation to imperialism.

The Call of the Wild: Degeneration in Individuals

The idea of degeneration as applied to individuals has a microcosmic relationship to the larger developmentalist–degradationist debate discussed in the previous chapter. As one of the foremost advocates of the idea of degeneration, George Dougal Campbell, the Duke of Argyll, wrote in *Primeval Man* (1869): 'nothing in the Natural History of Man can be more certain than that both morally, intellectually, and physically he can, and often does sink from a higher to a lower level. This is true of Man both collectively and

---

[53] John Buchan, 2.   [54] Ibid.

individually, of men and of societies of men'.[55] Examples of individuals or groups of men who had apparently relapsed into 'primitive savagery' provided anthropologists with the evidence they needed to support degeneration in cultures at large. Such stories of atavism also seem to have appealed to the macabre tastes of the Victorians. Even E. B. Tylor admitted that these individual cases of atavism were difficult to ignore:

Instances of civilized men taking to a wild life in outlying districts of the world and ceasing to obtain or to want the appliances of civilization, give more distinct evidence of degradation. In connection with this state of things takes place the nearest approach to an independent degeneration from a civilized to a savage state. This happens in mixed races, whose standards of civilization may be more or less that of the higher race (. . .) *One step beyond this brings us to cases of individual men being absorbed into savage tribes and adopting the savage life, on which they exercise little influence for improvement.*[56]

The last sentence here is especially relevant to *Heart of Darkness*, which portrays precisely this absorption of the civilized man into the savage tribe. Indeed this theme of primitivist absorption is a theme common in Conrad's writing; Jim is adopted similarly in *Lord Jim*. The African novella is particularly interesting, though, in light of Tylor's argument that the Europeans so adopted '*exercise little influence for improvement*'. Indeed this comment provides an ironic commentary on the barbarism Kurtz introduces or promotes among the Africans. The later popular version of this myth in the case of Tarzan and other similar heroes is treated much more darkly by Conrad, in keeping with Tylor's comment on degeneration.

Travellers' and missionaries' tales provided widely accepted examples of the individual and rapid decline to which Tylor refers. Indeed such degeneration was widely accepted as a logical and almost inevitable effect of the contact with primitive cultures and tropical climates. Environmental changes could cause reversion, in other words.[57] It is worth noting here that Conrad's Kurtz was to

[55] Campbell, 156.   [56] Tylor, *Primitive Culture*, i. 41, italics mine.

[57] Cesare Lombroso writes: 'The criminal is an atavistic being, a relic of a vanished race. This is by no means an uncommon occurrence in nature (. . .) The dog left to run wild in the forest will in a few generations revert to the type of his wolf-like progenitor, and the cultivated garden roses when neglected show a tendency to reassume the form of the dog-rose (. . .) This tendency to alter under special conditions is common to human beings . . . a return to characteristics peculiar to primitive

go even further in his degeneration than Tylor would have imagined. Tylor ended his discussion of degeneration in *Primitive Culture* by asserting the improbability of 'degeneration to the savage level' from a 'high-level civilization'.[58] This quotation provides an ironic gloss on Kurtz's degeneration because he is portrayed not only as a member of a 'high-level civilization' ('All Europe contributed to the making of Kurtz', *HD* 50) but as the epitome of that culture. Conrad remarks in one of his letters that 'I took great care to give Kurtz a cosmopolitan origin'.[59] In other words, Conrad chooses to make him not an aberration but the embodiment of all European culture. Kurtz by no means represents the only example of this sort of degeneration, nor is his case to be seen as an isolated one. Some scientists, in fact, believed that degeneration would be manifested precisely in the most highly developed individuals: 'we must occupy ourselves with the most highly developed state of man, since degeneration can be found only in the most fully developed specimens'.[60]

Walking on a Thin Crust: Naturvölker and Culturvölker

The notion that 'civilized' individuals might degenerate into 'savages' both derived from and added to the conception that the gap between so-called primitive people and their civilized relatives proved to be extremely narrow. If, it was argued, survivals of primitive culture were discovered even in the highest cultures; and if, moreover, the line between primitive and civilized man was not clearly demarcated, then a relapse into barbarism was taken as a *sine qua non*. 'The civilized European', wrote Theodor Waitz, 'is accustomed to look so much down upon the so-called savage that he deems it an insult to be compared with him; and yet, even in the midst of civilization we find traces of customs, manners, and modes of thinking which, like the relapse of man into a savage state, prove their intimate connection.'[61]

Waitz was a prominent German anthropologist whose *Intro-*

savages.' Cesare Lombroso, *Criminal Man* (London and New York: Putnam's, 1911), 135–6.

[58] Tylor, *Primitive Culture*, i. 49. [59] *Collected Letters of Conrad*, iii. 94.
[60] Maudsley, *Body and Will*, 243. [61] Waitz, i. 306.

duction to Anthropology was translated into English in 1863 as one of the first books published under the auspices of the 'Anthropological Society of London'. Waitz's book on the '*Naturvölker*', or natural man, seems to have been widely read by those interested in anthropology; certainly, the work was widely quoted.[62] Although many of the cultural assumptions upon which he based his works were still Eurocentric and even racist, Waitz refused to see the alleged savagery of primitive peoples as divorced from that of the civilized. In other words, while it would be absurd to overestimate Waitz's cultural relativism, it does provide us with a convenient analogy to Conrad's work. Like Conrad, Waitz writes of debased and savage Europeans in order to subvert Europeans' pretensions to civilization:

In contrasting these examples with the laziness and vulgarity into which small communities of civilized Europeans have sunk, when far removed from their native country, we are not merely cautioned against the assumption of specific differences between the white and the coloured races; but the question obtrudes itself whether, after all, it would be so very beneficial for all races to partake of our European civilization; or whether there are not certain states of culture which, though differing widely from ours, may not excel it in their moral aspect by the sum of happiness and well being they afford.[63]

In German anthropological theory the term *Naturvölker*, or primitive, was opposed to the *Culturvölker*, or civilized people. Waitz argued that the *Naturvölker* possessed an inherent aversion to culture, which he firmly resisted. At the same time, in the so-called advanced countries, Waitz posited, civilization is only a product of largely external circumstances, the accretions of time and accidents, which might easily be reversed. Clearly, Conrad shared many of these anthropological assumptions.

Civilization, Waitz argues, is extremely fragile, and cultural history reveals that either development or regression is possible for all races:

Civilization is a state which the uncultivated man be he European or African resists with all his power, according to the law of inertia; but it does not irresistibly lead to the conclusion that savage peoples are irreclaimable. If, on the other hand, the savage does not take freely to civilization, though surrounded by it, we find, on the other hand, that the

---

[62] See *Primitive Culture*, i. 1.   [63] Waitz, i. 386.

civilized man, living among savages relapses after a short time into a state of barbarism which, on that account, we must consider as the primitive condition of man.[64]

In other words, without the constant influence of civilization, Waitz, along with many of his contemporaries, believed the natural tendency of humanity was to degenerate into savagery.

These anthropological assumptions regarding degeneration were based on reports of Europeans living in other cultures. Waitz argued that colonies survived only because of the artificial constraints that the constant influx of European culture imposed on the foreign environment. Conversely, if the contact with the colonists' own culture were broken, then Waitz posited a rapid assimilation to the ways of the dominant foreign culture. Cultural norms alien to the 'primitive' environment could only be maintained with the greatest difficulty. Separate from European civilization, colonists, he warned, degenerated rapidly. Again, the relevance of these anthropological ideas to *Heart of Darkness* seems evident. Conrad's friend and editor, Edward Garnett, emphasized precisely this theme when he wrote of *Heart of Darkness*: 'it implies the acutest analysis of deterioration of the white man's morals when he is let loose from European restraint (. . .) degenerating whites staring all day and every day at the Heart of Darkness'.[65] The theory of colonists deteriorating provides a historical gloss on Conrad's portrait of the Congo. The rapid degradation that occurred when social constraints were lifted in the colonies confirmed for many Victorian anthropologists the narrowness of the gap between primitive and civilized people: 'We believe that we may be justified in concluding that the moral endowment of the white races differs in nothing from that of other races, for it is clearly shown that the rude primitive nature in man breaks out in the civilized man whenever wholesome restraints are removed.'[66] The phrase 'wholesome restraints' echoes Garnett's comment, and resonates with implications for Conrad's novella. Restraint, and the degeneration resulting from the loss of it, are two of Marlow's greatest concerns.

Interestingly, Waitz relates the idea of reversion to English culture specifically. He asks the question, 'What could have become of the transmarine colonies of the tough and almost indestructible

---

[64] Waitz, i. 312.   [65] Quoted in Sherry, *Critical Heritage*, 132.
[66] Waitz, i. 318.

English without a constant reinforcement from the mother country?' In a manner that must have caused concern among Victorian readers, he concludes that 'In spite of all the progressive tendency ascribed to the white race, we answer unhesitatingly, it would have either perished or returned to barbarism'.[67] Waitz gives many examples of how 'Europeans perfectly degenerate' in foreign climates. He cites accounts of Spaniards in Latin America lapsing into barbarism, as well as of Portuguese colonists in Africa and the 'horrors of their own dominion and their own degeneration'.[68] Waitz's predictions about the degeneration or re-barbarization of European colonists cut off from their own cultures illuminates the historical context of Conrad's portraits of Kurtz and other imperialists who 'returned to barbarism'. This character of the decaying colonist recurs in Conrad's work; indeed, Conrad's first novel, *Almayer's Folly* (1895), conjures up a portrait of a ghostly type who is to haunt all of his works. Inspired by a Eurasian inhabitant of Borneo whom Conrad claimed to have met, his portrait of Almayer draws upon many of these same preconceptions regarding the degenerative quality of exile in 'primitive' cultures. The novel is filled with images of decay and atrophy. Almayer, living in his 'new but already decaying house' surrounded by the 'triumphant savagery of the river', is the epitome of the decaying colonist (*AF* 7, 26).

Like many of his contemporaries, Waitz seems to have felt that civilization was a fragile inheritance, unlikely to be retained without external constraints. Just as Conrad's colonists will decline and fall in their exile amongst 'savage' people, so Waitz's isolated colonists regress to savagery. Waitz argued that even so-called civilized nations had comparatively recent primitive roots, while primitive cultures might well become civilized given a change in environment. In a way, this dictum reflects a nascent cultural relativism. Waitz wondered whether the accretions of civilization were to be desired. In the end, Waitz asserted that 'We dare not deny to any race the capacity for progress to a higher civilization'.[69] At the same time, Waitz warned, European meliorism rested upon a fragile base, for anthropological literature provided numerous examples of the decline and fall of individuals, as well as of empires.

[67] Waitz, i. 307.   [68] Ibid. i. 313.   [69] Ibid. i. 324.

5

'Going Native', Coming Home: 'Decivilization' in Heart of Darkness and Conrad's Malaysian Novels

> The thirst for the wilderness was on me; I could tolerate this place (England) no more (. . .) He begins to long—ah, how he longs!—for the keen breath of the desert air; he dreams of the sight of Zulu impis breaking on their foes like surf upon the rocks, and his heart rises up in rebellion against the strict limits of the civilized life.
>
> H. Rider Haggard, *Allan Quartermain*[1]

'Going Native', Coming Home

The theory of degeneration resembled very closely the more populist ideas of 'going native', or 'going fantee', with their racist overtones.[2] Such ideas could encourage a strict separation between natives and colonists for fear that the latter might be corrupted by the former. These ideas feed into much popular fiction of the time, by writers as varied as Kipling, Buchan, Haggard, and Conrad. A contemporary review of *Heart of Darkness* by Conrad's friend, Hugh Clifford, stressed this theme. He observed that the novella was

a sombre study of the Congo (. . .) the power of the wilderness, of contact with barbarism and elemental man (. . .) the demoralisation of the white man is conveyed with marvelous force. The denationalization of the European, the 'going Fantee' of civilized man has been often enough treated in fiction since Mr. Grant Allen wrote the story of the Rev. John Creedy, and before, but never has the 'why of it' been appreciated by any other author, as Mr. Conrad appreciates it, and never (. . .) has any writer

---

[1] H. Rider Haggard, *Allan Quartermain* (1887) (Reprinted Mattituck, NY: Ameron House, 1983), 11.

[2] See Watt, 144.

till now succeeded in bringing the reason, and the ghastly unreason of it all home to sheltered folk.[3]

The idea of imparting the degeneration of a colonist to the 'sheltered folk' in England shows how Conrad's tale would have fitted into the tradition of travel writing and ethnographic fiction. The goal of 'bringing the reason, and the ghastly unreason' of primitive cultures 'all home' was one of the professed desires of the authors of such books. In the view of many Victorians, Kurtz's denationalization would have inevitably carried with it the likelihood of moral degradation—a curious conflation dependent upon the idea that in transgressing national and ethnic boundaries, one inevitably transgressed moral boundaries as well.

A later review by Otto Lütken, a Danish sea captain who had commanded a steamer in the Congo for eight years, argued that

It is in the picture that Conrad draws of Kurtz, the *troppenkollered* white man, that his authorship rises supreme. The man is so lifelike and convincing—heavens, how I know him! I have met one or two 'Kurtzs' in my time in Africa, and I can see him now. Surely the touch in the Pamphlet on the means for civilising the Negroes and the last penciled note 'Exterminate the Brutes' is life. That happened.[4]

Lütken's statement is fascinating, for it suggests again that at least some of Conrad's contemporary readers would not have seen Kurtz in isolation, but in a typology of degenerative colonial figures. Indeed he calls Kurtz a 'type', though not a common type. Even by the time of Conrad's writing the late Victorian reader might have discerned, as does Lütken, not an individual in Kurtz but rather the embodiment of a class of men. '*Troppenkollered*' translates as 'maddened by the tropics', and represents a common belief in scientific circles. On one level, this is precisely what happens to Kurtz; and Conrad lends support to this view when he writes to Edward Garnett that *Heart of Darkness* rises above what is merely 'an anecdote of a man who went mad in the centre of Africa'.[5] Lütken writes of the Belgian agents: 'They were not gentle in their methods; it is very possible that some of them lost their mental balance a little in the savage environment in which they had to live

---

[3] Hugh Clifford, review in the *Spectator*, 828.

[4] Otto Lütken, 'Joseph Conrad and the Congo', *London Mercury* 22/130 (August 1930), 350. Watt quotes part of this passage, Watt, 145.

[5] Quoted in Watt, 244.

and fight—Lothaire, for instance, was according to Duhst's report, a brute'.[6] Lütken's comment here that 'some of them lost their balance a little in the savage environment' is all the more striking for its understatement. Like the Manager's remark that Kurtz's 'method is unsound' (*HD* 61) it is the more jarring for its understatement.

By the time the appalling atrocities in the Congo began to come to light after the turn of the century, it must have surely occurred to Conrad's contemporaries, if it had not already done so, that Kurtz was by no means a purely fictitious creation. E. D. Morel's scathing diatribe against Leopold's venture, *Red Rubber*, presents ample evidence that such brutal figures were, if not a commonplace in the Congo in the last decade of the nineteenth century, at least not unprecedented.[7] Morel cites an example of skulls brought to decorate an agent's flower garden, as well as the confession of a trader: 'I am going to appear before the Judge for having killed 150 men, cut off 60 hands; for having crucified women and children, for having mutilated many men and hung their sexual remains on the village fence.'[8] Even if exaggerated by Morel, such Kurtzian scandals must have brought home to the British public examples of the extreme moral degeneration which had already been captured in Conrad's novella. Although some of the examples cited by Morel were extreme, they were not apparently isolated. In 1893, the Governor-General of the Free State wrote to his agents in what sounds strangely like an account of Kurtz's actions:

From information which has reached the central government recently it appears that some of our agents settle, palavers, make war upon the native, burn villages without reporting their actions. Others have gone so far as to carry out with their own hands summary executions, and have thus become assassins (. . .) If individual caprice was to substitute itself for law, we should become in certain parts of the territory more savage than the natives whom we have to lead to civilization.[9]

The ironies and inversions of terms like 'savage' and 'civilized' are constantly revealed in Morel's scathing tract. When terms such as civilized and civilization collapse, the distinctions between high and

[6] Otto Lütken, 'Joseph Conrad and the Congo', *London Mercury*, 22/127 (May 1930), 42.
[7] See E. D. Morel's *Red Rubber* (London: T. Fisher Unwin, 1907).
[8] Quoted in *Red Rubber*, 46, 60.   [9] Morel, *Red Rubber*, 37–8.

low cultures, so insisted on by many Victorians, also begin to blur. Roger Casement, the Congo reformer whose relationship with Conrad has been well-documented,[10] wrote a letter in which he framed his aversion to Belgian rule in the Congo in these ironic tropes: Africa 'has been "opened up" (as if it were an oyster) and the Civilizers are now busy developing it with blood and slaying each other, and burning with hatred against me because I think their work is organized murder, far worse than anything the savages did before them.'[11]

'The Changes Take Place Inside'

The idea of colonists going mad in the tropics was a common stereotype in the Victorian era. Josiah Nott, an American doctor and amateur anthropologist had written similarly of the ill effects of the tropics on whites. An Englishman, he says, placed 'in the most healthful part of Bengal (. . .) soon ceases to be the same individual, and his descendants degenerate (. . .) both body and mind become sluggish; gray hairs and other marks of premature age appear (. . .) the average duration of life is shortened (. . .) and the race in time would be exterminated, if cut off from fresh supplies of immigrants'.[12] Nott here echoes Waitz's notion that only 'reinforcements' of other European immigrants prevent white colonists from utterly degenerating or even dying out in the alien environment. Conrad's 'An Outpost of Progress' similarly traces the effects of climate upon the two Belgian agents:

Now and then one of them had a bout of fever, and the other nursed him with gentle devotion. They did not think much of it. It left them weaker, and their appearance changed for the worst. Carlier was hollow-eyed and irritable. Kayerts showed a drawn, flabby face over the rotundity of his stomach, which gave him a weird aspect. But being constantly together, they did not notice the change that took place gradually in their appearance, and also in their dispositions.   (OP 6)

One recalls here the doctor's assertion in *Heart of Darkness* that it would be 'interesting for science to watch the mental changes

---

[10] See, for example, Meyers, 97–108 and Karl, 286–90.
[11] Quoted in Meyers, 102.
[12] Quoted in George W. Stocking, Jr, *Race, Culture and Evolution* (London: Collier-Macmillan, 1968), 48.

of individuals on the sport' (*HD* 15). 'An Oupost of Progress' illustrates Waitz's assertion that without the constant influx of new colonists to reinforce their own culture Europeans were prone to rapid degeneracy.

This idea of degeneration is closely connected with the idea of going native. Certainly, contemporary reviewers of Conrad's works were well aware of this theme of acclimatization and subsequent degeneration. As one reviewer remarked of *An Outcast of the Islands*, 'It was a favourite speculation of certain eighteenth century philosophers whether the civilised man tended to deteriorate under the condition of life in the tropic climates'. It is precisely this 'process of degradation', says this reviewer, that is 'set forth stage by stage' in Conrad's novel.[13] Judging from the abundance of material on such degeneration, it seems clear that the deterioration of white men in the tropics was still a 'favourite speculation' of the Victorian era.

The idea of physical debilitation in the tropics—the notion of the 'white man's grave'—is even more pervasive in *Heart of Darkness*. Marlow discusses this theme with a Swedish captain while travelling down the African coast:

'It is funny what some people will do for a few francs a month. I wonder what becomes of that kind when it goes up country?' I said to him I expected to see that soon. 'So-o-o!' he exclaimed. He shuffled athwart, keeping one eye ahead vigilantly. 'Don't be too sure,' he continued. 'The other day I took up a man who hanged himself on the road. He was a Swede too.' 'Hanged himself! Why, in God's name?' I cried. He kept on looking out watchfully. 'Who knows?' The sun too much for him, or the country perhaps.' (*HD* 18)

The theme of disease recurs often in the text: Marlow comments that 'I heard that men in that lonely ship were dying at the rate of three a day'; in the coastal station he sees a 'sick man (some invalided agent from up-country)'; of the pilgrims Marlow remarks that 'the only thing that ever came to them was disease'; 'The climate may do away with the difficulty for you,' says the uncle to his nephew; and Marlow recalls that when he returned to Europe his 'temperature was seldom normal' (*HD* 27, 22, 27, 33, 70). Finally, of course, Kurtz dies of fever, an incident that Ian Watt says

---

[13] Sherry, *Critical Heritage*, 64.

paralleled an actual experience during Conrad's trip—the death of the trader, Klein.[14]

It is important to emphasize here that the theme of physical deterioration in the tropics had many historical precedents. African colonists prepared almost fatalistically for the 'inevitable fever'.[15] Some European explorers in Africa, such as Paul Du Chaillu, even took pride in recounting 'fifty attacks of African fever'.[16] The prevalence of physical degeneration caused by the tropics would have been of more than passing interest for Conrad, who never fully recovered from the dysentery he contracted in the Congo. Indeed, the very real fear of tropical disease is a constant theme in the 'Congo Diary' and his letters from Africa. To cite but one example, he wrote to Karol Zagorski on 22 May 1890:

What makes me rather uneasy is the information that 60 per cent. of our Company's employees return to Europe before they have completed even six months' service. Fever and dysentery! There are others who are sent home in a hurry at the end of a year so they shouldn't die in the Congo. God forbid! It would spoil the statistics, which are excellent, you see! In a word, there are only 7 per cent. who can do their three years' service.[17]

In this black humorous statement about the danger of becoming one of the company's statistics, Conrad reveals the historical truth of records kept on tropical diseases. Nor was the fear of disease overstated. Phillip Curtin has written that 'European mortality was roughly four times as high in West Africa as it was in India or the West Indies'.[18] The idea of the intimate connection between climate and disease does not make reference only to colonialism in Africa, but is related to a larger historical pattern. In the analogy to the

[14] See Watt, 136, 141–2. Watt says that 'One can surmise that merely "seeing him die" gave Conrad an unbearably painful memory. From the departure on September 6th until Klein's death 15 days later, there would, in the very cramped quarters of the Roi des Belges, have been no escape from the sounds, the smell and the sight of a man in the last stages of dysentery—a disease peculiarly repulsive in its physical manifestations', 142.

[15] This is a theme common to a great deal of writing on tropical climates: 'In the tropics fever is a kind of curtain-fire put down by Nature, through which all have to pass and through which few come quite unscathed.' Owen Rutter, *British North Borneo: An Account of its History, Resources and Native Tribes* (London: Constable & Co., 1922), 8.

[16] Du Chaillu, *Adventures in Equatorial Africa*, pp. iii, v.

[17] Zdzislaw Najder (ed.), *Conrad's Polish Background: Letters to and from Polish Friends* (London: Oxford University Press, 1964), 211.

[18] Curtin, 71.

Roman soldiers Marlow speaks of the 'awful climate' and remarks, 'disease, exile and death,—death skulking in the air, in the water, in the bush. They must have been dying like flies here' (*HD* 10).

The pervasiveness of the disease theme may also be read on a symbolic level as a conflation of the senses of psychological and physical degeneration. Similarly, a chapter of Henry Drummond's *Tropical Africa* is entitled, 'The Heart Disease of Africa: Its Pathology and Cure'.[19] The 'primitivism' of Africa, Conrad seems to imply, is somehow infectious to the whites. On the other hand, the whites have brought the 'disease' of colonialism to Africa, a metaphor enacted in the grove of death. It is important to acknowledge the subtlety of the text because the disease metaphor resonates on many levels. Imperialism itself is viewed as potentially degenerative, a disease of Victorian culture. In this light, it is significant that J. A. Hobson subtitled his work, *Imperialism* (1902), *A Study of Social Pathology*.[20]

Climate and Acclimatization

Here it is necessary to discuss at some length an anthropological idea which paralleled that of degeneration, acclimatization. In the 'Preface' to the second edition of *Hereditary Genius* (1869, rvd., 1892) Francis Galton, Darwin's cousin, underscored the relevance of acclimatization to the imperial agenda: 'The recent attempts by many European nations to utilize Africa for their own purposes gives immediate and practical interest to inquiries that bear on the transplantation of races.' He continued:

They compel us to face the question as to what races should be politically aided to become hereafter the occupiers of that continent (...) Some of them must be more suitable than others to thrive under that form of moderate civilization which is likely to be introduced into Africa by Europeans, who will enforce justice and order, excite a desire among the natives for comforts and luxuries, and make steady industry almost a condition of living at all. Such races would spread and replace the others by degrees. Or it may prove that the Negroes, one and all, will fail as completely under the new conditions as they have failed under the old ones, to submit to the needs of a superior civilization to their own; in this case

---

[19] See Drummond, *Tropical Africa*.   [20] See Hobson.

their races, numerous and prolific as they are, will in course of time be supplanted and replaced by their betters.[21]

Galton's racist perceptions of the ill-adaptability of Africans in this influential scientific text obviously fuelled social-Darwinist arguments for 'survival of the fittest'. The last phrase ('replaced by their betters') underscores the theme of racial superiority which figured in Galton's eugenicist program. However, the issue of 'transplantation' that he addresses here also parallels the theme of degeneration in tropical climates discussed above.

Conrad's doctor is, in fact, representative of the ways in which science became implicated in the colonial project. In the letter already noted, Conrad mentioned the statistics which the company kept on the health of their employees. The doctor in *Heart of Darkness* whose 'little theory' the company men help him to prove closely parallels Galton's call for empirical data on adaptability:

It seems possible to assure ourselves as to the possibility of any variety of white men to work, to thrive, and to continue their race in the broad regions of the tropics. We could not do so without better knowledge of the different capacities of individuals to withstand their malarious and climatic influences (. . .) We require these records to enable us to learn hereafter what are the conditions in youth that are prevalent among those whose health subsequently endured the change of climatic influence satisfactorily, and conversely as regards those who failed.[22]

The examination scene in the novella makes perfect sense in this light. The doctor is concerned with gathering accurate data to further the kind of research that will perpetuate Galton's colonial agenda:

He gave me a searching glance and made another note. 'Ever any madness in your family?' he asked in a matter-of-fact tone. I felt very annoyed. 'Is that question in the interests of science too?' 'It would be,' he said without taking notice of my irritation, 'interesting for science to watch the mental changes of individuals on the spot, but' . . . 'Are you an alienist?' I interrupted 'Every doctor should be—a little,' answered that original imperturbably. 'I have a little theory which you Messieurs who go out there must help me to prove. This is my share in the advantages my country shall reap from the possession of such a magnificent dependency. The mere wealth I

[21] Francis Galton, *Hereditary Genius, an Inquiry into its Laws and Consequences* (1869) (Reprinted London: Watts & Co., 1950), p. xxvi.
[22] Ibid.

leave to others. Pardon my questions, but you are the first Englishman to come under my observation . . . Avoid irritation more than exposure to the sun (. . .) *Du calme, du calme. Adieu.'*   (*HD* 15)

If Galton and Conrad's doctor searched for the secrets of colonial success in the tropics, other Victorian thinkers argued that imperialism and colonialism in Africa and elsewhere in the tropics were doomed projects from the start. For example, Robert Knox, a Scottish anatomist, argued that the tropics were largely untamable because 'The tropical regions of the earth seem peculiarly adapted to him (the black); his energy is considerable; aided by the sun, he repels the white invader'.[23]

Obviously, acclimatization theory could serve the retrograde agenda of racism as well as imperialism. Those who argued, like Josiah Nott, an American doctor and amateur anthropologist, for the inability of human beings to become acclimatized to another geographical area were often reactionaries, bent upon retaining the status quo. As Nott wrote:

None of these plants and animals can be propagated out of the climate to which they are adapted by nature—and man forms no exception to the general law. The white man cannot live in tropical Africa, or the African in the frigid zone. Wherever colonies of Europeans have been formed, in temperate countries, they have soon flourished, and the white population has multiplied so fast as to encroach upon the native, and in many instances, entirely supersedes them. But in Africa, colonies of Europeans and Asiatics have dwindled away and become extinct (. . .) No black race in short has been or can be established at any great distance from the equator.[24]

The desire to marginalize certain cultures—to restrict blacks to the tropical regions of the globe—reflects both a fear of miscegenation, and a desire for white supremacy to be asserted in the temperate regions. Nott wrote prior to the rise of imperialism in Africa. On the other hand, he was an American southerner, deeply concerned about the possibility of blacks permanently adapting to 'temperate regions' such as the middle or northern United States. This represents the inverse of the imperialist notion that white men could adapt and succeed in other climates; such adaptability promised

[23] Quoted in Bolt, 22.
[24] Josiah Nott, *Two Lectures on the Natural History of the Caucasian and Negro Races* (Mobile, Ala.: Dade & Thompson, 1844), 19.

them the means to colonize much of the earth. Daniel Brinton, another contemporary writer, similarly argued that acclimatization was a myth: 'There is no such thing as acclimatization. A race never was acclimated, and in the present condition of the world, a race never can become acclimated.'[25] Such comments on acclimatization represent a common theme in the Victorian era, a theme closely allied to the growing 'science' of eugenics: in an age of increasing cultural contacts, writers worried about the loss of racial identity.

In the period before Conrad's *Heart of Darkness*, anxiety over contacts between cultures, with miscegenation often present as a subtext, seems to have been widespread. James Hunt, for example, argued that everywhere, including in the New World, 'the almost exterminated savage will be revenged by the slow gradual degeneracy, and perhaps final extinction of their (. . .) conquerors'.[26] Largely because of a pervasive racism in the attitudes of Victorian commentators, the contact of cultures seemed to be inherently infectious: 'degeneracy, and perhaps final extinction', were the results of such cultural displacement. The imperial theme elided here with this notion of acclimatization, for it was of more theoretical interest to countries sending colonists out to Africa what the impact of the climate would be.[27] In *Heart of Darkness* the ability to adapt to a new environment is the prerequisite for success in Africa; thus acclimatization theory squared with the social-Darwinist notion of 'survival of the fittest'. 'You stand the climate', the manager remarks in the novella, 'you outlast them all' (*HD* 34). Again, Marlow says that 'Once when various tropical diseases had laid low almost every "agent" in the station, he was heard to say, "Men who come out here should have no entrails"' (*HD* 25). Again, alluding to Kurtz's illness, the manager remarks of a hippopotamus: 'That animal has a charmed life (. . .) but you can say that only of brutes in this country. No man—you apprehend me?—no man here has a charmed life' (*HD* 31). This remark recalls a passage in Drummond's *Tropical Africa* (1888), which Conrad might well have read: 'The really appalling mortality of Europeans is a fact which all who have any idea of casting their lot with Africa

---

[25] Quoted in Bolt, 54.

[26] James Hunt, Untitled, *The Anthropological Review*, 8 (1870), 137. Bolt says that an article in this magazine in 1869 also asserted that 'Anglo-Saxon emigration to, and acclimatization in, the tropics, was a failure'. Bolt, 22.

[27] On this theme, see Bolt, 22.

should seriously reckon (. . .) the only known scientific test for it (malaria) at present is a human life. The test has been applied in the Congo region today with a recklessness which sober judgment can only characterize as reckless (. . .) And science has a duty in pointing out that no devotion or enthusiasm can give any man a charmed life.'[28]

The problem of adaptability to adverse climates had become a practical concern in the Victorian era because of imperialism, though, as Curtin has shown, it was a prominent issue from the eighteenth century on.[29] This theme of adaptability leads us to another issue related to climatic degeneration. Historically, the Victorians could point to the success of their English ancestors, both in terms of colonization and in advancement of culture; however, evolutionary theory implied that such success merely reflected adaptability. Contrasting this to the developmentalist theory in anthropology, the advance or decline of culture came to be seen as largely a result of external and accidental circumstances such as environment. Even Tylor, the quintessential progressionist, in his first work, *Anahuac*, supports this climatic argument: 'There is a theory afloat, that it is only in temperate climates that semi-barbarous nations make much progress in civilizing themselves. In tropical countries the intensity of the heat makes men little disposed for exertion, and the luxuriance of the vegetation supplies him with the little he requires.'[30] The environmental theory Tylor outlines here lends credence to the stereotype of the indolent 'savage'. Just as tropical climates tended to deter advance, so more temperate climates were thought to promote advance and hinder degeneration.[31]

Climate could induce decline as well as advance. Some anthropological degenerationists, for example, argued that so-called primitive tribes such as the Fuegians and Eskimos found at polar extremes represented degenerate groups that had been driven farther and farther off by strong competitors. The climates of these areas then led to the inevitable degeneration of these groups. Just as

---

[28] Drummond, *Tropical Africa*, 44.   [29] See Curtin, 187.
[30] E. B. Tylor, *Anahuac* (London: John Murray, 1861), 192.
[31] Henry Buckle argues that Europe has been dependent on a colder climate for its success. He writes: 'In Europe, for the first time, civilization arose in a colder climate: hence the reward of labour was increased, the distribution of wealth rendered more equal.' Henry Buckle, *The History of Civilization in England*, 2 vols. (London: John Parker & Son, 1858), 48. Also see Whatley, *Political Economy*, 130.

civilizations as a whole were impacted by climatic changes, so, it was believed, climate and environment would have a strong impact upon individual advance. Thus, the 'savage' removed to a different climate might become more civilized. Conversely, the extension of this sort of argument to the case of so-called primitive people seems clear: if environmental constraints are removed it is very easy for the native to degenerate again to his previous form.[32] This climatic theory supported, too, the idea of European degradation in a foreign environment. This brings us to the idea of 'cultural hybridity', another theory associated with Victorian anthropology.

The Case of the 'Cultural Hybrids'

Many zoologists and anthropologists in the Victorian era, including Waitz, debated whether or not the propensity to attain civilization might be an acquired characteristic.[33] An exception was often made in the case of 'primitive people' who were thought to progress slowly, if at all, and for whom such progress might not be passed onto the progeny. Waitz argues, for example, that primitive people must pass through 'transitional phases' in their cultural development; otherwise, they might 'relapse again into their original state'.[34] The theme of the reversion of primitive peoples, as we shall see, pervaded the anthropological and travel writing of the Victorian period; however, this theme also recurred in popular ethnographic novels. In one of G. A. Henty's novels, *By Sheer Pluck* (1874), a character who is Henty's mouthpiece for imperialism, Mr Goodenough, remarks that only by contact with Europeans can 'primitive' peoples be improved. Deprived of such ameliorative influences, the Victorians believed, the 'savages' would return to their original state: 'Living among white men, their imitative faculties enable them to attain a considerable amount of civilization. Left alone to their own devices they retrograde into a state little above their native savagery.'[35]

---

[32] Carl Vogt provides an example of this theme: 'In the same way as culture, wealth, aliment, and particular occupations may develop a cultured race from a natural race, so may the deprivation of such influences reduce a cultured race to its primary condition.' Cavl Vogt, *Lectures on Man*, James Hunt (ed.) (London: Longman, 1864), 427.

[33] See Waitz, i. 381.   [34] Ibid. i. 389.   [35] Quoted in White, 75.

The reversion of only partially assimilated people, or people of mixed culture, to savagery, was another common idea in the period, with clear racial undertones. Tylor argued that the contacts between primitive and civilized peoples had demonstrated the difficulties in attaining a higher level of development: 'Civilization is a plant much more often propagated than developed. As regards the lower races, this accords with the results of European intercourse with savage tribes.'[36] This idea inverted the theory of European degeneration in the tropics, and was based on a belief in the natural tendency of so-called primitive people to resist civilization. Many anthropologists thought, in addition, that civilization that had been only partially obtained could be easily lost again. This debate coincided with that regarding environment and heredity. In the terminology of the period, people who crossed cultural boundaries between savage and civilized became known as 'cultural hybrids'.[37] The idea of 'cultural hybridity' depended upon a botanical analogy. Plants that had been artificially cultivated over generations could only be sustained by constant breeding, whereas given a change in climatic conditions, they would tend to revert again to their dominant forms. Some Victorians extended this analogy to the acquisition of culture.

One famous example of the reversion of the cultural hybrid is provided by Darwin's account in his journal of the *Beagle*'s voyage, of the assimilation and degeneration of a Fuegian native. A group of Fuegians had been taken from Patagonia by Captain Fitzroy during an earlier voyage of the *Beagle*. Following in the long tradition of Pocahontas and other indigenous peoples being used as show-pieces, these 'natives' became celebrities in England. They lived in England for three years, where they were believed to have assimilated to European culture; Fitzroy then brings them with him on Darwin's voyage. From the start, Darwin is sceptical: 'Our three Fuegians, though they had been three years with civilised man, would, I am sure, have been glad to have retained their new habits; but this was obviously impossible. I fear it is more than doubtful, whether their visit will have been of any use to them.'[38] It comes as

[36] Tylor, *Primitive Culture*, i. 48.
[37] On 'cultural hybrids', see Street, 102–5.
[38] Charles Darwin, *Journal of Researches into the Natural History and Geology of the Countries Visited During the Voyage of the H.M.S. Beagle Round the World Under the Command of Captain Fitzroy, R. N.* (1839) (Reprinted London: John Murray, 1902), 232.

no surprise to Darwin, then, when the young Fuegian known as Jemmy Button strips off his European clothing and customs and 'reverts to savagery'. Darwin notes, in particular, the abandonment of European clothes as a sign of reversion. It is as if with the shedding of tie and starched collar, the Fuegian's reversion to savagery is visibly enacted.

Darwin's anecdote apparently became widely known as an example of the reversion of the cultural hybrid. Indeed, Max Nordau, whose book *Degeneration* will be examined at some length later, uses the character of Jemmy Button as a sort of icon of reversion and one, presumably, with whom his readers would have been familiar:

> We see savage races who die out when the power of the white man makes it impossible for them to shut out civilization; but we also see some who hasten with joy to tear off the stiff collar imposed by civilization, as soon as the constraint is removed. I need only recall the anecdote, related in detail by Darwin, of the Fuegian, Jemmy Button, who, taken as a child to England and brought up in that country, returned to his own land in the patent leather shoes and gloves, and what not of fashionable attire, but who, when scarcely landed, threw off the spell of his foreign slumber for which he was not ripe, and became again a savage among savages.[39]

The stiff collar of civilization is a perfect symbol for Nordau of the cultural constraints of which people, both primitive and cultured, would like to rid themselves.

The mirror image of the native who is uncomfortable in European clothes occurs in *Heart of Darkness* when Marlow points to the clothing of the company's chief accountant as a sign of discipline and a refusal to surrender to 'savagery': 'His appearance was certainly that of a hairdresser's dummy; but in the great demoralization of the land he kept up his appearance. That's backbone. His starched collars and got up shirt fronts were achievements of character' (*HD* 21). Conrad suggests here, only in part ironically that European clothing might be a guard against the incursions of savagery or primitive degeneration. As so often in Conrad, Marlow's response is ambivalent: On the one hand it partakes of the colonialist stereotype that 'dressing for dinner' is a guard against degeneration, on the other, Marlow's comment

---

[39] Max Nordau, *Degeneration* (1895) (Reprinted London: Heinemann, 1920), 542.

squares with occasional reports of those professional cultural relativists, anthropologists. Compare the passage in Conrad with the
account of Eleanor Bowen, an anthropologist doing fieldwork in
Africa. Experiencing a sense of 'culture shock', Bowen grounds
herself in the familiar signs and symbols which Oberg calls so
crucial in the process of identity maintenance:

It was merely a matter of hanging on to my resolution never again to forget
who and what I was: an anthropologist, an American, an heir to civilization. The English were quite right. One had to dress for dinner. One
needed a symbol, some external sign, to assist daily remembrance of what
one was. It did not occur to me that the need for such artificial aids was
alien to me and a sign that I was no longer myself.[40]

In this revealing passage, Bowen demonstrates what becomes clear
through the reading of anthropological diaries or fieldwork notes,
for example, in Malinowski's *Diary*, that even anthropologists are
not immune from this need to cling to the shreds of cultural identity
to maintain their balance.[41] Indeed, Bowen seems to invoke the
same self-distancing irony that is present in the Conrad passage;
she speaks of 'my resolution never again to forget who and what I
was: an anthropologist, an American, an heir to civilization'. The
word 'civilization' is particularly tinged with irony. Yet, at the same
time, Bowen recognizes that such apparently absurd actions are
necessary: 'I could escape my cultural isolation only by being alone
for a while every day with my books and my thoughts. It was the
one means of hanging on to myself, of regaining my balance, of
keeping my purpose in being out here before me, and of retaining
my own values.'[42] Clothing for Nordau, Conrad, and Darwin thus
represents the outward signs of the separation between primitive
and civilized people, though it is important to distinguish among
their views. To Darwin and Nordau, European clothing seems
ill-fitting on primitive people, a thin varnish over the savagery
underneath.[43] For Conrad, on the other hand, clothing is radically

[40] Quoted in Wengle, 22.
[41] The anthropological diary, indeed, may serve the same basic psychological
function as did Conrad's diary and letters from the Congo. Wengle quotes Rosemary
Firth: 'It (the diary) became for me a sort of lifeline, or checking point to measure
changes in myself . . . Mine was used as an emotional outlet for an individual
subjected to disorienting changes in his personal and social world.' Wengle, 24.
[42] Quoted in Wengle, 22–3.
[43] This is a common trope. Leo Frobenius, an ethnographer whose writing influenced D. H. Lawrence, writes similarly of this clothing theme; and his point is driven

decontextualized in a foreign environment, and stiff collars only point to the utter incongruity of the white colonist's presence in black Africa. Conrad recognizes the irony that colonialists must cling to those small cultural signs and symbols to retain their sense of self.

In *Heart of Darkness*, Marlow uses the image of clothing to show that 'civilization' is a threadbare garment on Europeans themselves, always in danger of disintegrating to leave them in primitive nakedness. He sees 'truth stripped of its cloak of time' and recognizes that civilization is only a matter of 'Acquisitions, clothes, pretty rags—rags that would fly off at the first good shake' (*HD* 38). But even in the novella European clothing and customs are viewed as unnatural impositions on the Africans, who are likely to return to 'primitivism'. Soon after the image of culture as a threadbare coat, Marlow takes a close look at his African fireman. In images very familiar to the readers of popular ethnographic fiction of this period, Marlow pokes fun at the assimilation of this character:

And meanwhile, I had to look after the savage who was a fireman. He was an improved specimen; he could fire up a vertical boiler. He was there below me, and upon my word, to look at him was as edifying as seeing a dog in a parody of breeches and a feather hat, walking on his hind legs. A few months of training had done for that really fine chap.   (*HD* 38)

The fireman is a familiar figure in Conrad, almost a stereotype of the cultural hybrid, one of those men and women whose inner impulse is to join in 'clapping his hands and feet on the band' to the sounds of primitive drums, 'instead of which he was hard at work' (*HD* 38–9). The comparison to a 'dog in a parody of breeches' has rightly been seen as dehumanizing, a surfacing of overt racism. The fireman also seems to be meant as a contrast to the unassimilated African fishermen Marlow sees in his voyage up the coast, and whom he respects for their dignity.

The idea of people of 'mixed-race' or 'hybrids' as being particularly prone to degeneration was another common feature of contemporary writing on so-called primitive cultures. Bolt speaks of this belief 'in the degeneracy and ferocity of hybrids'.[44] In a

home by a cartoon of an African chieftain in a top hat. See *Childhood of Man*, 21, 22–4.

[44] See Bolt, 23.

blatantly racist formulation, miscegenation was viewed as a terrible taboo, the prevention of which was justified by eugenicist notions of the sterility and fragility of those of mixed race. Tylor pointed to the degradation of mixed races or hybrids as evidence to support cultural degeneration: 'In connexion with this state of things take place the nearest known approach to an independent degeneration from a civilized to a savage state. This happens in mixed races, whose standards of civilization may be more or less that of the higher race.'[45]

The danger—almost the inevitability—of reversion to primitivism in persons of 'mixed race' is a common theme in Conrad's early novels, *Almayer's Folly* (1895) and *An Outcast of the Islands* (1896).[46] Indeed, the theme of the degeneration of a white trader in an alien environment is shared by both *Almayer's Folly* and *Heart of Darkness*. The thematic connections are hardly suprising. During his Congo journey Conrad carried with him the first seven chapters of the Borneo novel.[47] Contemplating the deterioration of Almayer might well have coloured his impressions of colonists in Africa. The implicit racism of this theme is tempered by the fact that Conrad does not tend to make the easy judgements about foreign cultures that some of his contemporaries made. But it would be wrong to see these early novels as divorced from the cultural assumptions of their time.[48] At times this theme has clearly racist overtones, as in *Almayer's Folly* when Captain Ford tells Almayer that despite his efforts to acclimate his daughter to European civilization: 'You can't make her white' (*AF* 28). Nina, the daughter of a Malaysian mother and a Dutch father, is educated in a convent, but when she returns home finds the allure of the so-called primitive culture irresistible. In a typical Victorian formulation, the half-civilized person throws off the constraints of

---

[45] Tylor, *Primitive Culture*, i. 41.

[46] One noteworthy study of the Malay novels is Heliéna Krenn's *Conrad's Lingard Trilogy: Empire, Race, and Women in the Malay Novels* (New York: Garland Publishing, 1990).

[47] Conrad wrote that he travelled in the Congo, 'always with *Almayer's Folly* amongst my diminishing baggage' (*PR* 14).

[48] The description of Mrs Almayer fits in with many of the racial stereotypes of so-called primitive people that Street examines in *Savage in Literature*: 'The squareness of lower jaw, the full red lips, the mobile nostrils, and the proud carriage of the head, gave the impression of being, half-savage, untamed, perhaps cruel, and corrected the liquid softness of the almost feminine eye, that general characteristic of the race' (*AF* 55).

civilization.[49] Conrad paints a picture of a person of 'mixed race' which is similar to those of popular contemporary writers.

Almayer worries about bringing his daughter into his own life of degradation: 'He could not take her back into the savage life to which he was condemned' (*AF* 27). However, in Victorian terms, she reverts easily to type: 'Nina adapted herself wonderfully to the circumstances of a half-savage and miserable life. She accepted without question or apparent disgust the neglect, the decay, the poverty of the household' (*AF* 29). The description of Nina may be compared with those of other writers whom Street discusses in *The Savage in Literature*.[50] The veneer of civilization, Conrad suggests, is very thin:

And listening to the recital of those savage glories, those barbarous fights and savage feasting; to the deeds valorous, albeit somewhat bloodthirsty, where men of her mother's race shone far above the Orang Blanda, she felt herself irresistibly fascinated and saw with vague surprise the narrow mantle of civilized morality, in which good meaning people had wrapped her soul, fall away and leave her shivering and helpless as if on the edge of some deep and unknown abyss (. . .) Her young mind had been unskillfully permitted to glance at better things, and then thrown back into the hopeless quagmire of barbarism.   (*AF* 37–8)

Again, Conrad depicts the morality imposed upon Nina as an ill-fitting garment.

Contemporary reviews of *Almayer's Folly* demonstrate how familiar Conrad's readers would have been with this theme of reversion. Indeed, Conrad seems to have welcomed this interpretation of the novel. He wrote to Wilfred Hugh Chesson, along with Garnett one of the readers of the novel, that *Almayer's Folly* might be characterized as a 'civilized story in savage surroundings'.[51] In keeping with this theme, the novel's reception in the *Daily News* should have come as no surprise to Conrad:

Mr Conrad says that he combines, 'the psychological study of a sensitive European living alone among semi-hostile Arabs and Malays with the vivid incidents attaching to the life of pirates and smugglers.' A merely 'sensitive' European has no business among the semi-savages of Borneo. What you want is an unbounded, reckless hospitality to all sorts of impressions.[52]

---

[49] As the reviewer in *Atheneum* described it, it is the story of the 'revolt of her half-tamed nature from the restraints of civilization'. Sherry, *Critical Heritage*, 52.

[50] See, for example, Street, 102–5.   [51] *Collected Letters of Conrad*, i. 99.

[52] Sherry, *Critical Heritage*, 47.

Perhaps most interestingly in relation to the anthropological theme, this reviewer commented on the 'reassertion of the old savage instinct in the pirate's lovely daughter—an atavistic fit'.[53]

The theme of the regression of the cultural hybrid, as Saveson notes, is a common theme in the early novels. In *Almayer's Folly*, Nina's 'action in deserting Almayer for Dain illustrates, although probably not in the usual pejorative sense, the law of evolutionary anthropologists that in any crossing of a higher with a lower strain, either of men or animals, the offspring will regress'.[54] In the novel, Nina's reversion is viewed as an almost inevitable facet of her mixed heritage: 'Her young mind having been unskillfully permitted to glance at better things, and then thrown back into the hopeless quagmire of barbarism, full of strong and uncontrolled passions, had lost the power to discriminate.'[55] The cultural degeneration of a half-European in Borneo was an issue raised in many of the reviews: 'The tragedy of it lies in the revolt of a half-savage daughter of a European—himself the husband of a Malay—to the passions of her mother's people'; 'The beautiful girl, educated as a Christian among white people, is the child of her mother as well as her father, and in the end it is the savage strain of her nature that conquers, and leads her to abandon the comparative civilisation of her father's house for the squalid luxury of a Malayan harem'.[56] H. G. Wells, in a favourable review of the novel, wrote that 'the central conception is the relapse of their daughter from the colonial version of civilization to barbaric life', while the *Speaker* emphasized the 'deterioration of character consequent upon his (Almayer's) life of semi-barbarism'.[57]

Another example of this theme in Conrad is the half-Portuguese family in *An Outcast of the Islands*. Conrad describes the Da Souzas as lazy and degenerate. A passage at the beginning of *An Outcast of the Islands* demonstrates that Conrad also subscribed to this view of primitivist reversion in his early works. He refers to Willems's relatives, the Da Souzas, as 'those degenerate descendants of Portuguese conquerors'.[58] This passage in Conrad closely resembles a passage in E. B. Tylor's *Anthropology*:

---

[53] Ibid.   [54] Cf. Saveson, 22.   [55] Quoted in Saveson, 23.
[56] Sherry, *Critical Heritage*, 51, 55.   [57] Ibid. 55.
[58] The theme of the degenerate 'half-caste' is very common in Conrad's works. In *Lord Jim*, Marlow's half-Portuguese servant is portrayed in this manner: 'The race—the two races rather—and the climate' (*LJ* 44–5).

Now the same rule applies both to taking in new civilization and keeping up old. When the new life of a people is altered by emigration into a new country, or by war and distress at home, or mixture with a lower race, the culture of their forefathers may be no longer needed or possible, and so dwindles away. Such degeneration is to be seen among the descendants of the Portuguese in the East Indies, who have married with natives and fallen out of the march of civilization, so that newly-arrived Europeans go to look at them lounging about their mean hovels in the midst of luxuriant tropical fruits and flowers, as if they had been set there to teach by example how man falls in culture where the need of effort is wanting.[59]

The idea of the reversion of 'half-civilized' people reinforced the Victorian conception that civilization was as difficult to keep as to gain. Degeneration is viewed as almost inevitable for persons of 'mixed race', while culture is seen to be extremely difficult to maintain. This passage represents a sort of lowest-common-denominator view of civilization—that the slide into primitivism for those only recently possessed of 'civilization' is almost inevitable. Atavism as a common feature of life in the East is an idea that is also present in Wallace's *The Malay Archipelago*, a work that Conrad read and respected: 'Next come the descendants of the Portuguese—a mixed, degraded and degenerate race.'[60] It seems very likely that Conrad culled the sense of the degeneracy of colonists in *Almayer's Folly* and *An Outcast of the Islands* in part from his reading of Wallace's book. A reviewer of the novel seems to have had Wallace in mind when he remarked that 'Hither the Portuguese came, and have since decayed'.[61] Willems's in-laws are described, in common Victorian tropes, as indolent, demoralized, and degenerate: 'They were a half-cast lazy lot, and he saw them as they were—ragged, lean, unwashed, undersized men of various ages' (*OI* 4–5).

Beneath the surface of anthropological objectivity often lurked the cultural taboo of miscegenation. The notion of miscegenation as a dangerous and inherently corrupting feature of the contacts among cultures underlay much writing of the period. Despite occasionally sympathetic treatments of miscegenation, it remained a

---

[59] E. B. Tylor, *Anthropology: An Introduction to the Study of Man and Civilization* (London: Macmillan, 1881), 19.
[60] Alfred Russel Wallace, *The Malay Archipelago* (New York: Harper & Brothers, 1869), 38.
[61] Sherry, *Critical Heritage*, 63.

largely taboo theme in colonial discourse.[62] When the notion was mentioned at all it was nearly always with disdain. At its most rabid, this idea of degeneration through intermarriage could be seen as a harbinger of cultural collapse. 'It is evident', wrote Josiah Nott, perhaps not coincidentally an American southerner of the mid-nineteenth century, 'that the superior races ought to kept free from all adulterations, otherwise the world will retrograde, instead of advancing, in civilization'.[63] Indeed, says Nott, 'Wherever in the history of the world the inferior races have conquered and mixed in with the Caucasian, the latter have sunk into barbarism'.[64] Again, he argues 'That the Negro and Indian Races are susceptible of the same degree of civilization that the Caucasian is, all history would show not to be true—that the Caucasian race is deteriorated by intermixing with the inferior races is equally true'.[65]

The theme of the degeneration of the European colonist in the East seems to have been of particular interest to Conrad, as Meyers says in his biography: 'He was strongly attracted to the theme of the degeneration of the white man in the tropics, and found it safer, for social and political reasons, to write about the Dutch rather than the English imperialists.'[66] Reviews of *An Outcast of the Islands* recognized the importance of this theme of the degeneration of colonists in primitive cultures in Conrad's works. The novel could be viewed as a portrait of 'two white men, outcasts from civilization', who 'stand out strongly in their isolation against the background of the tropical rainforest'.[67] The inherent conflict of character here is closely tied to the anthropological dilemma that has been traced in relation to *Heart of Darkness*. The colonists apparently have only two bleak choices in Conrad's view: to maintain their isolation from the indigenous culture and thus live as permanent outsiders, professional strangers in these 'primitive' cultures; or to choose the path of assimilation that for the Victorians was almost synonymous with degeneracy and demoralization. To attempt to remain 'aloof' presented almost impossible difficulties for a colonist so dependent on native people's support. In *An Outcast of the Islands*, Conrad portrays with a mixture of sympathy and disdain Willems's plight as a perpetual alien.

[62] See Bolt, 140–1.
[63] Quoted in Stocking, *Race, Culture, and Evolution*, 16.
[64] Quoted in Taylor, 16.   [65] Quoted in Taylor, 41.
[66] Meyers, 89.   [67] Sherry, *Critical Heritage*, 65.

Willems's relationship with Aïssa, which is all but doomed in the Victorian view because it is miscegenistic, is intimately bound up with Willems's recognition of his own degeneration.[68] Willems is disgusted because he views himself as 'a white man whose worst fault till then had been a little want of judgment and too much confidence in the rectitude of his kind. That woman was a complete savage (. . .) He seemed to be surrendering to a wild creature the unstained purity of his life, of his race, of his civilization' (OI 80–1). Conrad seems to be lampooning here Willems's pathetic racial pride when he writes of the 'unstained purity' of his life and race. The last word here, civilization, as we have already seen, often occupies an ironic place in Conrad's fictional lexicon. At the same time, Conrad is not merely satirizing the fear of racial degeneracy. As noted above, Willems, though often pathetic, receives some sympathy because of his marginalized status. Indeed, Conrad constantly stresses how extreme is Willems's disassociation from others: 'I shall never return. (. . .) I have done with my people. I am a man without brothers' (OI 131); 'I have no people of my own' (OI 143). Conrad sharply contrasts Lingard, a man who seems to need no ethnic safety net in order to maintain his sense of identity, to Willems. Lingard disdains racial distinctions; but he sees Willems as a man who has no loyalty to any culture or sub-culture: 'You are neither white nor brown. You have no color as you have no heart' (OI 276). On the other hand, all that Willems can cling to are the shreds of his perceived racial status; and yet, even this marks a pyrrhic victory, for he recognizes that he is actually the servant of 'native' interests. The theme of taboos regarding miscegenation which recurs in Conrad's Malaysian works apparently reflects a Victorian fear of sexual contacts as part of the process of 'going native'. Indeed, several historians have traced a change in sexual attitudes from early periods of contact between European traders and 'natives', when sexual relations are condoned, and a second stage of colonialism, when an attempt is made to establish in miniature a transplanted European world, including European

[68] Robert Louis Stevenson's narrator in *The Beach of Falesá* writes similarly of the dangers of 'mixed-marriages': 'I was one of those most opposed to any nonsense about native women, having seen so many whites eaten up by their wives' relatives and made fools of into the bargain (. . .).' Stevenson, *The Beach of Falesá: Being The Narrative of a South Sea Trader* in *Island Nights' Entertainment* (1892) Vailima edition of the works of R. L. Stevenson, 26 vols. (Reprinted London: Heinemann, 1922), vol. 15, pp. 295–6.

families. Is this problem, though, simply one of Victorian racism? This theme of sexuality is not widely discussed in anthropological literature, as John Wengle admits: 'The last point that I wish to consider here, (...) is the problem of sexuality for the fieldworker. Obviously, this is a touchy subject and little has been written about it.'[69] Wengle goes on, in a revealing passage:

An anthropologist's self-imposed celibacy can help him preserve his sense of identity by forcing him to direct his probably acute sexual needs and fantasies outside of the field environment and back to his home culture. By doing this, the anthropologist creates a 'strong and ever present link' with his home culture and so solidifies his sense of identity (...). The celibate anthropologist is, if nothing else, secure in his sense of identity.[70]

The maintenance of identity in celibacy, or the opposite—the loss of identity through 'miscegenation'—helps to explain, if not explain away, Willems's behaviour: 'He seemed to be surrendering to a wild creature the unstained purity of his life, of his race, of his civilization' (*OI* 80).

In a theme that was to become common in anti-imperial literature such as Hobson's *Imperialism* (1902), Conrad portrayed relationships among people in the colonies as infected by parasitism. All relationships seem to revolve around use. Thus, Willems is aware that his 'half-caste' and 'degenerate' relatives prey on him:

He was their providence; he kept them singing his praises in the midst of their laziness, of their dirt, of their immense and hopeless squalor: and he was greatly delighted. They wanted much, but he could give them what they wanted without ruining himself. In exchange he had their silent fear, their loquacious love, their noisy veneration. It is a fine thing to be a providence, and to be told so on every day of one's life. It gives one feeling of enormously remote superiority, and Willems reveled in it. He did not analyze the state of his mind, but probably his greatest delight lay in the unexpressed but intimate conviction that, should he close his hand, all those admiring human beings would starve. His munificence had demoralized them. An easy task... This was power. Willems loved it.

(*OI* 4)

The phrase 'in exchange' may well be charged with Conradian irony, for, as Conrad and other writers of the period suggest, the imperial trade infects all human interchanges and renders them mere exchange mechanisms. At the same time, as Hobson

---

[69] Wengle, p. 25.   [70] Ibid.

demonstrates, the whole imperial venture is a process of one culture feeding on another in the name of capitalism. Stevenson invokes this theme in his fiction when he writes of his characters in *The Beach of Falesá*: 'Trade and station belonged both to Randall; Case and the negro were parasites; they crawled and fed upon him like the flies, he none the wiser.'[71] Stevenson's culturally shipwrecked characters parallel Conrad's Willems, whose almost hysterical insistence on the purity of his race is presented as pathetic; he clings to an ethnic identification because of his lack of personal integrity. Willems betrays Lingard and is punished by being left by Lingard in his perpetual exile among people who will never accept him. When Willems's wife returns, the novel ends in Willems's almost farcical murder by Aïssa. Until the end of the story he is constantly searching for a racial identification that he equates with understanding: 'There were ships there—ships, help, white men. Men like himself. Good men who would rescue him . . . take him far away where there was trade, and houses, and other men that could understand him exactly' (*OI* 329).

Denationalization

The Victorian lexicon reserved a scornful term for those who thus transgressed both cultural and moral boundaries—such people were called denationalized. The concatenation of 'denationalization' (losing one's national loyalty) and 'degeneration' (losing one's moral centre) is a common feature of writing on the colonial experience. Conrad's friend Hugh Clifford, a Malaysian district officer and later governor, who often wrote with great sensitivity and cultural relativism about the 'East' also painted portraits of whites who had 'gone native'. In his novel *A Freelance of Today* (1902), Clifford writes about Martin Curzon, a brilliant young district officer who goes native and takes a native wife. When he departs for England on leave and returns with a white fiancée, he is faced with the consequences of having become denationalized. At the beginning of the story Clifford writes of his protagonist:

circumstances and inclination had combined to well-nigh denationalise him, to make him turn from his own kind, herd with the natives, and

---

[71] Stevenson, *Falesá*, p. 291. Brantlinger notes this theme, *Rule of Darkness*, 40.

conceive for them such an affection and sympathy that he was accustomed
to contrast his countrymen unfavourably with his Malayan friends. This,
be it said, is not a wholesome attitude of mind for any European, but it is
curiously common among such white men as chance has thrown for long
periods of time into close contact with Oriental races, and whom Nature
has endowed with imaginations sufficiently keen to enable them to live into
the life of the strange folk around them.[72]

Clifford's passage is fascinating for its anthropological resonances;
the phrase 'whom nature has endowed with imaginations sufficiently keen to enable them to live into the life of the strange folk
around them' recalls the goals of fieldwork. The anthropological
fieldworker attempts similarly to 'live into the life' of his or her
subjects. Ironically, Clifford suggests that the 'talent' (for such
cultural sensitivity seems to be, in part, a talent) for cultural assimilation that he invokes here is ultimately degenerative, a 'not wholesome attitude of mind for any European.' Indeed, Curzon is initially
a prototype for the rare kind of colonial administrator whose talent
for languages and whose sensitivity to the customs and traditions of
indigenous people linked him or her with the later anthropological
fieldworker. He has the capacity to 'live into the life' of the
Malaysians. In some ways, this portrait seems semi-autobiographical, for Clifford himself as a young district officer seems to have
possessed many of these same qualities as his hero; he pursued what
might be called a participant-observer strategy in an admirable
way.[73] Indeed, although Clifford praised Conrad's *Almayer's Folly*,
he often contrasted his own intimate acquaintance with Malaysia
with Conrad's 'superficial acquaintance with the Malayan customs,
language and character'.[74]

In his writing, Clifford demonstrates his pride in his 'opportunity
of entering into the lives of the people' of Malaysia.[75] Again,
Clifford writes of his cultural assimilation among the Malays:

This meant that I was privileged to live for nearly two years in complete
isolation among the Malays in a native state which was annually cut
off from the outside world (. . .) I was afforded an unusual opportunity
of completing and perfecting my knowledge; and that circumstances

---

[72] Quoted in Goonetellike, 22.
[73] Richard Allen writes of Clifford's importance as a colonial administrator. See
Richard Allen, *Malaysia, Prospect and Retrospect: The Impact and Aftermath of
Colonial Rule* (London: Oxford University Press, 1968).
[74] Quoted in Goonetellike, 58.   [75] Quoted in Goonetellike, 58.

compelled me to live in a native hut, on native food, and in native fashion, in the company of a couple of dozen Malays—friends of mine, from the Western side of the Peninsula, who had elected to follow my fortunes. Rarely seeing a white face or speaking a word of my own tongue, it thus fell to my lot to be admired to *les coulisses* of life in a native state, as it was before the influence of Europe had tampered with its eccentricities.[76]

Clifford here embodies the assimilationist desire that would become an inherent goal of anthropological fieldwork; this sort of cultural relativism is worlds away from the brutality of a Kurtz. Yet, the Victorian fears of degeneration and loss of cultural identities caused many colonists and anthropologists themselves to resist crossing such boundaries. Indeed, although Clifford seems to have been able successfully to pursue such cultural assimilation, he can only go so far in support of such cultural relativism. Ironically, his novel portrays Curzon's denationalization and subsequent degeneration through a disastrous relationship with a Malaysian woman. In other words, Clifford's Martin Curzon, to an extent like Conrad's Almayer and Willems, degenerates because of his 'going native'.

One way in which contemporary readers might have perceived Conrad's early novels was as stories of the degenerative impact of denationalization—of being cut off from one's culture. In *An Outcast of the Islands*, this theme of the loss of racial or cultural solidarity figures in relation to Willems's relationship with Aïssa:

He sought refuge within his ideas of propriety from the dismal mangroves, from the darkness of the forests and of the heathen souls of the savages that were his masters (. . .) would his ideas ever change so as to agree with her own notions of what was becoming respectable? (. . .) She would never change! This manifestation of her sense of proprieties was another sign of their hopeless diversity; something like another step downwards for him. She was too different from him. He was so civilized! It struck him suddenly that they had nothing in common. (. . .) and he could never live without her.   (*OI* 128)

Again, Willems thinks:

It was the unreasoning fear of this glimpse into unknown things, into those motives, impulses, desires he had ignored, but that had lived in the hearts of despised men, close by his side, and were revealed to him for a second,

---

[76] Hugh Clifford, 'Preface' to *The Further Side of Silence* (New York: Doubleday, Page and Co., 1916), p. ix.

to be hidden again behind the black mists of doubt and deception. It was not death that frightened him: it was the horror of bewildered life where he could understand nothing and nobody round him; where he could guide, control, comprehend nothing and no one—not even himself.   (*OI* 149)

In order historically to contextualize the theme of the decivilization or degeneration of Europeans in tropical climates it is useful to compare Conrad's portrait to Stevenson's South Sea island tales.[77] The idea of degeneracy is already enshrined as a literary motif by Conrad's time. Stevenson's tales of the South Seas abound in images of 'broken white folk living on the bounty of the natives'.[78] For example, in *The Ebb Tide* (1896), Stevenson portrays a group of degenerate Europeans living in the South Pacific:

Throughout the island world of the Pacific, scattered men of many European races and from almost every grade of society carry activity and disseminate disease. Some prosper, some vegetate. Some have mounted the steps of thrones and owned islands and navies. Others, again, must marry for a livelihood; a strapping, merry chocolate-coloured dame supports them in sheer idleness; and, dressed like natives, but still retaining some foreign element of gate or attitude, still perhaps with some relic (such as a single eye-glass) of the officer and gentleman, they sprawl in palm-leaf verandahs, and entertain an island audience with memoirs of the music-hall. And there are still others, less pliable, less capable, less fortunate, perhaps less base, who continue, even in these isles of plenty, to lack bread.[79]

Stevenson's *The Beach of Falesá* provides another example of the clear parallels between Stevenson and Conrads' tales of 'going native'. As Brantlinger writes, 'In *Falesá*, adventure has given way to trade (. . .) A felt contradiction between trade and the heroic, aristocratic significance of adventure results in a narrative that links together imperial domination, the profit motive, moral degeneracy, parasitism, and ultimately murder or attempted murder'.[80] By the end of the story, the narrator, a trader named John Wiltshire, has settled down with a native woman. Like Almayer, he worries about his physical and psychological distance from Europe, and fears for

[77] David Thorburn makes a very different comparison between Conrad and Stevenson. See *Conrad's Romanticism*. See also Batchelor, *Lord Jim*, 25–31.

[78] Robert Louis Stevenson, *In the South Seas* (1891), Vailima edn. (London: Heinemann, 1922), xvi. 23.

[79] Robert Louis Stevenson, *The Ebb Tide: A Trio and a Quartette* (1896); Vailima edn. (London: Heinemann, 1922), xviii. 5

[80] Brantlinger, *Rule of Darkness*, 40.

the prospects of his 'half-caste' children: 'I'm stuck here, I fancy. I don't like to leave the kids (. . .) they're better here than what they would be in a white man's country, though Ben took the eldest up to Auckland, where he's being schooled with the best. But what bothers me is the girls. They're only half-castes, of course; I know that as well as you do, and there's nobody thinks less of half-castes than I do; but they're mine, and about all I've got. I can't reconcile my mind to their taking up with Kanakas, and I'd like to know where I'm to find the whites?'[81] Once again, the theme of miscegenation enters the fiction; in the Victorian mindset such 'half-castes' or 'cultural hybrids' are inherently suspect.

A reviewer of *An Outcast* in the *Nation* helps to clarify the historical importance of this theme not only in Conrad's writing, but in the Victorian *Zeitgeist*.

In this trio of tales there is a single theme—the degeneracy of the white man under the influence of the South Sea islands (. . .) In essentials, however, one does not detect any variations from the type studied by Robert Louis Stevenson in Samoa. There is always the Caucasian enslaved by the forces he came to conquer, the non-militant, alluring, poisonous forces which insidiously sap the courage and manhood of the superior alien (. . .) The white man, confronted in his idleness by great solitudes, tempted by the seductions of gluttony, cannot maintain a sufficient hold upon himself to preserve his individuality. His environment softens and disintegrates him. Through delirium tremens, or simple madness or some other of the abhorrent rear gates which it is civilization's task to keep closed, he degenerates.[82]

The motif which this critic detects in Conrad's work is a common one in the travel writing, ethnographic fiction, and anthropology of the late nineteenth century. Faced with the unrestrained native, living in a condition of *anomie*, the European degenerates. The image of this primitivism entering through the 'abhorrent rear gates which it is civilization's task to keep closed', is profoundly relevant to the writings of a German writer, Max Nordau, who claimed to have discovered the seeds of the degeneration in Europe itself.

[81] Stevenson, *Falesá*, 391.   [82] Sherry, *Critical Heritage*, 65.

6

Nordau's Degeneration *and Lombroso's Atavism in* Heart of Darkness *and 'Falk'*

Nothing can save society then except the clear head and the wide purpose; war and competition, potent instruments of selection and evolution in one epoch, become ruinous instruments of degeneration in the next. In the breeding of animals and plants, varieties which have arisen by selection through many generations relapse precipitously into the wild type in a generation or two when selection ceases (. . .)

We must therefore frankly give up the notion that Man as he exists is capable of net progress. There will always be an illusion of progress (. . .) forgetting that most of the evils we see are the effects, finally become acute, of long-unnoticed retrogressions (. . .) that on the lines along which we are degenerating, good has become evil in our eyes.[1]

Nordau, the Cultural Physician

The great success of Max Nordau's *Entartung*, published in Germany (1892) and translated into English under the title *Degeneration* (1895), depended upon cultural assumptions concerning 'primitive' and 'civilized' cultures for which anthropology had paved the way. Nordau envisioned a Europe in which the anarchic desires associated with primitive peoples, or what Durkheim would call *anomie*, had become rampant. The seemingly illimitable passion of modern man, Nordau argued, could only be checked through a return to strict moral limits. This state of unrestricted desire, Nordau labelled degeneration. Although Nordau popularized the idea of degeneration in culture, the lineage of the idea is

---

[1] Shaw, *Man and Superman*, 235.

much longer, dating back to the French psychologist, B. A. Morel.[2] Eugene S. Talbot wrote confidently of the authority of the theory in *Degeneracy, Its Causes, Signs, and Results* (1898):

With the close of the year 1883 the degeneracy doctrine may be regarded as having been practically accepted in biology, in anthropology, in sociology, in criminology, in psychiatry, and general pathology. Debate was thenceforth not as to its existence, but to its limitations.[3]

Talbot rightly traces the genealogy of Nordau's doctrine back at least ten years, to 1883. The fact that the dominance of the 'degeneracy doctrine' could be so clearly stated in 1898 shows just how important the theory was in the late Victorian and Edwardian eras. There is no satisfactory account of Nordau's reception in England. The book is too often known second-hand. Therefore, it is worth exploring *Degeneration* in light of contemporary versions of the degenerationist theory, and then suggesting some parallels and distinctions between Nordau's account of primitivistic degeneracy and Kurtz's reversion in *Heart of Darkness*.[4] Nordau's warning of the dangers of unimpeded and unrestrained appetites in man paralleled criminological studies such as those of Cesare Lombroso and Havelock Ellis. *Degeneration* called for a reconsideration of the moral imperative to restrict man's desire; as Durkheim wrote later, 'Morality is . . . like so many molds with limiting boundaries, into which we must pour our behavior'.[5] In the late nineteenth century, Nordau believed that these delimiting moulds had begun to disintegrate, leaving unbounded and irrational forces to flow into society.

Given the controversy surrounding Nordau's work, it is likely that Conrad would have been aware of *Degeneration*, at least in its general outline.[6] The thesis must have been of particular interest to Conrad because it attacked some of the French writers who so influenced him. More importantly for my purposes, though, *Degeneration* did not merely represent a *fin de siècle* world weariness; rather, it was the product of a scientific movement which had begun much earlier in anthropology, psychology, and criminology,

---

[2] See Pick, *passim*.

[3] Eugene S. Talbot, *Degeneracy, Its Causes, Signs, and Results* (London: Walter Scott, 1898), 26.

[4] John Batchelor writes: 'Nordau's central thesis, that man as a species is irreversibly degenerating (. . .) underlies the figure of Kurtz.' *H. G. Wells* (Cambridge: Cambridge University Press, 1985), 5–6.

[5] Quoted in Herbert, 73.   [6] See Watt, 161.

the purpose of which was to eradicate primitivistic elements in contemporary society. Conrad, who responded with anxiety to the notion of the degenerative contact with unrestrained 'primitive' cultures, may well have found, not just in Nordau but in the whole degenerationist argument, the roots of atavism of which Kurtz was his principle avatar. As Hans Kurella, a protégé of the Italian criminologist Cesare Lombroso, wrote darkly of the possibility of atavism: 'the occasional appearance of one or two additional atavistic characters (. . .) is hardly so incredible an occurrence (. . .) Modern man has freed himself from much that was rooted in the blood and bone of his forefathers. But unquestionably he has not freed himself from all that was so rooted'.[7]

Upon its appearance in England in 1895, *Degeneration* was sometimes ridiculed, sometimes emulated, but certainly not ignored. In English it ran to seven impressions in its first year. It spurred a lengthy anonymous reply, *Regeneration* (1896), enjoyed numerous reviews (mixed) and elicited a strong response from Bernard Shaw, *The Sanity of Art: An Exposure of the Current Nonsense about Artists Being Degenerates*, first commissioned by the American radical, Tucker, for his newspaper *Liberty*. Shaw related the origin of the reply: 'In the Easter of 1895, when Nordau was master of the field (. . .) Mr. Tucker, seeing that nobody had answered Dr. Nordau', invited Shaw to review *Degeneration* for *Liberty*.[8] In this account, written in 1895 and revised in 1907, Shaw distorted the actual history, downplaying the importance of the book and recasting it as a historical anomaly. In fact, as has been noted elsewhere, the book received a great deal of attention and was widely reviewed, though often critically. The critic in the *Saturday Review*, for example, complained that 'Nordau has been soaked up to his neck in Darwinism'.[9] The reviewer for the *Bookman* suggested, not entirely facetiously, that Nordau had become hysterical as a result of the time he had spent in hospitals and asylums.[10] The *Fortnightly Review* critic did not discount the thesis, but felt that degeneration remained a limited phenomenon: 'In a generation or more, the degenerate may be a mere sporadic survival, little likely to persist amid a race endowed with sound minds

---

[7] Hans Kurella, *Cesare Lombroso: a Modern Man of Science*, trans. M. Eden Paul (London: Rebmen, Ltd., 1911), 23–4.

[8] George Bernard Shaw, *The Sanity of Art: An Exposure of the Current Nonsense about Artists Being Degenerates* (London: Constable & Co., 1911), 7–8.

[9] Quoted in Pick, 53.   [10] Ibid.

and healthy bodies.'[11] The *Blackwood's* reviewer thought the thesis suffered from overstatement but agreed with the general diagnosis: 'we should be grateful to Dr. Max Nordau for his striking and powerful book, *Degeneration*'. While noting that the theory had been 'violently assailed', this writer agreed that the modern age had its degenerative perils: 'ours may be an age of progress, but it is a progress which, if left unchecked, could land us in the hospital or the lunatic asylum'.[12] This warning is particularly interesting in the way that it corresponds to Conrad's subversion of the idea of progress. Progress and degeneration could be closely allied.

Although George Bernard Shaw's review often ridiculed Nordau, it was a humour tempered with deep concern. Nordau's book, as Shaw described it, argued that 'all the leaders of art movements of our time are degenerate, and, consequently, retrogressive lunatics'.[13] The fact that he was even called upon to attack the book showed that in England a rearguard action was being fought against the influential book. He grudgingly admitted Nordau's influence when he wrote that 'in the main he is received as a serious authority on the subject; and that is why we two (Shaw and Tucker) without malice and solely as a matter of public duty are compelled to take all this trouble to destroy him'.[14] As the anonymous writer of *Regeneration* commented:

Dr. Max Nordau has by his book entitled 'Degeneration' produced no small sensation throughout the world, and not least in this country. Though his work may not have made the stir of a sensational novel read by millions, there can be little doubt it has imposed itself on every educated mind in the country.[15]

This claim for Nordau's impact given by a contemporary—that it had 'imposed itself on every educated mind in the country'—may be somewhat sensational, but it underscores the status of *Degeneration* as more than a short-lived *succès-de-scandale*.

Degeneration summarized contemporary movements in science, but also lent positivistic support to the criticism of contemporary 'decadence' in Europe:

---

[11] Quoted in Pick, 53.
[12] Hugh M. Stutfield, 'Tomyrotics', *Blackwood's Edinburgh Magazine*, 157/956 (June 1895), 833.
[13] Shaw, *Sanity of Art*, 38.   [14] Ibid. 103.
[15] Anon., *Regeneration: A Reply to Max Nordau* (London: Constable, 1895), 9.

It is no wonder that his work has become as it were a nightmare to millions of minds. If its diagnosis and its conclusions are as irrefutable as to most people they appear to be, we indeed live in a fool's paradise (...) the progression we vaunted is a slippery plane sliding us back to bestiality (...) unbridled animal appetites threaten to take the place of law and religion; all social order is being undermined; and the vilest instincts press for gratification in lust, rapine and murder.[16]

The receptiveness of Nordau's audience to these themes of bestiality and primitivism suggests that the time was especially ripe for such anxieties. The notion of the *anomie* of primitive peoples was, after all, a common trope in Victorian anthropology and travel literature. As the writer of *Regeneration* explains the impact of Nordau's thesis, degeneration subverted all pretensions to European 'progression'. Bestiality, unbridled animal appetites, vilest instincts: Victorians willingly accepted such a diagnosis of their time.

A widely-read cosmopolitan German trained in medicine, and with a tendency toward reductionism in his writing, Max Nordau looked around at contemporary culture in the last decade of the nineteenth century and became profoundly frustrated at what he saw—the corruption which he believed resulted from urbanization, the debasement of morals, and, particularly, the degeneration of a segment of society to a more primitive state. Nordau asserted that degenerates 'have the name of liberty on their lips when they proclaim their corrupt self, and call it progress when they extol crime, deny morality, raise altars to instinct, scoff at science, and hold up loafing aestheticism as the sole aim of life'.[17] The vaunted secularization of the era and the displacement of religion by science seemed to many Victorians to have opened the floodgates of primitivism. Fearing the transvalutation of values—the Nietzschean philosophy which had apparently filled the void left by the erosion of religion—Nordau combatted this incipient primitivism. This fear of the incursions of the primitive into modern culture included many common anxieties: the degenerate rejected 'progress' in favour of 'instinct', 'civilization' in favour of 'savagery'.

Degeneration presented a watered-down version of Haeckel, Morel, Lombroso, and others whose own theories depended upon Darwinism and anthropology. He made this debt clear in his

---

[16] *Regeneration*, 9–10.   [17] Nordau, 554.

obsequious dedication to Cesare Lombroso, the Italian psychologist who applied Darwinist and anthropological theory to criminology:

the notion of degeneracy, first introduced into science by Morel, and developed with so much genius by yourself, has in your hands already shown itself fertile (. . .) Degenerates are not always criminals, prostitutes, anarchists, and pronounced lunatics; they are often authors and artists. These, however, manifest the same mental characteristics and for the most part the same somatic features, as the members of the above mentioned anthropological family.[18]

Degeneration appeared by its very nature atavistic—that is, it implied a reversion to a more primitive state of man. The 'somatic features' of degenerates were frozen at an early evolutionary level. It is therefore not surprising that he should speak of degenerates as an 'anthropological family', for anthropologists, as I have demonstrated, long argued over the degeneration of cultures, both primitive and civilized. In the popular mind Nordau and Lombroso seem to have been closely linked.

Nordau's thesis relied on a peculiar application of Darwinism to the arts. The arts had developed along evolutionary lines similar to those in biology, this theory held, and new degenerate artists threatened to reverse the course of natural selection:

Retrogression, relapse—this is in general the ideal of this band who dare to speak of liberty and progress. They wish to be the future. That is one of their chief pretensions (. . .) We have, however, seen in all individual cases that it is not the future but the most forgotten, far-away past, (. . .) They confound all the arts, and lead them back to the primitive forms they had before evolution differentiated them. Every one of their qualities is atavistic, and we know, moreover, that atavism is one of the most constant marks of degeneracy.[19]

The Measure of Man: Craniologists and Cranks

Lombroso, like so many cultural critics of the late nineteenth century, depended upon anthropology to support his theories. Indeed, Lombroso's principal theory—that criminals represented a particular physiological type, can be traced back to Pieter Camper's

[18] Nordau, p. vii   [19] Ibid., pp. vii–viii.

(1722–89) and J. F. Blumenbach's interest in phrenology in the late eighteenth and early nineteenth centuries, as well as the theories of Paul Broca, J. Gall and C. Spurzheim later.[20] These early anthropologists set out theories of race which correlated physiological and racial types with moral and physical development. Although Blumenbach's theory attributed physiological differences to environment rather than race, this aspect of the theory was largely disregarded by later writers. What later theorists assimilated from Blumenbach's work was the notion of a hierarchy of races, with the Caucasian squarely at the centre: 'The Caucasian must, on every physiological principle, be considered the primary or intermediate of these five principal Races.'[21] Blumenbach helped to introduce the idea of craniometry—that cranial size and shape largely determined intelligence. Other writers such as T. H. Huxley originally subscribed to these theories, and only later disregarded craniology. Although Huxley's support for craniology gradually diminished, his status as a comparative anatomist and lecturer in craniology in the 1860s was so great that John Lubbock sought his advice in preparation for *Pre-historic Man*.[22] Alfred Russel Wallace followed Huxley in declaring craniometry to be an anthropological dead end:

A few years ago it was thought that the study of Crania offered the only basis for the classification of man. Immense collections have been formed; they have been measured, described and figured; and now the opinion is beginning to gain ground that for this special purpose they are of very little value. Professor Huxley has boldly stated his views to this effect, and in a proposed new classification of mankind gives scarcely any weight to characteristics derived from the cranium.[23]

Conrad, who had read Wallace, similarly disregarded the idea of craniometry. In nearly one hundred years, the theory of craniometry did not disappear, but had become reinforced by pseudo-scientists like Lombroso. Lombroso attempted to isolate the regressive physiological characteristics which he believed existed in criminals.

[20] Christine Bolt writes of the resurgence of these theories in the late nineteenth century: see Bolt, 15. See also Gould, *Mismeasure of Man*, and Street, 51–5.

[21] J. F. Blumenbach, A *Manual of the Elements of Natural History* (London: W. Simpson & R. Marshall, 1825), 37.

[22] Leonard Huxley (ed.), *Life and Letters of Thomas Henry Huxley*, 2 vols. (London: Macmillan, 1900), i. 237–8, 287–9.

[23] Wallace, 599. See Hunter, 184.

In a scene in *Heart of Darkness*, Conrad parodies the craniological theories of pseudo-scientists such as Lombroso. The doctor who works for the trading company examines Marlow before his journey: 'then with a certain eagerness (he) asked me whether I would let him measure my head. Rather surprised I said Yes, when he produced a thing like calipers and got the dimensions back and front and everyway, taking notes carefully (. . .) "I always ask leave, in the interests of science, to measure the head of those going out there" ' (*HD* 15). Conrad's doctor is a composite of many of the scientific interests of his day: craniology, incipient alienism, phrenology, and physical anthropology. Here Conrad seems to be satirizing the craniological ideas of Lombroso. One element in the scene seems to be the anthropological concern with the impact of climate upon physiognomy. The measurement of Marlow's head in the interest of science may be seen as an attempt to ascertain physiological changes caused by the foreign environment of Africa. The doctor seems to be particularly interested in Marlow's racial background: 'You are the first Englishman coming under my observation' (*HD* 15).

Conrad had a personal connection with this tradition of physical anthropology. As Frederick R. Karl has noted in *Joseph Conrad: The Three Lives*, in 1881 Conrad's uncle, Tadeusz Bobrowski wrote on behalf of an old tutor of Conrad's, Izydor Kopernicki, a prominent Polish anthropologist, doctor, and social scientist who had written a book on craniology, *Comparative Studies of Human Races, Based on Types of Skulls*.[24] Interestingly, Kopernicki, who, like Lombroso, was both an anthropologist/ethnologist and a medical doctor, suggesting the blurring of scientific interests during the Victorian era. Bobrowski remarked in this letter:

Mr. Kopernicki was most solicitous in inquiring about you. I read out your letters to him, having found one waiting for me. He is engaged upon a great work which has already brought him European fame: 'Comparative studies of human races based on types of skulls.' This particular branch of science is called 'Craniology.' He earnestly requests you to collect during your voyages skulls of the natives, writing on each whose skull it is and the place of origin. When you have collected a dozen or so of such skulls write to me and I will obtain from him information as to the best way of dispatching them to Cracow where there is a special Museum devoted to Craniology.

[24] Karl, *Three Lives*, 80.

Please do not forget this, and do your best to fulfill the request of this scientist.[25]

Although there is evidence to suggest that Conrad aided Kopernicki to the extent that he provided names of correspondents, it is clear from his writing that his reaction to craniology was sceptical.[26] However, the subject of craniology should not be dismissed as merely the province of cranks; craniology developed as an important and widely-known science in the Victorian era, given support by prominent anthropologists such as Lubbock and Huxley. Indeed, the prominence and popularity of craniology is suggested by Bobrowski's allusion to a museum of craniology in Cracow. One of the chief proponents of this 'science' during Conrad's lifetime was Cesare Lombroso.

Kurtz and Lombroso: Criminal or Man of Genius?

Following phrenologists and physical anthropologists, Lombroso applied the same general theories, with somewhat different implications, to the study of criminal psychology. He found that *l'uomo delinquente*, or criminal, resembled a nearly morphological duplicate of the types of primitive man. Drawing loosely upon anthropological sources, Lombroso and his followers compared the behaviour of criminals with that of so-called primitives. The fear of the primitive, the instinctive, and the unconscious impulses in humanity could thus be identified with a particular group. As Lombroso explained in *The Female Offender*, the criminal was 'only a reversion to the primitive type of his species'.[27] Interpreted in a Darwinist light, both criminals and 'savages' represented either evolutionary 'throw-backs', or those whose development had been arrested at a primitive level. Criminals therefore challenged prevalent Spencerian notions regarding the development of morality through the evolutionary process. William Douglas Morrison, an English penologist, wrote in the introduction to Lombroso's *The Female Offender* (1895):

These mental anomalies are visible among the criminal population in an absence of moral sensibility, in general instability of character, in excessive

[25] Ibid.   [26] Ibid.
[27] Cesare Lombroso and William Ferrero, *The Female Offender* (London: T. Fisher Unwin, 1895), 112–13.

vanity, excessive irritability, a love of revenge, and, as far as habits are concerned, a descent to customs and pleasures akin in their natures to the orgies of uncivilized tribes. In short, the habitual criminal is a product, according to Dr. Lombroso, of pathological and atavistic anomalies; he stands midway between the lunatic and the savage; and he represents a special type of the human race.[28]

Criminals represented 'atavism', a word which implied primitive ancestry or lineage (atavist, from the Latin *atavus* meaning 'ancestor'). This elision of primitivism and criminality became one of the most controversial and widely debated implications of Lombroso's studies; it was also, undoubtedly, the most influential, and was eagerly seized on by many of his contemporaries. Although reviled by some, the theory of atavism was the hallmark of late nineteenth-century criminology. The author of the entry under criminology in the 1910 version of the *Encyclopaedia Britannica*, for example, credits Lombroso with seeing the intimate relationship between the psychology of 'born criminals' and their physiognomy, 'due partly to degeneration, partly to atavism'. The writer then paraphrases Lombroso: 'The criminal is a special type of the human race, something midway between the lunatic and the savage.'[29] This aspect of Lombrosan theory seems to have gained wide currency in part because it coincided with implications of Darwinism in the popular mind: the notion of 'descent' from an ape-like progenitor carried with it the dangers of reversion, atavism, regression, and degeneration, all of which in their different manifestations fascinated the Victorians. As Bernard Shaw's John Tanner comments, 'the wild beast breaks out in Man and casts him back momentarily into barbarism under the excitement of war and crime'.[30] This theme might be similarly applied to H. G. Wells, who also conceived of man as an animal poised only tenuously on the verge of civilization—a culminating ape. Although he was ambivalent about the notion of degeneration, Darwin's own brief comment in *The Descent of Man* gave support to this view: 'With mankind some of the worst dispositions which occasionally without any assignable cause make their appearance in families, may perhaps be reversions to a savage state, from which we are not removed by many genera-

---

[28] Cesare Lombroso and William Ferrero, *The Female Offender*, p. xvi.
[29] Anon., 'Criminology', *Encyclopaedia Britannica*, 11th edn. (1910), vii. 465.
[30] Shaw, *Man and Superman*, 242.

tions.'[31] This reversion, on one level, is precisely the theme of Kurtz's fall in *Heart of Darkness*.

Lombroso's seminal work, *Criminal Man* (1876) was widely known on the continent, and in England through Havelock Ellis's summary in *The Criminal* (1890). It was only later translated into English by his daughter (1911). In this work, Lombroso explained that the theory of atavism had occurred to him as a sort of revelation in December 1870. In looking at the skull of the Brigand Villella, Lombroso began to see it as a map of primitive emotions and impulses:

This was not merely an idea but a revelation. At the sight of the skull, I seemed to see all of a sudden, lighted up as plain as day under a flaming sky, the problem of the nature of the criminal—an atavistic being who reproduces in his person the ferocious instincts of primitive humanity and inferior animals. Thus were explained anatomically the enormous jaws, high cheek bones, prominent supercillary arches, solitary lines in the palms, in criminals, savages and apes, insensibility to pain, extremely acute sight, tattooing, excessive idleness, love of orgies, and the irresponsible craving of evil for its own sake, he desire not only to extinguish life in the victim, but to mutilate the corpse, tear its flesh and drink its blood.[32]

Although I would not press the point too far, there seems to be an element of this Lombrosan atavism in Conrad's Gentleman Brown:

Brown was a latter-day buccaneer, sorry enough, like his more celebrated prototypes; but what distinguished him from his contemporary brother ruffians (...) was the arrogant temper of his misdeeds and a vehement scorn for mankind at large and for his victims in particular. The others were merely vulgar and greedy brutes, but he seemed moved by some complex intention. He would rob a man as if only to demonstrate his poor opinion of the creature, and he would bring to the shooting or maiming of some quiet unoffending a stranger a savage and vengeful earnestness fit to terrify the most reckless of desperadoes.   (*LJ* 352–3)

Again, in a later passage Marlow describes the 'natural senseless ferocity' (*LJ* 370) of Brown.

According to Lombroso's theory, contemporary criminals could thus be divided into strata of social savagery; they represented, in anthropological terms, 'survivals' of a previous stage of man, but

---

[31] Charles Darwin, *The Descent of Man and Selections in Relation to Sex*, 2 vols. (1871) (Reprinted London: John Murray, 1891), i. 137.
[32] Lombroso, *Criminal Man*, pp. xiv–xv.

their lineage could stretch back even further, to that of primates: 'In other words, the human brain is an advanced type of the brain of the primate in general, but in the brain of the criminal the resemblance to the simian type are much more strongly marked.'[33] The biologist Rudolf Virchow (1822–1902) influenced Lombroso by developing a theory of organic regression. Virchow coined the term 'theromorphism,' or the idea that man could take on bodily peculiarities of lower animals. Lombroso also referred to the 'primatoid features' of criminals.[34] We have already seen this notion of theromorphism, or animalistic regression, in reference to the more extreme assertions of Nordau. If not an animal, the criminal was certainly deemed a primitive. *L'uomo dilinquente*, in other words, was a savage in the midst of civilization, acting quite naturally as a primitive man, but subverting the constraints of a society that could not tolerate the threat of his existence. The dangers of primitivistic atavism, in short, lurked both within and without. Criminals represented, Lombroso argued, 'veritable savages in the midst of this brilliant European civilization'.[35]

The grotesque image of drinking the victim's blood in the passage quoted above suggested that at worst criminals might represent a regression to cannibalism of the most 'primitive' sort, an idea which is perhaps suggestive in relation to the 'unspeakable rites' in *Heart of Darkness*. Indeed, in speaking of the criminal tendencies of gipsies, Lombroso noted that 'they were formerly suspected of being cannibals', an accusation that Lombroso neither supports nor refutes.[36] The most 'unspeakable crime', then—the eating of human flesh—links the born criminal with the exaggerated reports of cannibalism among primitives. Lombroso's study of criminals resulted in the discovery, he wrote, of 'the cannibalistic instincts of primitive anthropophagists and the ferocity of beasts of prey'.[37] The image that Marlow calls up of Kurtz's voracity hints at the connection with these marks of Lombrosan atavism: 'I saw him open his mouth wide—it gave him a weirdly voracious aspect, as though he had wanted to swallow all the air, all the earth, all the men before him' (*HD* 59). Such an extreme image of cannibalism—the desire to swallow 'all the men before him'—links Kurtz with the Lombrosan

[33] Kurella, 43–4.   [34] Ibid. 29–30.
[35] Cesare Lombroso, *Crime: Its Causes and Remedies*, trans. Henry B. Horton (London: Heinemann, 1911), 12.
[36] Quoted in Stephen Jay Gould, 126.   [37] Lombroso, *Criminal Man*, p. xv.

degenerate. Indeed, the parallel is perhaps more convincing because Conrad distinguishes Kurtz's voracity from the 'restraint' of the cannibal crew. Lombroso repeatedly uses the image of the enlarged jaw and mouth as a consummate sign of primitive reversion; he writes repeatedly of 'enormous jaws (. . .) common to carnivores and savages, who tear and devour raw flesh'.[38]

Cannibals and Criminals

The Victorians knew of many episodes of degeneration from high culture to the most animalistic level. Among the contemporary examples of degeneration with which Victorian readers would have been familiar were several particularly explicit cases. For example, Douglas Hewitt has argued that readers of *Heart of Darkness* probably would have understood the allusion Marlow makes at the beginning of the novella, in the list of explorers, to the fate of Captain John Franklin. Franklin's ship, the *Erebus and Terror*, was caught in the ice in the Arctic, and his men were rumoured to have succumbed to cannibalism. 'There can, I think', says Hewitt, 'be little doubt that when in the February, 1899 number of *Blackwood's* the first readers of *Heart of Darkness* began that story of the dark continent where cannibalism was to be expected, many were reminded of that oft-denied but never disproved account of cannibalism by their own countrymen. It would be for them the first hint that the story was to be a little more perturbing than they might have expected.'[39] In 'Geography and Some Explorers', Conrad recounts reading Sir Leopold McLintock's book on Franklin, *The Voyage of the Fox in the Arctic Seas*, at the age of ten. Conrad refers to the incident as 'the darkest drama played behind the curtain of Arctic mystery' (*LE* 11). Clearly, the image impressed Conrad, and he recalled it many years later, in 1903. In the story 'Falk', which will be discussed below, the theme of cannibalism is also placed in the Polar regions, though perhaps in order not to recall the *Erebus* incident too exactly, Conrad locates his story in the South Pole:

---

[38] Ibid. 7.
[39] Douglas Hewitt, '*Heart of Darkness* and Some "Old and Pleasant Reports"' in *Nineteenth Century Fiction*, no. 38 (1987), 374–5.

Then after the report of the two shots, followed by a profound silence, there crept out into the cold, cruel dawn of the Antarctic regions, from various hiding-places, over the deck of that dismantled corpse of a ship floating on a gray sea ruled by iron necessity and with a heart of ice—there crept into view one by one, cautious, slow, eager, glaring, and unclean, a band of hungry and livid skeletons.   (FA 234)

Similarly, many Victorians would probably have been familiar with the rumours of the degeneration of the rearguard of Stanley's Eman Pasha expedition into brutality, and allegations of cannibalism in the Benin expedition.[40] Moreover, Conrad would probably have been aware of the ostensible arguments for Leopold's 'civilizing mission' in Africa. The suppression of cannibalism figured prominently in such propaganda. Stanley remarked in the introduction to Guy Burrows' *Land of the Pigmies* that

King Leopold found the Congo 'stained by wasteful deformities, tears, and heart's blood of myriads', cursed by cannibalism savagery and despair; and he has been trying with a patience, which I can never sufficiently admire, to relieve it of its horrors, rescue it from its oppressors, and save it from perdition.[41]

Ironically, however, the 1890s brought back to England disturbing reports on the Free State. Not only was anthropophagy still practised but, according to some accounts, rampant. Reviewing a book by Sidney Hinde, a doctor working with the troops during the Arab revolt, an anonymous critic in the *Academy* wrote: 'Captain Hinde, who has given special attention to this subject, describes many other almost incredible horrors associated with anthropophagy, which he assures us is not only rampant but even on the increase in the Congo Free State.'[42] Indeed, rather typically for his time, Hinde

[40] See Tony Gould, *In Limbo: The Story of Stanley's Rear Column* (London: Hamish Hamilton, 1979).

[41] Burrows, 81.

[42] Unsigned Review, 'Among Cannibals' in *Academy*, 51/1294 (20 February 1897), 228. Such tales of cannibalism abound. Hinde writes: 'So far as I have been able to discover, nearly all the tribes in the Congo basin either are, or have been, cannibals.' Hinde, 66. Richard Burton commented: 'Anthropophagy, either as a necessity, a sentiment, or a superstition, is known to sundry, though by no means all, the tribes dwelling between the Nun (Niger) and Congo Rivers (. . .).' Burton, *Two Trips to Gorilla Land*, i. 216. Stanley's rear column officer, James S. Jameson, writes: 'The Bangalas (. . .) are cannibals and file their teeth in points', which recalls Conrad's fireman (*HD* 38). Again, Jameson observes: 'We passed great numbers of villages, the inhabitants of which are a really savage-looking people, of whom it is easy to believe all the stories of cannibalism.' James S. Jameson, *Story of the Rear*

dwelt at some length upon the subject of anthropophagy; and it is fascinating to see how often in these late nineteenth-century travel books the morbid fascination with this theme, given such disproportionate treatment in relation to other customs and rites, masquerades as ethnological curiosity. The Bongala, many of whom worked on the steamboats in the Congo, were reported to be cannibals: 'The Bongala (. . .) are largely employed on the steamers (. . .) they are, however, cannibals and are constantly giving trouble in this respect.'[43] Although Conrad should not be fully excused for anthropological errors and misunderstandings, we must situate the novella in such a tradition of travel writing in which the leitmotif of primitives as the embodiments of unrestrained desire recurred in numerous works. Indeed, there are few images in *Heart of Darkness* that do not have some corollary in the vast amount of travel literature on Africa. Consider, for example, Hinde's morbid description of a village: 'This village (. . .) was oval in form and strongly fortified (. . .) the whole top being surrounded by a palisade. The top of every tree in this palisade was crowned with a human skull (. . .) The approach to each of these six gates was ornamented by a pavement of skulls.'[44]

Cannibalism represented an extreme form of atavism for many Victorians because it involved the suspension of the most basic moral codes which had been formed as man advanced.[45] Primitive peoples were associated with boundless desire, or what Durkheim called *anomie*, unchecked by moral restraints; and thus primitives could be credited with being utterly devoid of civilized checks against anthropophagy.[46] If civilization only placed artificial restrictions on this state of boundless desire, then the extreme result of being disassociated from European culture might be the degeneration even to cannibalism. W. Cooke Taylor, the degenerationist writer mentioned previously, examined the case of a European victim of a shipwreck who not only reverted to cannibalism, but who found, in this unrestricted state of *anomie*, a taste for human

Column of the Emin Pasha Relief Expedition, Mrs. J. S. Jameson (ed.) (London: R. H. Porter, 1890), 31, 63.

[43] Hinde, 25.   [44] Ibid. 91.

[45] On Victorian notions of cannibalism in anthropology and ethnographic fiction, see Andrea White, 14, 22, 50, 147–8; Knox-Shaw, 139, 158–9, 186, 188–91; and Brantlinger, *Rule of Darkness*, 185–6.

[46] Cf. Herbert, 62–3.

flesh that never left him. Taylor writes of the 'desire strangely mixed with loathing' which this character later felt in regard to cannibalism.[47] Although the subject of cannibalism is veiled in *Heart of Darkness*, Conrad made explicit use of the theme in a short story, 'Falk' (1903), a tale of Darwinistic atavism. At the beginning of the story, Conrad carefully evokes the atmosphere of primitivism and suggests an analogy between the sailors who sit around telling tales and primeval men gathered around fires. This device, which is similar to the comparative method in anthropology, is a common one in Conrad's work. Just as at the beginning of *Heart of Darkness* the listeners aboard the 'Nellie' are implicitly implicated in the savagery of the Roman colonists, so at the beginning of 'Falk', the narrator reminds the reader of the sailors' proximity to primitive man:

The wooden dining-room stuck out over the mud of the shore like a lacustrine dwelling (. . .) the chops recalled times more ancient still. They brought forcibly to one's mind the night of first ages when the primeval man, evolving the first rudiments of cookery from his dim consciousness, scorched lumps of flesh at a fire of sticks in the company of other good fellows; then, gorged and happy, sat him back among the gnawed bones to tell his artless tales of experience—the tales of hunger and hunt—and of women, perhaps!   (FA 145–6)

The 'night of the first ages' is a direct quotation from *Heart of Darkness* (*HD* 37), and thus reveals the affinities between the two works. Both are temporal and psychological journeys back to a more primitive condition of humanity. After this reminder of the continuity between primitive and modern cultures, the narrative comes back to the theme of the beast within. The whole story turns upon Falk's confession that he had been forced by self-preservation into cannibalism: 'Imagine to yourselves (. . .) that I have eaten man' (FA 218). The confession ensures Falk's ostracism from human society, and his identification as a 'Beast' (FA 218). The act of cannibalism transgresses the most basic moral codes of society, ensuring that Falk, like Kurtz, must be cast out. By his act he has become a criminal, a word which is so often tinged with irony in Conrad's fiction. Can the accordance with basic instinct be considered criminal? the story asks, or is it natural? The narrator's

---

[47] Taylor, i. 127. Cf. Herbert, 62.

friend, Hermann, with whose daughter Falk is in love, adheres to a strict moral code:

According to his ideas no circumstances could excuse a crime—and certainly not such a crime. This was the opinion generally received. The duty of a human being was to starve. Falk therefore was a beast, an animal; base, low, vile, despicable, shameless, and deceitful (. . .) He would have preferred not to know that such an unclean creature had been in the habit of caressing his children. He hoped I would say nothing of all this ashore, though. He wouldn't like it to get about that he had been intimate with an eater of men—a common cannibal. (FA 221–2)

The black humour of the last phrase—the notion of cannibalism as a social stigma—shows that the idea was not particularly shocking to Conrad.[48] Hermann's condemnation partakes, perhaps intentionally, of the somewhat hysterical language of a Nordau or Lombroso: 'Falk therefore was a beast, an animal; base, low, vile, despicable, shameless, and deceitful' (quoted above). The notion that he has become a 'beast, an animal' through his actions would have squared with Victorian notions of the vestigial remains of the primitive, and even the beast, in 'civilized' cultures. Falk has followed the Lombrosan pattern of atavism back into a more 'primitive' form of being. The narrator is able to discern this 'primitivism' merely from his appearance: 'the remembrance of Falk's words, looks, gestures, invested it not only with an air of reality but with the absolute truth of primitive passion' (FA 223). Hermann's final judgment on Falk's act sounds like a muted version of Kurtz's self-condemnation: 'Horrible! Horrible!' (FA 223).

Falk's bestiality is apparently stressed by Hermann in order to distance himself from the dark possibility of such vestigial remains of savage and brutal instincts in humanity generally. Falk's action must be labelled as bestial, and the knowledge of it must be suppressed, in order to maintain the sustaining illusion of morality. Hermann asks the narrator not to repeat the story partly in order to shore up the fragile edifice of 'civilization', just as Marlow suppresses the truth about Kurtz. The well-known Victorian psychologist, Henry Maudsley, provides an interesting response to the theme of humanity's innate bestiality, and the attempt to mask it:

[48] Conrad adopts a similarly joking tone in a letter to William Blackwood. He remarks that 'his behaviour (Falk's), if cannibalistic, is extremely nice throughout—or at any rate perfectly straight forward'. *Collected Letters of Conrad*, ii. 357.

Amazed and aghast at such brutal explosions of the natural man when they befall from time to time (...) men cry out that they are monstrous, unnatural, inhuman, incredible, and hasten either to draw a veil over them or to put a falsely fair face on them, or to ignore and forget them, in any case to say little about them. Meanwhile they are not incredible (...) nor unnatural.[49]

Maudsley constantly emphasizes 'the relative nature of morality', the fact that it is dependent upon the type and stage of society.[50] Under stress, or in the grip of instinct, people revert to an earlier stage of being. The structure of society, and the Marlowian values of solidarity, sympathy and restraint break down. As the narrator remarks, 'The organized life of the ship had come to an end. The solidarity of the men had gone. They had become indifferent to each other' (FA 231). The image of prehistoric people at the beginning of the story is thus illuminated. As Conrad must have been aware, the 'primal horde' was viewed by many Victorian anthropologists as being utterly devoid of these social mores; and cannibalism represented the utter lack of ethical social organization.[51] Indeed, as Maudsley remarked, the higher moral attributes would be disadvantageous to 'primitive' people: 'Roaming savages, naked or nearly so in body and mind, destitute of social organization (...) have not the mental qualities of the social man in them; indeed, they need not, and are better without, qualities which would be a detriment or destruction to them.'[52]

Conrad's narrator is reserved in his judgment of Falk, finding in this cannibalistic incident the morality of a Spencerian survival of the fittest. This is, indeed, one of the most explicit acknowledgements in Conrad's work of his knowledge of Darwinism and its offshoots. The passage is not very well known; therefore, I will quote at length:

He wanted to live. He had always wanted to live. So we all do—but in us the instinct serves a complex conception, and in him the instinct existed alone. There in such simple development a gigantic force, and like the pathos of a child's naive and uncontrolled desire (...)

[49] Henry Maudsley, *Life in Mind and Conduct* (London: Macmillan, 1873), 140.
[50] Ibid. 160.
[51] Guy Burrows writes: 'Cannibalism seems to have prevailed to a considerable extent among the primitive inhabitants of Europe, and still more in America.' Burrows, 144. Burton argues that 'The "unnatural" practice (...) has at different stages extended over the whole world.' Burton, *Two Trips to Gorilla Land*, 213.
[52] Maudsley, *Life in Mind and Conduct*, 138.

I said—'You were then so lucky in the drawing of lots?'

'Drawing lots?' he said. 'What lots? Do you think I would have allowed my life to go for the drawing of lots?' (. . .)

'Many heads went wrong, but the best men would live.'

'The toughest you mean,' I said. He considered the word. Perhaps it was strange to him, though his English was so good.

'Yes,' he asserted at last. 'The best. It was everybody for himself at last and the ship open to all.'   (FA 223–7)

In a misunderstanding that is partly linguistic ('Perhaps it was strange to him, though his English was good'), the words 'toughest' and 'best' elide in the conversation. This passage plays on the confusion in social Darwinism to which T. H. Huxley often alluded, the conflation of fitness with virtue. Huxley wrote in *Evolution and Ethics* (1894), a work which will be considered at some length later, and of which, as I will argue, Conrad was probably aware:

I suspect that this fallacy has arisen out of the unfortunate ambiguity of the phrase 'survival of the fittest.' 'Fittest' has the connotation of 'best'; and about 'best' there hangs a moral flavour. In cosmic nature, however, what is 'fittest' depends upon the conditions (. . .) The struggle for existence tends to eliminate those less fitted to adapt themselves to the circumstances of their existence. The strongest, the most self-assertive, tend to tread down the weaker.[53]

Indeed, 'Falk' can be read as an allegory of Darwinist notions of competition and survival of the fittest. There is, perhaps, even a black joke in the description of the victim of Falk's cannibalism: 'He had been the best man of the lot (. . .) had preserved to the last some vigour and decision of mind.' Preservation, though of individuals rather than species, is precisely the subject of the tale; and self-preservation is what motivates Falk's act. Although, in general, the notion of self-preservation at all costs is not regarded as a virtue in Conrad's writing, there is a suspension of moral judgement in this tale over the issue of restraint. Does self-abnegation include the imperative to die of starvation rather than, as the Victorians would have seen the action, to regress to a more primitive or instinctive level? In the extreme, Hermann argues that self-preservation must be set aside in favour of social constraints: 'The duty of a human being was to starve' (quoted above).

[53] Huxley, *Evolution and Ethics*, 80–1.

The motif of cannibalism, though apparently a peripheral concern in Conrad's writing, is nevertheless an important theme. Degeneration into cannibalism is again hinted at in *Lord Jim*, when the old sailor, Chester, speaks to Marlow: 'He put his lip to my ear. "Cannibal?—well, they used to give him the name years and years ago. You remember the story? A shipwreck on the west side of Steward Island; that's right, seven of them got ashore (. . .) Alone? Of course (. . .) the Lord God knows the right and wrong of the story"' (*LJ* 12–13). Again, Guy Burrows's writing on the Congo provides a parallel here. Explaining African cannibalism he observes: 'Fierce hunger has driven men of our own race, as a last resort in the pinch of hunger, to satisfy their craving in this terrible way. Sailors in a boat or on a raft have killed their fellow for food, and it is a sailor's gruesome tradition that the liver alone in such cases should be eaten, as being the most digestible.'[54] All of these cannibalistic episodes, which appealed to Victorian taste for the macabre, apparently had wide currency and would have provided Conrad's contemporaries with glosses on the deterioration of 'civilized' people in contact with 'primitive' cultures.

Atavism and Living Anachronisms

Victorian criminologists frequently associated the atavism of criminals with 'savage' traits of childishness, amorality, vanity, violence, irrationality, lasciviousness, etc. The criminal, like the primitive, occupied a world of Durkheimian *anomie*, unrestricted and untethered in the pursuit of his desires. Like the true primitive, the urban savages of Europe—the poor, children, and criminals—were unchecked by moral constraints.[55] 'Garofolo,' remarks Lombroso, 'has admirably summed up the psychical characteristics of the born criminal as being the absence of feelings of shame, horror, and pity, which are those that are lacking in savages also. We may add to these the lack of industry and self-control.'[56] It is precisely the suspension of self-control or discipline that links the criminal to the

[54] Burrows, 141.

[55] Herbert discusses at some length this theme of anomie in relation to sociologists such as Henry Mayhew. See especially his chapter on 'Mayhew's Cockney Polynesia' in Hebert, 204–52.

[56] Lombroso, *Crime*, 366.

child and the 'primitive' according to Lombroso: 'Thus the psychology of the criminal is summed up in a defective resistance to criminal tendencies and temptations, due to that ill-balanced impulsiveness which characterizes children and savages.'[57] In short, the criminal exists in a world of *anomie*; he lacks *restraint*, precisely the quality in which Marlow finds Kurtz to be deficient: 'They [the heads] only showed that Mr. Kurtz lacked restraint in the gratification of his various lusts, that there was something wanting in him—some small matter which, when the pressing need arose, could not be found under his magnificent eloquence' (*HD* 57).

Lombroso often compared the criminal with the child, and found both to be, in effect, little savages. Moreover, he suggested that the lack of social constraints (education, fear of others' opinion, fear of punishment) in early childhood and in 'primitive' cultures corresponded to the impairment of these constraints in the criminal. For example, he implies a moral relativism which has interesting implications for Kurtz's behaviour:

These facts prove clearly that their most horrible crimes have their origin in those animal instincts of which childhood gives us a pale reflection. Repressed in civilized man by education, environment, and the fear of punishments, they suddenly break out in the born criminal without apparent cause, or under the influence of certain circumstances, (...) when we take into account the short distance that separates the criminal from the savage, we come to understand why convicts so easily adopt savage customs, including cannibalism.[58]

Christopher Herbert had demonstrated the pervasiveness of this theme of *anomie* in nineteenth-century culture. Thus, in *Moral Education*, a series of lectures delivered in 1902–3, a few years after the publication of *Heart of Darkness*, Durkheim warned of the need to place boundaries on our behaviour: 'Moral rules are genuine forces, which confront our desires and needs, our appetites of all sorts, when they promise to become immoderate.'[59] Kurtz, who possesses the 'power to charm or frighten rudimentary souls into an aggravated witch-dance in his honour' (*HD* 58) thus partakes of the condition of *anomie* identified with criminals and primitives by Conrad's contemporaries. The sense of childish egoism seems to be hinted at by Marlow: 'Sometimes he was contemptibly childish. He

---

[57] Enrico Ferri, *Criminal Sociology* (London: T. Fisher Unwin, 1895), 11.
[58] Lombroso, *Crime*, 366.   [59] Quoted in Herbert, 73.

desired to have kings meet him at railway stations on his return from some ghastly Nowhere, where he intended to accomplish great things' (*HD* 67).

The criminal's 'primitivism' linked him or her with other groups: children, the insane and, as has been remarked with reference to Nordau, geniuses.[60] Such conceptions drew upon a changed perception of children largely due to the 'new psychology' of Ribot, Charcot, Morel, and others, as well as on a common theme of anthropology—the child-like and unrestrained nature of 'primitive' peoples. The criminal was perceived as a man-child, the child as a nascent savage. As Havelock Ellis expresses this notion: 'In the criminal we may often take it, there is an arrest of development. The criminal is an individual who, to some extent, remains a child his life long—a child of larger growth and with a sinister capacity for evil.'[61] Again, in his textbook, *Criminology* (1893), Arthur MacDonald writes: 'The criminal approaches more the savage; the moral sense of the savage is animal or extinct but in impetuosity and instability they are much alike; the savage is a child with the physical powers of a man.'[62] Perhaps it is not too far-fetched to suggest that Kurtz's behaviour marks him out as a Lombrosan man-child, not only in his savagery but in his acquisitiveness. In the following passage one is reminded of a child's assertions of control and possession: ' "My Intended, my ivory, my station, my—" Everything belonged to him'. This is perhaps not surprising when we recall that the regression to a 'savage' state paralleled in the minds of Conrad's contemporaries a sort of return to childhood. The 'primitive', after all, was merely considered to be a cousin to the 'civilized' child; both displayed egoism and a lack of self-control.

In other words, the criminal is predisposed to savage reversion, but environment may also be a factor in atavism. This claim seems relevant to Kurtz's regression, for Conrad implies that the African environment merely brings to the surface Kurtz's latent savagery. I am not suggesting a simplistic analogy: in Victorian terms Kurtz is not simply a 'criminal type'. The borders between criminality,

---

[60] Cf. Cesare Lombroso, *The Man of Genius*, trans. and ed. Havelock Ellis (London: Walter Scott, 1891).

[61] Havelock Ellis, *The Criminal* (1890), (Reprinted London: Walter Scott, 1891), 260.

[62] Arthur MacDonald, *Criminology* (New York: Funk & Wagnalls, 1893), 91.

insanity, and genius in this period were constantly blurred. For this reason, Kurtz's primitivism does not have to be strictly labelled according to one of these categories.

Ellis demonstrates how common this belief regarding the continuity between primitive peoples and criminals was at the end of the nineteenth century.[63] Ellis quotes, for example, an essay from the *Journal of Mental Science* (1885):

Such a man as this is a reversion to an old savage type, and is born by accident in the wrong century. He would have had sufficient scope for his bloodthirsty propensities and been in harmony with his environment, in a barbaric age, *or at present in certain parts of Africa.*[64]

Written at the height of the scramble for Africa, in 1885, the last part of this quotation is particularly relevant to a discussion of Kurtz's degeneration. Africa was seen, in other words, as a potential lure for those who dwelt on the moral fringes of European society. This is not to argue that Kurtz merely stood for the European outcast. On the contrary, he is ironically portrayed as someone who went to Africa with a moral code of some sort. Victorians argued, though, that an environment such as Africa would give scope for the realization of innate 'primitive' tendencies held in check in Europe. Placed in 'certain parts of Africa', a man like Kurtz, 'would have had sufficient scope for his bloodthirsty propensities and been in harmony with his environment.'

Victorian writers seem not to have been disdainful of such aggressive and violent tendencies at all, but rather to have viewed the criminal as merely a natural throw-back. Seen in this cynical light, men such as Kurtz could be viewed as not evil but only displaced, their talents wasted in the present age. Born into another time, or into an altered environment, such men would be natural leaders like Kurtz. As Tarde puts it, 'Some of them at least would have been the ornament and the moral aristocracy of a tribe of Red Indians'.[65] Again, Ellis quotes another contemporary writer:

Of a very great number of modern habitual criminals it may be said that they have the misfortune to live in an age in which their merits are not

---

[63] 'As regards psychical atavism', wrote Ellis in an orthodoxly Lombrosan manner 'we have to recognize that the criminal, being often a person of underdeveloped psychic constitution, often tends to revert to the underdeveloped modes of thought and feeling common among primitive people, such reversion being frequently aided by the conditions of environment.' Ellis, 253.

[64] Quoted in Ellis, 254–5, italics mine.   [65] Quoted in Ellis, 254.

appreciated. Had they been born in the world a sufficient number of generations ago, the strongest of them would have been chiefs of a tribe. (. . .) With the dispositions and the habits of uncivilised men which he has inherited from a remote past, the criminal has to live in a country where the majority of inhabitants have learned new lessons of life, and where he is regarded more and more as an outcast as he strives more and more to fulfill the yearnings of his nature.[66]

The image of criminals as displaced tribal chiefs or barbarian leaders is a common image in criminological writings of this period: 'The criminal of to-day is the hero of our old legends. We put in prison to-day the man who would have been the dreaded and respected chief of a clan or a tribe.'[67] The imagery from such criminological writing closely parallels, I would argue, the description of Kurtz's reign of terror. 'Kurtz got the tribe to follow him, did he?' Marlow asks. The Harlequin replies, 'They adored him. (. . .) he came to them with thunder and lightning, you know—and they had never seen anything like it—and very terrible' (HD 56). Again, in describing Kurtz's position amongst the Africans, Marlow says, 'He was not afraid of the natives; they would not stir until Mr. Kurtz gave the word. (. . .) The camps of these people surrounded the place, and the chiefs came every day to see him. They would crawl . . .' (HD 58).

Statements regarding the amorality of criminals in this context suggest the Nietzschean 'transvaluation of values' carried on throughout this period. In almost all of these quotations the authors betray a grudging respect for the 'pluck' and power of the criminal, his 'fitness' to survive in savage conditions. Although perhaps not the *Übermensch* of Nietzsche's theories, the criminal could be viewed as a sort of natural aristocrat, a perfect savage leader. One is reminded here of the ironic description of Kurtz as a natural leader of an 'extreme party' (HD 71). Although it is unclear whether or not Conrad was familiar with Ellis's transcription of Lombrosan doctrines in *The Criminal*, the work was widely known and readily available before the composition of the novella.

The theme of Kurtz's ascendency to the position of chiefdom would have also been prepared for by claims of anthropology and travel literature. For example, in *Pre-historic Times* (1865), Lubbock wrote that 'we must remember that savages regarded the

[66] Quoted in Ellis, 254.   [67] Ibid.

white men as beings of a superior order to themselves. Thus (. . .) Du Chaillu tells us, that some of the African savages looked upon him as a superior being; and the South Sea islanders worshipped Captain Cook as a deity'.[68] Lubbock noted that 'Europeans hold, in fact, almost the same position in public estimation as did the (. . .) deities of ancient mythology'.[69] The passage in Paul Du Chaillu's work to which Lubbock refers casts an interesting light on Kurtz's rise in the African tribe. Although there is no indication that Conrad read Du Chaillu's travel books, the incident is suggestive:

I was formally invested with the kendo, which is here, also the insignia of the head-man or chief ruler (. . .) 'You are one of those whom we have often heard of who comes from nobody knows where, and whom we have never hoped to see. You are our king and ruler; stay with us. We love you, and will do what you wish.'[70]

In another work, Du Chaillu relates that the Africans shouted at him: 'Spirit, you are our king. You have come to our country to do us good. You can do everything.'[71] This recalls, on one level, Jim's position among the Malays: 'Already the legend had gifted him with supernatural powers' (LJ 266). Similarly, Marlow remarks of Jim:

He dominated the forest, the secular gloom, the old mankind. He was like a figure set on a pedestal to represent in his persistent youth the power, and perhaps the virtues, of races that never grow old, that have emerged from the gloom.   (LJ 265)

The claim which Kurtz makes in his 'Report' corresponds to this belief in European deification by 'savages', and should be seen in this historical context:

He began with the argument that we whites, from the point of view of development we had arrived at, 'must necessarily appear to them in the nature of supernatural beings—we approach them with might as of a deity,' and so on. 'By the simple exercise of our will we can exert a power for good practically unbounded,' etc.   (HD 50)

Marlow's 'so on' and 'etc.' suggest that these arguments for the virtual apotheosis of whites by 'less developed' Africans were commonplace arguments; and, indeed, there are many sources for such

[68] Lubbock, Pre-Historic Times, 460.   [69] Ibid.
[70] Du Chaillu, Adventures in Great Forest, 343–4.
[71] Du Chaillu, Explorations and Adventures in Equatorial Africa, 441.

a view in the travel literature and anthropology with which Conrad might well have been acquainted. Certainly, this theme of apotheosis and worship seems to have been one that concerned Conrad. In a letter to H. Devray in 1902 concerning the translation of some of his works, Conrad described *Heart of Darkness* as a story that 'happens in the Belgian Congo. A wild story of a journalist who becomes manager of a station in the interior and makes himself worshipped by a tribe of savages'.[72]

---

[72] *Collected Letters of Conrad*, i. 407.

7

Anthropology's Impact on Evolution and Ethics in the Victorian Era

You said also (. . .) that 'giving your life up to them' (*them* meaning all of mankind with skins brown, yellow, or black in colour) 'was like selling your soul to a brute'. You contended that 'that kind of thing' was only endurable and enduring when based on a firm conviction in the truth of ideas racially your own, in whose name are established the order, the morality of an ethical progress. 'We want its strength at out backs,' you had said. 'We want a belief in its necessity and its justice, to make a worthy and conscious sacrifice of our lives' (. . .) The point . . . is that of all mankind Jim had not dealings but with himself, and the question of whether at last he had not confessed to a faith mightier than the law of order and progress.

(*LJ* 339)

Morals in Evolution

The Victorian period witnessed an astounding proliferation of works on the evolution of ethics.[1] Influenced and encouraged by Darwinism, many Victorians came to believe that 'After Darwin it has become inevitable that moral conceptions should be systematically related in terms of our new conception of the moral destiny of man'.[2] Coinciding with this post-Darwinian challenge, many Victorians began to speculate on the issue of moral evolution. To name but a few, an educated reader prior to 1900 might have been familiar with W. E. Lecky's *A History of European Morals* (1869), Herbert Spencer's *Data of Ethics* (1879), Leslie Stephens's *The*

[1] On the theme of Conrad and the evolution of ethics, several works must be noted. See particularly Allan Hunter, *Joseph Conrad and the Ethics of Darwinism* and John E. Saveson, *Joseph Conrad: The Making of a Moralist.* .
[2] H. G. Wells, 'Human Evolution: Mr. Wells Replies', in *Natural Science: A Monthly Review of Scientific Progress*, 10 (May 1897), 244.

Science of Ethics (1882), T. H. Green's *Prolegomena to Ethics* (1883), Henry Maudsley's *Body and Will* (1883), W. R. Sorley's *The Ethics of Naturalism* (1885), Henry Sedgwick's *Outline of the History of Ethics* (1886), J. G. Romane's *Mental Evolution in Man, the Origin of Human Faculty* (1888), Henry Drummond's *The Ascent of Man* (1894), T. H. Huxley's *Evolution and Ethics* (1894), and Paul Topinard's *Science and Faith* (1899).[3] Conrad's friend, H. G. Wells, revealed this interest in the science of ethics in *The War of the Worlds* (1898), in which Wells's narrator is introduced as a prototypical Victorian ethicist, 'busy upon a series of papers discussing the probable development of moral ideas as civilization progressed'.[4] In addition to works explicitly on the 'development of moral ideas', a huge number of anthropological works, several of which have already been mentioned, also surveyed the vast field of ethics and customs, mapping out the 'extremes' of behaviour in various cultures. In a sense, these works fulfilled E. B. Tylor's hope that anthropology, the identification of diverse customs, would enable modern man more objectively to judge ethical standards: 'When the ethical systems of mankind from the lowest savagery upwards have been analyzed and arranged in their stages of evolution, then ethical science (. . .) will put its methods to fair trial on the long and intricate world-history of right and wrong'.[5] We should take note here of the view of morality as a natural product of evolution, and a corresponding belief that the history of ethics could be traced in the same manner that fossils in a rock formation revealed the evolution of species. The phrase 'ethical evolution' is made here to take on a profound neutrality.

[3] W. E. Lecky, *A History of European Morals from Augustus to Charlemagne* (London: Longman, 1869); Herbert Spencer, *The Data of Ethics* (London: Williams & Norgate, 1879); Leslie Stephen, *The Science of Ethics* (London: Smith, Elder & Co., 1882); T. H. Green, *Prolegomena to Ethics* (1883) (Reprinted Oxford: Oxford University Press, 1924); Maudsley, *Body and Will*; W. R. Sorley, *The Ethics of Naturalism* (Edinburgh and London: Blackwood's, 1885); Henry Sedgwick, *Outline of the History of Ethics* (1886) (Reprinted London: Macmillan, 1954); J. G. Romane, *Mental Evolution in Man, the Origin of Human Faculty* (London: Kegan, Paul, Trench, 1888); Henry Drummond, *The Ascent of Man* (London: Hodder & Stoughton, 1894); T. H. Huxley, *Evolution and Ethics*; and Paul Topinard, *Science and Faith: Man as an Animal and Man as a Member of Society*, trans. Thomas McCormack (London: Kegan, Paul, Trench, 1899).

[4] H. G. Wells, *The War of the Worlds*, in *The Invisible Man, The War of the Worlds, and A Dream of Armageddon*, The Atlantic Edition of the Works of H. G. Wells, 24 vols. (London: T. Fisher Unwin, 1924), iii. 220.

[5] Tylor, *Primitive Culture*, i. 449.

At the opening of his published Romanes lectures, T. H. Huxley wrote: 'My attention, (. . .) has been much directed to the bearing of modern scientific thought on the problems of morals'.[6] The notion that ethics could be reduced to a science, as both Tylor and Huxley assert, exemplifies the secularization of morality in the Victorian era. Even the subtitle of Tylor's *Primitive Culture* indicates the change in emphasis: *Researches into the Development of Mythology, Philosophy, Religion, Art, and Custom*. Religion is only one element in Tylor's definition of that complex system known as 'culture', and it is by no means clear that it is the most important element. In his obituary for the Orientalist and theologian Robertson Davies, James Frazer suggests that the scientific study of religion would dispel erroneous theological and ethical views:

Now the careful and dispassionate analysis to which the comparative study of religion subjects the religious beliefs and practices of mankind, leads inevitably to the conclusion that a great proportion of them are false and foolish (. . .) And as the rules of conduct which have guided and still guide men in the affairs of life are to a large extent deduced from religious or ethical premises, it follows that the comparative study of religion (. . .) calls for a reconsideration of the speculative basis of ethics as well as of theology.[7]

What is interesting here is the way in which many Victorian thinkers radically revised their views of ethics by wresting these issues from theology. One striking example is Huxley's comment on his preparation of the Romanes lectures which became *Ethics and Evolution*: 'I have long had fermenting in my head, some notion about the relation of Ethics and Evolution (or rather the absence of such as are commonly supposed).'[8]

The secularization of ethics, influenced both by Darwinism and anthropology, deflated the argument for Christianity as the central civilizing force, and for morality as dependent upon divine sanctions. Instead, anthropologists such as Tylor relied on what they argued was a natural theory of ethics, with no recourse to Christian theology. George Stocking summarizes this transformation: 'Victorian anthropologists were willing to contemplate the possibil-

---

[6] Huxley, *Evolution and Ethics*, vi.

[7] James G. Frazer, 'Robertson Smith', in *Fortnightly Review*, 60/330 (June 1894), 803.

[8] Quoted in Leonard Huxley (ed.), *Life and Letters of Thomas Henry Huxley*, ii. 350.

ity that the world as they knew it was the result of purely natural processes, and even to join in extending the revolt against patriarchal authority to the cosmos as a whole. But the weakening of their religious belief had not been accompanied by a loss of moral commitment.'[9] The response included the kinds of explorations of ethics cited above; however, there remained a paradox: 'granted that moral values varied in time and place—perhaps in Darwinian terms, were "adapted" to different environmental situations—this could mean that there was no standard by which they might be evaluated.' The socio-cultural evolutionary writers such as McLennan, Tylor, and Lubbock solved this problem by reference to a natural evolution of societal ethics, predicated upon a Lamarckian belief in inheritance: 'If the devil in the form of a baboon was to be our grandfather, then the moral guides and goals that had once been provided by the creator had to find some evolutionary derivation and justification.'[10] The history of ethics, in other words, did not partake of any divine plan. As Henry Maudsley put it, 'conscience was not implanted ready-made in man from his beginning on earth, it is not a constant quantity or quality, but was the slow and painful acquisition of development through past ages'.[11]

'Virtue Is One All Over the World'

Regarding the issue of the universality of ethics, we discover a paradox in the Victorian period. The search for universal standards of ethical evolution inevitably conflicted with the revelation of vast diversity in ethics in various cultures. In particular, the growing science of anthropology brought home to Conrad's contemporaries the relentlessly relativistic nature of cultural mores and morals. As H. G. Wells, put it in 'Morals and Civilization' (1897):

Now, it is scarcely necessary to say that, in accordance with this view, there is no morality in the absolute. It is relative to the state, the civilisation, the corporate existence to which the man beast has become adapted on the one hand, and to the inherent possibilities of the man on the other. And the data of morality must vary with the state, the social environment rather, in

[9] Stocking, *Victorian Anthropology*, 222–3.   [10] Ibid. 224.
[11] Maudsley, *Life in Mind and Conduct*, 138.

which the man exists; the alternative judgments of right and wrong in action, that is, must vary.[12]

We should note here the sense of morality as a natural product of evolution, and a corresponding belief that the history of ethics could be traced in the same manner that fossils in a rock formation revealed the evolution of species. We should also recognize the fact that the phrase 'ethical system' is made to take on a profound neutrality. 'Ethical science' became the catch-phrase in the period, as, for example, in Huxley's *Evolution and Ethics*: 'The science of ethics professes to furnish us with a reasoned rule of life.'[13] Given the admitted diversity of ethical codes, though, it is profoundly unclear how this reasoned rule would be constructed. Ethics were contingent and tentative rather than proven. The anthropological study of religion and law among so-called primitive and barbaric peoples revealed vastly disparate systems of ethics. Many Victorians nevertheless attempted to construct unified patterns of ethical evolution; however, for now I am interested in how these issues of cultural and ethical relativism relate to Conrad's work.

Conrad seems to have been profoundly aware of the ways in which the sciences of anthropology and Darwinist biology subverted the easy moral codes of Victorian theology. In *Lord Jim*, for example, Conrad's protagonist transcends individuality to stand for a complex of cultural and biological issues. Marlow hints at the significance attached to Jim when he comments that 'The mystery of his attitude got hold of me as though he had been an individual in the forefront of his kind, as if the obscure truth involved were momentous enough to affect mankind's conception of itself' (*LJ* 93). His actions rupture Marlow's faith in the very basis of ethical conduct and raise 'doubt of the sovereign power enthroned in a fixed standard of conduct' (*LJ* 50). It is precisely this 'fixed standard of conduct' that was rapidly being undermined in the Victorian era. Jim's background and experiences suggest a fundamental conflict regarding ethical relativism at the end of the nineteenth century.

The letter which Marlow discovers from Jim's father, almost a parody of the country vicar, the 'good old parson' (*LJ* 341), points

[12] H. G. Wells, 'Morals and Civilisation', in *Fortnightly Review*, 61 (February 1897), 263. This essay is reprinted in Robert M. Philmus and David Y. Hughes (eds.) *H. G. Wells*.

[13] Huxley, *Evolution and Ethics*, 52.

to this disparity between an easy complacency over ethical standards and the uncomfortable cultural relativism imposed by travel
in so-called primitive cultures. The vicar represents those Victorians
who have read little and seen less of other cultures, who inhabit
'that quiet corner of the world as free of danger or strife as a tomb
and breathing quietly the air of undisturbed rectitude' (*LJ* 342).
Marlow is amazed that Jim should belong to this narrow world:
'Nothing ever came to them; they would never be taken unawares'
(*LJ* 342). The letter is full of an 'easy morality' (*LJ* 341) that seems
precarious, a relic of a moral world that Darwinist biology and
anthropology had irrevocably overthrown. The irony of this passage is palpable and somewhat pathetic. The vicar 'goes on equably
trusting Providence and the established order of the universe' in a
manner that seems utterly anachronistic in a work of 1900. The
complacent conclusion of the letter regarding the basis of ethics is
clearly intended to evoke a sense of rupture between mid- and late
nineteenth-century views:

One can almost see him, grey-haired and serene in the inviolable shelter of
his book-lined, faded, and comfortable study, where for forty years he had
conscientiously gone over and over again the round of his little thoughts
about faith and virtue, about the conduct of life and the only proper
manner of dying; where he had written so many sermons, where he sits
talking to his boy, over there, on the other side of the earth. But what of the
distance? Virtue is one all over the world, and there is only one faith, one
conceivable conduct of life, one manner of dying.   (*LJ* 341)

The phrase, 'Virtue is one all over the world, and there is only one
faith (. . .)', is particularly tinged with irony. Comparing this with
the conclusion of a prominent nineteenth-century anthropologist,
Theodor Waitz, we are immediately struck by the disparity between
such a faith in universal codes and the relativism that anthropology
necessitated:

The atrocities we see committed by savages (and sometimes by ourselves)
in cold blood, without the least scruple, and their insensibility to all moral
relations, has something so repulsive to civilized man, that he feels inclined
to assume that they are specifically different beings. We, however, soon
learn that such a theory is not tenable. (. . .) In our own time even we find
moral judgment very elastic, and just adapted to the prevailing practice;
habit makes us so familiar with this that only striking deviations become
perceptible.[14]

[14] Waitz, i. 313–15.

A Victorian psychologist who will be considered at some length later, Henry Maudsley, writes similarly: 'Therefore it always has been, and still is, the case that the moral sense of our age or place or people approves that which is an offense to another age or place or people. (. . .) in the domain of real things its sense of right and wrong fluctuates, is not constant, makes convenient accommodations.'[15]

The beliefs that 'Virtue is one all over the world' and the 'moral judgment very elastic' are utterly incompatible, as Marlow is clearly aware. Such smug sentiments are born of provincialism, 'that quiet corner of the world as free of danger or strife as a tomb, and breathing equably the air of undisturbed rectitude' (*LJ* 342); they are utterly at odds with an increasingly variegated world, inhabited by a vast array of peoples with conflicting codes and customs. A great irony exists in the sense of Jim's betrayal as a 'breach of faith with the community of mankind' (*LJ* 157). What *Lord Jim* calls into question, though, is the very idea of the community of mankind. The community to which Jim, along with Marlow, belongs is a tiny sub-section of humanity, the moral values of which only hold good for that particular culture. Conrad suggests elsewhere that the very idea of community may be a fiction, though a necessary fiction. In *The Nigger of the 'Narcissus'*, Conrad writes that moral conduct depends on what he calls the 'common bond', the 'strong, effective and respectable bond of a sentimental lie' (*NN* 155) that we call community.

One answer the Victorians gave to the question of cultural relativism, an answer that Marlow is loathe to accept, is that in a world becoming aware of cultural diversity, ethics can only be a by-product of a *particular* culture: 'You contended that "that kind of thing" was only endurable and enduring when based on a firm conviction in the truth of ideas racially your own, in whose name are established the order, the morality of an ethical progress' (*LJ* 338–9). Jim's desertion of the pilgrims on the Patna apparently derives, in part, from an ethnocentric disregard for those who make no claim on ethnic or cultural solidarity; they are not, to use Marlow's phrase in its latent racial context, 'one of us'. Before he makes his 'jump', Jim fails to distinguish the faceless mass of pilgrims as kindred spirits. He even denies the very basic claim

---

[15] Maudsley, *Life in Mind and Conduct*, 136–7.

made on his conscience by the pilgrim who asks him only for water. Ironically, Jim's transformation to the position of a tribal leader, responsible for 'his people' in Patusan, is shattered by the racial claim made on him by Brown. Thus, Jim never truly escapes from the bonds of ethnicity.

At least one original reviewer of *Lord Jim* distrusted Conrad's ethnographic empathy but found the theme of ethnic solidarity to be redeeming:

Mr. Conrad, beyond all others, has identified himself with the standpoint of the natives. (. . .) Such an achievement (. . .) seems to indicate a denationalisation that might inspire a certain amount of distrust. But in the volume before us, though the 'noble savage' is once more prominent, the story is half finished before we reach the Malaya, and the central figure (. . .) throughout all his long exile never loses touch with the sentiment, the ideas, the ethos of his race.[16]

This is the other side of cultural relativism—one's racial 'ethos' or loyalties should be taken with one abroad. Despite experiences in foreign cultures, Marlow argues at one point, it is to their own cultures that travellers must eventually return to render their accounts of themselves:

We wander in our thousands over the face of the earth (. . .) but it seems to me that for each of us going home must by like going to render an account (. . .) Each blade of grass has its spot on earth whence it draws its life, its strength; and so is man rooted to the land from which he draws his faith together with his life.   (*LJ* 221–2)

This theme must have been particularly poignant for Conrad, whom James Clifford has called a 'polyglot refugee'.[17] Jim might be seen to be doomed precisely because he is, in Victorian terms, denationalized—one of those who is cut off. 'He would never go home now', says Marlow (*LJ* 222). In the end, though, even Jim cannot escape the idea of ethnic solidarity; and his cultural bond with Gentleman Brown ensures his fate. Brown reminds him of this link: 'You have been white once, for all your talk of this being your own people and you being one with them' (*LJ* 381). In fact, Brown is perspicacious in pointing out Jim's tenuous place in the Patusan community; the ethnic appeal is somehow irresistible for Jim: 'there ran through the rough talk a vein of subtle references to their

[16] Sherry, *Critical Heritage*, 119.   [17] Clifford, *Predicament of Culture*, 10.

common blood, an assumption of common experience,' (*LJ* 387). Although Jim believes that the Malaysians are his people, his death indicates that he has not truly assimilated the traditions of another culture which he does not fully understand, and which does not understand him. Marlow remarks: 'People had trusted him with their lives—only for that; and yet they could never, as he had said, never be made to understand him' (*LJ* 409). His death occurs largely as a result of cultural misunderstanding—over the clash of one system of ethics with another, 'their creed' and 'his truth' (*LJ* 393).[18]

This problem of cultural or ethical relativity (two terms that often elide) is one of the fundamental problems at the heart of anthropology, both historical and modern. In an essay entitled 'The Impact of Culture on the Nature of Man', Clifford Geertz warns of 'becoming lost in a whirl-wind of cultural relativism', and decries Ruth Benedict's famous work of anthropology, *Patterns of Culture*, 'with its strange conclusion that anything one group of people is inclined toward doing is worthy of respect by another'.[19] Even in Conrad's time, not only formal anthropology but the popular fiction associated with imperialism and the accounts of travellers had made painfully clear that ethical systems might be utterly irreconcilable.[20] This disparity between cultures or races figures prominently at the end of *An Outcast of the Islands* as well: 'Hate filled the world, filled the space between them—the hate of race, the hate of hopeless diversity, the hate of blood; the hate against which the man born in the land of life and of evil from which nothing but misfortune comes to those who are not white' (*OI* 359). The contact of cultures led to the recognition of this 'hopeless diversity', and did little to alleviate the sense of the ethical incompatibility of competing systems. Willems's relationship with Aïssa in *An Out-*

[18] John Batchelor writes: 'the belief that there is an unbridgeable gulf between the races is so prevalent, so widely shared, that it takes on the status of a historical fact. After the complexity and the absence of "systems" of Chapters 5–35, Marlow has returned to a simpler world, which does have systems, and the systems are of the period: there is a moral system with clear distinctions between good and evil, honour and dishonour, courage and cowardice, and there is also a racial system with an equally clear distinction between white and non-white. It is a mark of the process of simplification that has taken place that the phrase "one of us", which has had so many meanings in Marlow's spoken narrative, here narrows down to a single meaning: "white man"'. Batchelor, *Lord Jim*, 143–4.

[19] Geertz, *Interpretation of Cultures*, 43–4.

[20] See Brantlinger, *Rule of Darkness*, 173–97, *passim*.

cast constantly causes him to ruminate on this theme of hopeless diversity:

> He sought refuge within his ideas of propriety from the dismal mangroves, from the darkness of the forests and of the heathen souls of the savages that were his masters (. . .) Would his ideas ever change so as to agree with her own notions of what was becoming, proper and respectable? (. . .) She would never change! This manifestation of her sense of proprieties was another sign of their hopeless diversity; something like another step downwards for him. She was too different from him. He was so civilized! It struck him suddenly that they had nothing in common (. . .) and he could not live without her.   (*OI* 128)

The idea of the incompatibility of ethical or cultural norms, of course, circles around the sense of racial associations. Diversity can be a code-word for racial difference: 'He was carried away by the flood of hate, disgust, and contempt of a white man for that blood which is not his blood, for that race which is not his race (. . .) This feeling of repulsion overmastered his reason in a clear conviction of the impossibility for him to live with her people' (*OI* 152).

The assurance of the universality of ethical codes could be not only foolish but dangerous. As Waitz again remarked, 'Whosoever (. . .) acquires his notion of human nature from the study of the Caucasian race (. . .) obtains thus a code of laws and morals which is only binding for one part of humanity.'[21] Such a statement could have ramifications for imperialism, for an empire that failed to take into account this ethical and customary diversity risked failure in its imperial project. Jim's death may be attributed, in the end, to this incompatibility of vastly different codes of law and morality between Europeans and so-called primitives, a grim lesson for contemporary imperialists, who often set out to impose their own morality onto other cultures. Conrad was profoundly uneasy about this apparent irreconcilability between a desire to construct universal standards and a belief that accommodations made between cultures could result in the destruction of both cultures.

The other danger of the decentring of universal ethical standards due to the recognition of diversity lay in the rise of egoistic philosophy. The kind of ethical diversity that anthropology recognized could devolve into a Nietzschean relativism in which the only standard of conduct would be purely egoistic. Conrad, who strug-

---

[21] Waitz, i. 12.

gled to cling to a notion of community must have feared such a philosophy. Consider Remy de Gourmont's statement:

We have learnt from Nietzsche to pull down the old metaphysical structures built upon a basis of abstraction. All the ancient corner-stones are crumbled to dust, and the whole house has become a ruin. What is liberty? A mere word. No more morality, then, save aesthetic or social morality: no absolute system of morals but as many separate systems as there are individual intellects.[22]

Such radical individualism in the sphere of ethics utterly subverted Conrad's necessary fiction of community. If the ego is paramount, then all of the Victorian efforts to trace an evolutionary pattern in morality must be fruitless. Few Victorians were willing to accept such a radical transvaluation of values.   .

Altruism vs. Egoism: Transvaluations

In a well-known letter to Cunninghame Graham, written not long before the publication of *Heart of Darkness*, Conrad struggled over one of the most profound ethical debates of his time:

It [Gabriela Cunninghame Graham's *Santa Teresa*] is indeed old life revived. And old life is like new life after all—an uninterrupted agony of effort. Yes. Egoism is good, and altruism is good, and fidelity to *nature* would be best of all (. . .)[23]

Egoism, altruism, truth to nature: these are all crucial elements of the debate over the evolution of ethics in the Victorian period; and Conrad here displays an awareness of these issues which were of such concern to anthropologists, historians, and Darwinian biologists. Conrad may well have approached the problem of egoism and altruism, or sympathy, through a Schopenhauerian model; but Schopenhauer was not the only likely source for his views.[24] There

[22] Quoted in Michael Levenson, *A Genealogy of Modernism* (Cambridge: Cambridge University Press, 1984), 67.

[23] Conrad to Cunninghame Graham, 31 January 1898, *Collected Letters of Conrad*, ii. 30. Allan Hunter cites this letter in relation to *Lord Jim*. See Hunter, 75–6.

[24] Bruce Johnson quotes Schopenhauer: 'The Will, the macrocosm, is objectified in each individual, the microcosm, and the inner nature of the individual is shown in his fundamental egoism: because he is the objectification of the will, indeed is the Will, acts as if he alone matters (. . .) Knowing that the sufferings of others are, metaphysically, his own sufferings, he will do what he can to alleviate those

existed a vast Victorian literature on altruism vs. egoism. Many philosophical arguments of the period centred around the notion of the 'higher moral attributes', altruism or sympathy, and how they came into being; and of their relation to egoism.[25] For example, in *Science and Faith: Man as an Animal, and Man as a Member of Society* (1899), the French theologian Paul Topinard granted 'primitive' peoples certain attributes: 'Savages surely do not understand morals as we do, but they have their morality nevertheless, and one which though different from ours yet has its value. They are straightforward, frank, loyal, and not wicked.'[26] However, Topinard writes, 'primitives' lack one crucial ethical attribute: 'In altruism they are at the same stage as the average run of birds and of herbivorous animals.'[27] In other words, Topinard argues that we cannot search for the origin of altruism in some inherent animal instinct, but rather only in people as social creatures. The very title of Topinard's book suggests as much: Man is seen either as an 'Animal' or as a 'Member of Society'. In much of his fiction, Conrad similarly represented people as social creatures, products of a 'culture' or 'society', and seems to have been concerned, like many Victorian scientists, that the social instinct in man was not inherent. If man were not simply a creature for whom society were the natural mode of life, then societal virtues like altruism could be negligible and subject to erosion. Like Topinard, Conrad seems to have allied himself with the belief that altruism is not a natural instinct at all, but represented the suspension of instinct. In *Lord Jim*, for example, Marlow remarks that Dain Warris, 'had also a European mind', as evidenced by the fact that, unlike *naturvölker*, he had attained social attributes such as restraint, discipline and altruism: 'You meet them sometimes like that, and are surprised to discover unexpectedly a familiar turn of thought, an unobscured vision, a touch of altruism' (*LJ* 261). Conrad implies here that altruism might be, in a Lamarckian sense, an acquired character-

---

sufferings. Sympathy, then is an essential grade of morality.' Bruce Johnson, *Conrad's Model of Mind* (Minneapolis: University of Minnesota Press, 1971), 44. For a different interpretation of this issue of altruism see Hunter, 75–6.

[25] Drummond quotes Benjamin Kidd: 'The process of social development, which has been taking place, and which is still in progress, is not the product of the intellect, but the motive force behind it has its seat and origin in the fund of altruistic feeling with which our civilization has become equipped.' Quoted in *Ascent of Man*, 71.

[26] Topinard, 252–3.   [27] Ibid. 253.

istic inherited by Europeans over generations; however, it is not inherent precisely because it is lacking in 'primitives'.

One factor in this Victorian debate over the development of altruism was Nietzsche's influence and reception in England in the late nineteenth century. Nietzschean philosophy challenged common Victorian views on the importance of sympathy or altruism in the course of human evolution.[28] In a transvaluation of values, Nietzsche argued that social instincts, viewed by many as crucial markers on the path to civilization, represented instead unfortunate detours. As Alexander Tille, an early adherent of Nietzschean philosophy in England put it in his preface to the English translation of *A Genealogy of Morals* (1899), published in the same year as *Heart of Darkness*, English studies of ethics typically rested upon the 'enunciation of selfishness as something morally better than egotism; of the welfare of the neighbour (. . .) of the happiness of the many'.[29] According to Tille, these English ethicisists were merely 'intoxicating themselves with phrases like altruism, charity, social justice'.[30] Indeed, 'there is not doubt, that the altruistic ideals, everywhere on British soil, are spoken of and regarded as infinitely greater than the egotism which characterizes everyone in the business of actual life'.[31] To this deluded English philosophy of ethics, says Tille, Nietzsche provided the counter-weight.[32]

Max Nordau's work probably preconditioned English attitudes towards Nietzschean philosophy, and the initial contact many English readers might have had with Nietzsche's thought might well have been through the vitriolic chapter devoted to him in *Degeneration*.[33] As William Wallace wrote in the *Academy* (1 August 1896), 'Perhaps the majority of such English readers as take an interest in these matters have gained their acquaintance with him (Nietzsche), and their estimate of his ideas, from the chapter devoted to him in Max Nordau's *Degeneration*.[34]

While most critics have merely dismissed Nordau's thesis, his critique of Nietzsche illustrates how important the debate over

---

[28] On Nietzsche's reception in England, see David S. Thatcher's *Nietzsche in England, 1880–1914: the Growth of a Reputation* (Toronto: University of Toronto Press, 1970), and Patrick Bridgewater's *Nietzsche in Anglosaxony* (Leicester: Leicester University Press, 1972).

[29] Alexander Tille, 'Preface' to Friedrich Nietzsche, *A Genealogy of Morals, Poems* (London: T. Fisher Unwin, 1899), p. xi.

[30] Ibid., p. xiii.   [31] Ibid.   [32] Ibid., p. xiv

[33] See Thatcher, 27–29, 184–5 and *passim*.   [34] Quoted in Thatcher, 184.

altruism and egoism was in the Victorian study of ethics. One of the principal points of disagreement between Nordau and Nietzsche lay precisely in this issue of altruism vs. egoism.[35] According to Nordau, Nietzsche's version of prehistoric anthropology and the development of ethics inverted notions of altruism as a natural instinct, and asseverated, on the contrary, that 'primitive' man must have been a 'beast of prey, the splendid blond beast, lustfully roving in search of spoils and victory'.[36] In this formulation, a sort of Kurtzian egoism gained pre-eminence, and the master morality of the few *Übermensch* was allowed free play. Of course, this represents only a brief and inevitably reductive account of what is a more complex problem; on the other hand, this was precisely the sort of interpretation being placed on Nietzsche's works at the time of his introduction into England in the 1890s. In the Nietzschean paradigm, altruism would only have arisen as a late development, once 'primitive' master morality had been replaced by slave morality. Such an event would have had a degenerative impact, for altruism was incompatible with a primal egoism; and thus man would be deluded regarding his inherent impulses. Civilization attempted to 'change and rear the beast of prey of "man" into a tame and civilized animal, a domestic animal'.[37] Although Conrad's position on the debate over egoism and altruism was not as static or didactic as Nordau's, Conrad's position in arguing for restraint, discipline, and sympathy as essential to societal development closely resembled Nordau's arguments in *Degeneration*. The support for Nordau's own version of prehistory, he argued, lay in anthropology. He decried the Nietzschean version of prehistory in *Degeneration* as anthropologically inaccurate:

Firstly, the anthropological assertion. Man is supposed to have been a freely roaming solitary beast of prey, whose primordial instinct was egoism and the absence of any consideration for his congeners. This assertion contradicts everything that we know concerning the beginnings of humanity. (. . .) As far as our view penetrates into prehistoric time, every discovery shows us primitive man as a gregarious animal, who could not possibly have maintained himself if he had not possessed the instincts

[35] Thatcher writes that 'Nietzsche was not opposed to altruism since he valued altruism and egoism alike according to the doer and the consequences of his deed; it would be more acceptable to regard Nietzsche not as the apostle of egoism in oppostition to altruism, but as the apostle of true aristocracy as opposed to democracy'. Thatcher, 57.
[36] Nietzsche, *Genealogy*, 39.   [37] Ibid. 108.

which are presupposed in life in a community, viz., sympathy, the feeling of solidarity and a certain degree of unselfishness. (. . .) Hence, it is not true that at any time man was a 'solitary roving brute'.[38]

Interestingly, Nordau's version of prehistory includes two virtues that have a particularly Conradian tone—'sympathy' and 'solidarity'. The picture of the evolution of ethics painted here is much more common in the Victorian era than that sketched by Nietzsche. Sympathy, solidarity, and restraint seemed to many Victorians to be the cornerstones of society; and Nordau's criticism of Nietzsche here places him in the Huxleyan camp. Evolutionary theory and Darwinian science supplied the underlying authority for such a position:

The biological truth is, that constant self-restraint is a necessity of existence as much for the strongest as for the weakest. (. . .) If these are not exercised they waste away, i.e., man ceases to be man, the pretended over-man becomes sub-human—in other words, a beast. By the relaxation or breaking up of the mechanism of inhibition in the brain the organism sinks into irrecoverable anarchy, (. . .) this leads, with absolute certainty, to ruin, to disease, to madness and death, even if no resistance results from the external world against the frenzied egoism of the individual.[39]

Conrad probably knew of Nietzsche's work at second hand.[40] Although this must remain speculative, Conrad, like so many of his contemporaries, might well have been introduced to Nietzsche's work through *Degeneration*, or through the many reviews of the work which appeared in 1895. In particular, he might well have read a review of Nordau's book in *Blackwood's* in which the critic extolled the 'restraints and conventions which civilised mankind have set over their appetites', and labelled Nietzsche a 'German imbecile'.[41] Other possible links to Nietzschean philosophy include Conrad's friends, Cunninghame Graham, who wrote an article for the Nietzschean journal, *The Eagle and the Serpent* in 1898, and Edward Garnett, who wrote an essay on Nietzsche in *Outlook* in 1899.[42] Certainly, by 1899 Conrad knew something of Nietzsche, for in July of this year he wrote a letter to Helen Sanderson which was critical of both Nietzsche's radical egoism and Christian altruism. Conrad imagines both types struggling in rough waters: 'The

[38] Nordau, 426-7.   [39] Ibid. 108.
[40] See Thatcher, 81-3, 170-1, 227-31.
[41] Hugh E.M. Stutfield, 'Tomyrotics', 833.   [42] See Thatcher, 30.

mad individualism of Niet(z)sche, the exaggerated altruism of the next man tainted with selfishness and pride comes with their noise and froth, pass away and are forgotten.'[43] In this letter, he abjured both what he perceived to be the anarchic individualism of Nietzsche and the extreme Christian renunciation which Conrad apparently took to be merely another form of egoism. Again, much later, in his essay 'The Crime of Partition', Conrad identified Nietzsche with the 'barbaric' German tribes as well as the modern German state: 'The action of Germany, however cruel, sanguinary, and faithless, was nothing in the nature of a stab in the dark. The Germanic tribes had told the whole world in all possible tones carrying conviction, the gently persuasive, the coldly logical; in tones Hegelian, Nietzschean, war-like, pious, cynical, inspired, what they were going to do to the inferior races of the earth, so full of sun and all unworthiness.'[44] This later passage makes clear that Conrad associated Nietzsche with barbarism and cruelty.

The subjugation of individual to communal concerns is one of the dominant themes of Nordau's book. To Nordau, man seemed a herd animal, though he did not invest this phrase with Nietzschean scorn. Rather, man represented a herd animal in that community must take precedence over egoistic individualism:

The man whom the healthy-minded moralist has before his eyes is one who has attained a sufficiently high development to extricate himself from the illusion of his individual isolation, and to participate in the existence of the species, to feel himself one of its members, to picture to himself the states of his fellow creatures—i.e. to be able to sympathize with them. (. . .) The truth is that this herding animal—i.e., man whose 'I' consciousness has expanded itself to the capacity of reviving the consciousness of the species—represents the higher development, to which mental cripples and degenerates, for ever enclosed in their diseased isolation, cannot ascend.[45]

The word 'ascend' at the end of this passage was charged with particular significance in this period. Henry Drummond's *The Ascent of Man* is only one example of the way in which Victorian thinkers revised the theory of natural selection and evolution in order to give this theory a melioristic tinge.[46] It is important to take note of Nordau's emphasis on sympathy, or empathy, as one of the

[43] *Collected Letters of Conrad*, ii. 188.
[44] Conrad, 'The Crime of Partition' (*NL* 24–5).   [45] Nordau, 435.
[46] Huxley uses images of ascent and descent to describe the process of the evolution of ethics. See *Evolution and Ethics*, 48.

primary social attributes, for in Conrad's view as well sympathy was a crucial factor in societal development, and the lack of sympathy led to social deterioration.

Although the theme of egoism is only one facet of Nietzsche's works, it seems to have been one idea that was anxiously seized upon by both advocates and opponents in England. In opposition to T. H. Huxley, who argued for the necessary existence of altruism as a precondition for 'civilized' society, some Nietzscheans launched vitriolic attacks on this 'higher moral attribute': 'A race of altruists is necessarily a race of slaves (. . .) Egoism spells justice and freedom as surely as altruism spells charity and slavery.'[47]

[47] 'Untitled', *The Eagle and The Serpent*, 1 (15 February 1898), 3.

8

Tribes and Detribalization: Gemeinschaft *and* Gesellschaft

The ethnographics of the modern world system (. . .) also suggest that anthropologists revise their image of the discontinuous world, breaking up the boundaries of their cherished tribes and villages (. . .)

The futuristic image of the global village need not, however, be a particularly realistic one. We should not underestimate the human capacity for reinforcing existing barriers, inventing new ones, or reinventing those of the past.[1]

When reduced to its plot elements, *Heart of Darkness* traces the journey of an individual who attempts to rescue an estranged European and bring him back to his own community; this attempt to reinstate the resistant *émigré* back into his own culture irrevocably calls the values of the rescuer into question.[2] This plot summary inevitably begs the question of what the relationship is between an individual and his community, a question which was of particular concern in the late nineteenth century. In recent years, anthropology has destabilized, and perhaps even obliterated, many of the notions of the world as divisible into clearly bounded individual communities or cultures; however, for Victorian anthropology the notion of tribes or cultures as separate homogeneous entities was relatively stable.[3]

In the nineteenth century the word 'community' in its German form—*Gemeinschaft*—began to take on a peculiar anthropological meaning. As defined by the anthropologist Ferdinand Tönnies in

---

[1] Pálsson, 38.

[2] See Levenson, who makes a striking and unusual comparison between the summary of this plot of the voyage to the alien community in *Heart of Darkness* and in Henry James's *The Ambassadors*. *Modernism and the Fate of Individuality*, 2.

[3] See, for example, A. P. Cohen, *The Symbolic Construction of Community* (London: Tavistock, 1985), and Fabian.

1887, this term referred to a community of intimate inter-relation-ships. *Gemeinschaft* contrasted sharply with *Gesellschaft*—the im-personal association of people as distinct individuals, especially in cities.[4] These notions of cultural hermeticism and separateness often elided with nationalistic rhetoric in the Victorian era. Nation-alism and imperialism may be said to have implicitly aligned them-selves with the *Gemeinschaft* ideal because they viewed the communal self as contrasted with those cultural 'others'. The dangers of degeneration, atavism, and 'going native' were that these ideas threatened this sense of national or cultural homogeneity. Degeneration, in the Victorian view, paradoxically both causes and is caused by the erosion of this stable sense of community, an ideal which was a cultural fiction for Conrad.[5] This ideal of community is crucial, also, in the defence of that other fiction—of the indi-vidual as bounded or secure in his or her identity. If cultural identifications are necessary in defining and maintaining what we call the 'self' in relation to the 'other', as cultural anthropology seems to imply, then the dissolution of a personality in atavism is a danger.[6] After all, the borders of cultures are often demarcated by showing what they are not; people often distinguish themselves

---

[4] These categories are explained with more clarity in Tönnies's work. See F. Tönnies, *Community and Association* (1887), trans. C. P. Loomis (Reprinted London: Routledge & Kegan Paul, 1955). Cf. Tim Ingold, who discusses these terms in 'The Art of Translation in a Continuous World', in Pálsson, 225–6. Ingold poses the question, 'Why does the invocation of community immediately intimate the presence of boundaries?' Ibid. 228. The categories of *Gemeinschaft* and *Gesellschaft* have largely broken down in anthropology because they are viewed as patronizing equivalents of 'savage' and 'civilized', 'primitive' and 'modern'; however, these categories are useful historically for framing my discussion of the Victorian sense of community.

[5] An important work, in this regard, is Avrom Fleischmann's *Conrad's Politics: Community and Anarchy in the Works of Joseph Conrad* (Baltimore: Johns Hopkins University Press, 1967). See also Jeremy Hawthorn, *Joseph Conrad: Narrative Technique and Ideological Commitment* (London: Edward Arnold, 1990).

[6] The problem of defining 'culture' is an anthropological and sociological Gordian knot. For a few works on the subject see Ruth Benedict, *Patterns of Culture* (Cambridge: The Riverside Press, 1934); Roy Wagner, *The Invention of Culture* (Englewood Cliffs, NJ: Prentice-Hall, 1975); Raymond Williams, *Culture and Society, 1780–1950* (New York: Columbia University Press, 1983); Eric Gans, *The End of Culture: Toward a Generative Anthropology* (Berkeley: University of California Press, 1985); Margaret S. Archer, *Culture and Agency: The Place of Culture in Social Theory* (Cambridge: Cambridge University Press, 1988); and Morris Frelich (ed.) *The Relevance of Culture* (New York: Bergin & Garvey Publishers, 1989).

against the background of 'otherness'.[7] Cultural identity is often actually identity-by-contrast.[8]

Maintenance of one's cultural identity in the face of a fear of disintegration or fragmentation is a commonly-expressed goal in many works of the late nineteenth century.[9] The mistake we make is in thinking that this kind of binary opposition between self and other is simply a product of European society. Julia Kristeva writes of this theme of clan identification in relation to Freud's seminal work, *Totem and Taboo*.

Of course, Freud has demonstrated to what extent the conglomeration of men and women into sets is oppressive and death-bearing. 'Society is founded on a common crime', he wrote in *Totem and Taboo*, and the exclusion of 'others', which binds the identity of a clan, a sect, a party, or a nation, is equally the source of the pleasure of identification ('This is what *we* are therefore it is what *I* am') and of barbaric persecution ('That is foreign to me, therefore I throw it out, hunt it down, or massacre it').[10]

Ethnocentricity may be one of the most common features in the studies of culture; it is through ethnocentricity that the self as a cultural construct is often defined.

The notion of tribal identification is not simply a rarefied subject. Unfortunately, events of the last few years have, as Edward Said reminds us in *Culture and Imperialism*, demonstrated that the recourse to tribal or ethnic identifications, a neo-nationalism, has had disastrous consequences: 'There is no question (. . .) that in the

---

[7] The comment of a social anthropologist, I. M. Lewis, is relevant here: 'Ethnocentricity is the natural condition of mankind. Most peoples of the world do not, in their conservative heart of hearts, like foreigners and display feelings of hostility (often tinged with fear) towards them. This indeed is one of the most widespread ways in which people declare and affirm their identity—by saying who they are not.' I. M. Lewis, *Social Anthropology in Perspective: The Relevance of social Anthropology* (1976) (Reprinted London: Penguin, 1981), 15. Ingold writes similarly, '*We* are all the same by virtue of our contrast to *them*.' In Pálsson, 228. Clearly, Said is crucial to the issue of defining oneself against the background of 'otherness'. See Edward Said, *Orientalism* (New York: Pantheon, 1978).

[8] This phrase is Ingold's. See Pálsson, 227.

[9] Malinowski seems to have used his Trobriand *Diary*, written in Polish, as a means of setting out a boundary defence against fragmentation: 'This morning . . . it occurred to me that the purpose in keeping a diary and trying to control one's life and thoughts at every moment must be to consolidate life, to integrate one's thinking, to avoid fragmenting themes.' *Diary*, 175. One underlying theme in the *Diary* is the fear of loss of self: 'I dissolved in the landscape.' *Diary*, 82.

[10] Kristeva, 50.

past decade the extraordinarily intense reversion to tribal and religious sentiments all over the world has accompanied and deepened many of the discrepancies among polities that have continued since—if they were not actually created by—the period of high European imperialism.'[11] The theme of tribalism is one to which Said returns several times:

> We are all taught to venerate our nations and to admire our traditions: we are taught to pursue their interests with toughness and in disregard for other societies. A new and in my opinion appalling tribalism is fracturing societies, separating peoples, promoting greed, bloody conflict, and uninteresting assertions of minor ethnic or group particularity. Little time is spent not so much in 'learning about other cultures'—the phrase has an inane vagueness to it—but in studying the map of interactions, the actual and often productive traffic occurring on a day-to-day, and even minute-by-minute basis among states, societies, groups, identities.[12]

While Said writes with a humane sympathy for this current trend toward tribalism, the truth may be that such virulent tribal identifications are not 'new' at all. Conrad delineated the essentially tribalistic nature of man as a recurring and crucial theme in his writing; he would therefore have found such a reversion to tribalism to be intelligible, though certainly not admirable.

Unlike anthropologists, who often projected tribal status onto 'primitive' cultures, while reserving the separate and superior terms culture, civilization, or society to describe their own polities, Conrad often implied that Europe is not far removed from tribalism. Paradoxically, the imperialism at the centre of *Heart of Darkness* is portrayed as a form of only slightly elevated tribalism, while at the same time, it is viewed as destructive of the tribal integrity of African cultures. Almost by definition, imperialism attempts to extend the boundaries of one culture into another; in order to justify this invasion, the values of ones own culture must be held up as supreme. The idolatry with which the 'tribe' of imperialist adventurers bow down to their gods of trade and civilization is explicitly parodied in the text.[13] Indeed, Marlow debunks the rhet-

---

[11] Said, *Culture and Imperialism*, 35–6.   [12] Ibid. 20.
[13] Benita Parry writes that 'by revealing the disjunctions between high-sounding rhetoric and sordid ambitions and indicting the purposes and goals of a civilization dedicated to global (. . .) hegemony, Conrad's writings (are) more destructive of imperialism's ideological premises than (are) the polemics of his contemporary opponents of empire'. Parry, 10. Perhaps the most explicit statement of this disparity

oric of imperialism through portraying it as a modern version of tribal war: 'The conquest of the earth, which mostly means the taking it away from those who have a different complexion or slightly flatter noses from ourselves, is not a pretty thing when you look into it too much' (*HD* 10). The justification for imperialistic conquest, in other words, is risible. The underlying justification for conquest, Marlow implies, lies in an almost comical racial or tribal difference: Those people do not look like us, therefore our conquest of them is justified. Even the redeeming idea which he then famously describes is predicated upon a view of the Europeans imperialists themselves as a 'tribe' who superstitiously worship in a sort of elevated ancestor cult: 'What redeems it is the idea only. An idea at the back of it, not a sentimental pretense but an idea; and an unselfish belief in the idea—something you can set up, and bow down before, and offer a sacrifice to. . . .' (*HD* 10). In the light of this imagery of what Europeans would have described as 'fetishism', the saving 'idea' seems to disintegrate. The sacrifices to Kurtz referred to later in the text (the 'unspeakable rites') cast this language of 'primitive' worship in a darkly ironic light.[14] Indeed, the ironies in this passage, which has oddly been seen as a justification for imperialism, are rampant. One of the fundamental cultural justifications for imperialism is the spread of Christianity; however, the imperialists themselves are imagined as 'pagans', setting up false idols. Conrad implies that both kinds of sacrifice involve bloodshed in the pursuit of a tribal ideal; yet, the Europeans constantly decried what they believed to be the bloody rituals of African tribes.[15] All

between imperialist cant and reality occurs not in *Heart of Darkness*, but in *The Inheritors: An Extravagant Story*, which he co-wrote with Ford Maddox Hueffer. 'More revolting to see without a mask was that falsehood which had been hiding under words which for ages had spurred men to noble deeds, to self-sacrifice, to heroism. What was appalling was . . . that all the traditional ideals of honor, glory, conscience, had been committed to the upholding of a gigantic and atrocious fraud' (*I* 282). Cf. Brantlinger, *Rule of Darkness*, 259.

[14] Herbert convincingly demonstrates that the 'superstitions' of 'modern' societies centre around the very idea of culture itself. In other words, there is no inherent difference, he argues, between those nineteenth-century anthropologists who presented portraits of 'savages' and the anthropologists themselves, whose works were predicated upon superstitious notions. See especially the introduction, 'Superstitions of Culture', 1–28.

[15] On the common theme of the bloodiness of African religions see Brantlinger, *Rule of Darkness*, 182–3. A great deal of blood was shed in the Congo venture, most of it African. As the Congo reformer E. D. Morel noted, 'From 1890 onwards the record of the Congo State had been literally blood-soaked'. *King Leopold's Rule in*

of these ironies seem to subvert the reading of this passage as a rationalization of the imperialist adventure.

Imperialism is imbricated with the same superstitions and rituals which Europeans so commonly abjured in other cultures. Marlow constantly reminds the reader that the Europeans he observes are no less bound up in superstitions than are their 'primitive' counterparts. For example, the company clerk uses his clothing as a sort of talisman against the dangers of degeneracy. Indeed, all of the 'principles' on which European society are predicated do not differ significantly from the bases of African tribal identification. In his discussion of hunger Marlow blends together 'superstitions, beliefs, and what you may call principles' (*HD* 43). The reasons why some ideas or ideals are revered are unclear; superstitions, beliefs, and principles are indistinguishable. Marlow's narrative often acts as an anthropological account of his own European tribe; he analyses the beliefs and customs of the Europeans in Africa as if they were a tribal culture. The tribal loyalty of the colonialists in the novel, though, is a cynical veil for rapacity.

Kurtz's real 'sin', in the eyes of the Manager and others, seems to be that he has become detribalized; he has adopted a different tribe. After all, Kurtz was originally a kind of tribal chieftain in his own European world. As the chief accountant tells Marlow: 'Oh, he will go far, very far (. . .) He will be a somebody in the Administration before long. They, above—the Council in Europe, you know— mean him to be' (*HD* 22). In a comical way, the administrators in the Congo speak of those remote figures in Brussels in the hushed tones of idolatry. As a tribe, they worship gods which become apparent to Marlow: 'They wandered here and there with their absurd long staves in their hands like a lot of pilgrims bewitched inside a rotten fence. The word "ivory" hung in the air, was whispered, was sighed. You would think they were praying to it' (*HD* 26). When Kurtz makes the fatal decision to turn his canoe around and return to his new 'tribe', he has irrevocably broken his communal loyalty to Europe; he has challenged the *Gemeinschaft*.

Africa (1904) (Reprinted Westport, CT: Negro Universities Press, 1970), 103. Cf. Brantlinger, *Rule of Darkness*, 260. See Hunt Hawkins, 'Joseph Conrad, Roger Casement, and the Congo Reform Movement', *Journal of Modern Literature* 9 (1981), 65–80; 'Conrad and Congolese Exploitation', *Conradiana* 13/2 (1981), 94– 100; and 'Conrad's Critique of Imperialism in *Heart of Darkness*', *PMLA* 94/2 (1979), 286–99. See M. M. Mahood, *The Colonial Encounter: A Reading of Six Novels* (London: Rex Collings, 1977).

The parameters for the ethnocentricity of the *Gemeinschaft* may be narrow, the identification with a family, group, or tribe; or broad, a nation, or ethnic group.[16] Marlow implies the narrowness of tribal associations when he refers to the Congolese crew who 'were as much strangers to that part of the river as we, though their homes were only eight hundred miles away' (*HD* 41). People are the products, Marlow implies, of a particular place; even the African crew are strangers or foreigners in relation to other tribes. Geertz writes of the genealogy of the idea of culture as particularization: 'there is no such thing as a human nature independent of culture (. . .) We are, in sum, incomplete or unfinished animals who complete or finish ourselves through culture—and not through culture in general but through highly particular forms of it'.[17] Geertz implies here, as does Marlow in *Heart of Darkness*, that people are the products of a particular culture; and that they are largely identified by their association with place and 'tribe'. Marlow's listeners on the 'Nellie' are safe because they 'all are, each moored with two food addresses, like a hulk with two anchors' (*HD* 48). In other words, these people are saved from the fate of those who remain culturally adrift, or who have no ties to a particular group.[18]

The anxiety over the disintegration of personality in the face of the 'other' was a common concern in Conrad's age, in part because, even by Conrad's time, people were beginning to view themselves as cultural constructs and not simply as products of some universal humanity. In many ways, Conrad seems 'modern' to us because he portrayed the borders at which cultural identities seem to be in danger of disintegrating. The solidarity and fidelity that are such common themes in Conrad's works are, in part, responses to this fear of dissolution. Solidarity or fidelity, both of which involve allegiance to a community or culture, are Conrad's barriers to dissolution; they are what prevent *Gemeinschaft* from degenerating

---

[16] On the imaginary quality of such identifications, see Benedict R. Anderson, *Imagined Communities: Reflections on the Origin and Spread of Nationalism* (London: Verso, 1991).

[17] Geertz, *Interpretation of Culture*, 49.

[18] In part, Conrad's concern over this issue of cultural identification may have been personal, for, as Najder writes, he led a rather isolated life in England: 'Conrad did not live within a community. He was not a member of a group or coterie; he stayed in the country, led an almost isolated and atypical life, without a stable social environment until his last years.' Najder, *A Chronicle*, p. ix.

into *Gesellschaft*. One must remain firm in one's sense of belonging to a group, Conrad's characters constantly assert. At times, this sense of division can be seen in a clearly racist context; for example, Almayer's daughter, Nina, bitterly informs him that 'I am not of your race. Between your people and me there is . . . a barrier that nothing can remove' (*AF* 179). Again, racial boundaries are clearly delineated; solidarity is the act of observing these boundaries, while betrayal is the act of crossing them. Although the notion of solidarity has a cultural matrix in Conrad, the matrix is not *always* ethnic. For example, in *Heart of Darkness* Marlow feels a bond with the Africans on the ship because they have become part of his sub-culture, sailors; the crew forms an integral component of the workings of the steamer: 'We had enlisted some of these chaps on the way for a crew. Fine fellows—cannibals—in their place. They were men one could work with, and I am grateful to them' (*HD* 36). The Africans become part of the community that Marlow elsewhere calls the 'community of inglorious toil' (*LJ* 50); they enter into the 'solidarity of the craft' (*LJ* 131). The Africans, in other words, broadly 'belong' to Marlow's community of the sea, or the ship, while the 'pilgrims' seem to evoke little loyalty or camaraderie in Marlow. This is not a community identified by race or ethnicity but by work, or what Conrad would call service. Conrad suggests at one point in *The Mirror of the Sea* that sailors have almost 'primitive' or 'tribal' loyalties which transcend ethnic or national identities: 'in a sense, all sailors belong to one family; all are descended from that adventurous and shaggy ancestor who . . . accomplished the first coasting trip in a sheltered bay ringing with the admiring howls of his tribe' (*MS* 148–9).

Marlow's narrative emerges out of a sense of community: He tells the story to a group of friends who share, as the frame-narrator tells us, 'the bond of the sea' (*HD* 7). In other words, there is a presumption of shared values. Thus, from the beginning, the importance of the community, or the sub-culture, and the corresponding dangers of the community breaking down are important themes. Again, the bonds that form a community or sub-culture, though, do not necessarily rest on ethnic identification. For example, when the helmsman dies, Marlow remarks:

I missed my late helmsman awfully—I missed him even while his body was still lying in the pilot-house. Perhaps you will think it passing strange this regret for a savage who was no more account than a grain of sand in a black Sahara. Well, you don't see, he had done something, he had steered; for months I had him at my back—a help—an instrument. It was a kind of partnership. He steered for me—I had to look after him, I worried about his deficiencies, and thus a subtle bond had been created of which I only became aware when it was suddenly broken. And the intimate profundity of that look he gave me when he received his hurt remains to this day in my memory—like a claim of distant kinship affirmed in a supreme moment.

(HD 51)

The 'subtle bond' that is created stems not from ethnic identification but from another source—a kinship of work. Clearly, there is an underlying racism in some elements of this passage. While I would not overemphasize the cultural relativism implied in the novella, I would stress this linkage.

In his attack on Conrad, Achebe suggests that Conrad intentionally makes the Africans anonymous and indistinct, 'Africa in the mass'; and he argues that this generalizing is inherently dehumanizing.[19] In part, this criticism may stem from the anthropological notion of the structure of African society as essentially tribal and not individual. While Achebe's criticism has force, it may be argued that Marlow's narrative distinguishes the Africans' sense of community, or what I have already termed *Gemeinschaft*, from the rabid egotism and fragmentation of the Europeans with whom Marlow comes into contact—the *Gesellschaft*. Conrad suggests that imperialism tests the bonds of tribal loyalties by asserting the importance of individual economic competition. For example, Dennis Brown suggests this opposition of communality and individuality:

As a contrast to the hollow egotism of the Imperialists, the native Africans of the tale assert a dignified form of 'natural' selfhood—when they are uncorrupted by Western culture. They are represented in terms of mystery, simplicity, otherness. They are neither unitary selves not fragmented selves but suggest a tribal self-in-community quite outside Western conceptions. So, where the egotism of the whites causes them to inhabit a social realm of constant intrigue and backbiting, each willful self plotting to reorder affairs to its own advantage—the natives on the river-bank merge into harmonious communality, expressed in drumming, dancing and shared gesticulation whose meaning is quite closed to Western observation (. . .) Those unlucky enough to have fallen afoul of the Imperialist endeavour

[19] Achebe, 254.

sink, with bleak dignity, into a deathly despair, cut off from their tribal relationship and so drained of all sense of self or even life.[20]

Detribalization, the forced dissociation of African peoples from their tribal roots, is viewed as a brutal process by Marlow because the tribe is seen to be so central to the African culture.[21] In the 'grove of death' Marlow begins to understand the effects of being wrenched out of one's tribe: 'Brought from all the recesses of the coast in all the legality of time contracts, lost in uncongenial surroundings, fed on unfamiliar food, they sickened, became inefficient, and were then allowed to crawl away and rest' (*HD* 20). We see here that the theme of people as products of culture is not limited to the Europeans. Marlow sympathetically portrays the plight of Africans cut off from the sense of the 'familiar'. People, he seems to imply, are only truly at home in the community; disassociation from the community brings despair, or even death.

Many Victorian writers recognized and admired in 'primitive' peoples the sense of community which they found to be profoundly lacking in an increasingly fractured urban and cosmopolitan Europe. While cohesive communities were believed to exist outside of urban areas, the occupants of cities had become increasingly alienated. Thus, A. R. Wallace, whom Conrad deeply admired, ended his account of the Malay Archipelago with an encomium to the values of 'tribal' community—what Tönnies would have called the *Gemeinschaft*. Europe, which has degenerated into a *Gesellschaft* of competing individuals, Wallace warns, could learn from the example of the Dyaks, which he portrays in an idealized fashion as an almost utopian community:

We most of us believe that we, the higher races, have progressed and are progressing (. . .) Now it is very remarkable, that among people in a very low stage of civilization, we find some approach to such a perfect social state. I have lived with communities of savages in South America and in the East, who have no laws or law courts but the public opinion of the village

[20] Dennis Brown, *The Modernist Self in Twentieth-Century English Literature. A Study in Self-Fragmentation* (New York: St. Martin's, 1989), 23.
[21] Several contemporary anthropological studies of detribalization might be mentioned in this regard. See Peter Claus Wolfgang Gütkind (ed.), *The Passing of Tribal Man in Africa* (Leiden: Brill, 1970); Robert H. Bates, *Ethnicity in Contemporary Africa* (Syracuse, NY: Syracuse University Press, 1973); and Louise S. Spindler, *Culture Change and Modernization: Mini-Models and Case Studies* (New York: Holt, Rhinehart & Winston, 1977); all of these studies trace the theme of detribalization as a much more subtle and complex phenomenon.

freely expressed. Each man scrupulously respects the rights of his fellow, and any infraction of those rights rarely or never takes place. *In such a community*, all are nearly equal. There are none of those wide distinctions, of education, and ignorance, wealth and poverty, master and servant, which are the product of our civilization; there is none of that widespread division of labor, which, while it increases wealth, produces also conflicting interests; there is not that severe competition and struggle for existence, or for wealth, which the dense population of civilized countries inevitably creates. All incitements to crimes are wanting, and petty ones are repressed, partly by the influence of public opinion, but chiefly by that natural sense of justice and of his neighbors right, which seems to be, in some degree, inherent in every race of man.[22]

Wallace stresses the sense of community—*Gemeinschaft*—in the Malay Archipelago as a principal virtue which separates the Dyaks from Europeans. It should come as no surprise to us that Joseph Conrad, who presented such bleak portraits of urban alienation and degeneracy as *The Secret Agent*, may have culled from Wallace's work his sense of the value of community.

Wallace's commentary on the barbarism of modern urbanization provides a gloss on Conrad's dark view of the *Gesellschaft* of modern society: 'Our vast manufacturing system, our gigantic commerce, our crowded town and cities, support and continually renew a mass of human misery and crime absolutely greater than has ever existed before. They create and maintain in life-long labor an ever-increasing army, whose lot is the more hard to bear, by contrast with the pleasures, the comforts, and the luxury which they see all around them, but which they can never hope to enjoy; and who, in this respect, are worse off than the savage in the midst of his tribe.'[23] The process of alienation which Wallace perceives in the city may be viewed as a function of detribalization, of people being dissevered from any sense of community. In effect, he echoes the sentiments of Victorian social reformers such as Mayhew. The imagined degeneracy of urban populations, which I have mentioned elsewhere in relation to Nordau and Lombroso, fuelled Wallace's accusation of 'social barbarism' in Europe: 'We allow over a hundred thousand persons to have no means of subsistence but by crime, to remain at large and prey upon the community . . . This in a country which boasts of

---

[22] Wallace, 595–6, italics mine.   [23] Ibid. 598.

its rapid increase in wealth, of its enormous commerce and gigantic manufactures, of its mechanical skill and civilization, of its high civilization and its pure Christianity, I can but term a state of social barbarism.'[24]

The idea of disintegration concomitant with separation from one's 'clan' is a common theme in Conrad's writing. In 'An Outpost of Progress', the Africans are removed from familiar surroundings:

Belonging to a tribe from a very distant part of the land of darkness and sorrow, they did not run away, naturally supposing that as wandering strangers they would be killed by the inhabitants of the country; in which they were right. (. . .) They were not happy, regretting the festive incantations, the sorceries, the human sacrifices of their own land; where they also had parents, brothers, sisters, admired chiefs, respected magicians, loved friends, and other ties supposed generally to be human. Besides, the rice rations served out by the Company did not agree with them, being a food unknown to their land, and to which they could never get used. Consequently they were unhealthy and miserable.   (OP 100)

Aside from the erroneous and racist reference to human sacrifice, Conrad displays here his sympathy for the detribalized Africans; and he suggests the deterioration that arises from being cut off from one's surroundings.

Such a theme of detribalization is intimately bound up with imperialism, for what happened in the process of imperialism was an eradication of the very traditions and cultural roots that characterized pre-imperial Africa. Mary Kingsley, a Victorian travel writer schooled in anthropology, wrote sensitively of the process of breaking down African institutions without any regard for consequences: 'The white race seems to me to blame in saying that all the reason for its interference in Africa is the improvement of the native African, and then proceeding to alter African institutions without in the lease understanding them (. . .) who would not destroy native independence and institutions if they but knew what those things really were.'[25] Of the decimation of African culture through slavery and forced migration, Kingsley writes:

Those Africans had a culture of their own—not a perfect one, but one that could be worked up towards perfection, just as European culture could be worked up. I do not say that if Europe does break down the nationality of

[24] Ibid. 598n.
[25] Mary Kingsley, 'Introductory Note to Second Edition', *West African Studies*, p. xvii.

Africa she will utterly destroy Africans or African culture, but I do say that if she does it, she will make the Africans a people like the Jews—a landless people and an unhappy people.[26]

The result of such forced dislocations is 'seedy, demoralised natives'.[27] The community, or *Gemeinschaft*, disintegrates. Clearly, the notion that the Africans' culture is 'not a perfect one' may be patronizing; however, what Kingsley is defending is a nascent notion of cultural relativism—of respect for those distinct cultures of Africa.

Conrad's 'detribalized' African guard exists as an icon of the disjunctive forces of imperialism that wrenched people from their own cultures, and imposed alien cultural standards on diverse people.[28] Indeed, it might be argued that the rupture that imperialism causes is essentially that between *Gemeinschaft* and *Gesellschaft*. Unlike the 'cannibal crew', who maintain their identity through community, the guard is a product of the new order, the imperialism which was wrenching Africans from their homelands. As such, he is a portrait of a cultural exile, a border dweller who no longer exists in the African community or in the colonialist society. Marlow satirizes him as 'one of the reclaimed, the product of the new forces at work' (*HD* 19). Interestingly, even in this portrait we see some of Conrad's cultural relativism. The man looks at Marlow as just a faceless white, the 'other': 'He had a uniform jacket with one button off, and seeing a white man in his path, hoisted his weapon to his shoulder with alacrity. This was simple prudence, white men being so much alike at a distance that he could not tell who I might be' (*HD* 19). This is one example of Marlow's attempts, however rudimentary, to reconstruct imaginatively another cultural perspective: What must I look like, he thinks, to the guard?

Detribalization is a concept that might usefully be applied as much to the colonists in Conrad's stories as to the 'natives'. Imperialism can be viewed as one of the most disjunctive movements in modern history. Although it may be difficult to summon up sympathy for those imperialists who imposed European will on subjugated people, Conrad constantly shows us that for the colonist the experience of colonialism is as disorienting as for the 'native'. Perhaps the clearest statement of this sense of cultural

---

[26] Mary Kingsley, p. xviii.   [27] Ibid. 326.   [28] Cf. Brown, 23–4.

dissociation or detribalization leading to the degeneration of colonists occurs in 'An Outpost of Progress':

They had been in this vast and dark country only a very short time, and as
yet always in the midst of other white men, under the eye and guidance of
their superiors. (. . .) They were two perfectly insignificant and incapable
individuals whose existence is only rendered possible through the high
organization of civilized crowds. Few men realize that their life, the very
essence of their character, their abilities, and their audacities, are only the
expression of their belief in the safety of their surroundings. The courage,
the composure, the confidence; the emotions and principles (. . .) belongs
not to the individual but to the crowd: to the crowd that believes blindly in
the irresistible force of its institutions and of its morals, in the power of its
police and of its opinion. But the contact with pure unmitigated nature and
primitive man, brings sudden and profound trouble into the heart.

(OP 89)

The behaviour of people such as Kayerts and Carlier is based upon
the constrictions of the 'crowd' or tribe—a stable sense of
Gemeinshaft. Conrad suggests here that, like the Africans in the
outpost who have been taken from their tribal homelands, Kayerts
and Carlier deteriorate in isolation. Of course, there is no moral
equation here between the detribalization of these Belgian colonists
and the African slaves—Kayerts and Carlier choose their fate as
colonialists; however, what Conrad is suggesting is that most ethical systems rely on a sort of tribal identification: 'Society, not from
any tenderness, but because of its strange needs, had taken care of
these two men, forbidding them all independent thought, all initiat-
ive, all departure from routine; and forbidding it under pain of
death' (OP 91). People in so-called civilized societies are just as
dependent upon unwritten codes of behaviour—routine—as are
those in primitive societies, which Victorian anthropology had
demonstrated to be strictly controlled by customs and taboos.

If tribalism is an essential condition of mankind, even among
Europeans, then the detribalization of colonists must lead to degeneration. The portrait of the Belgians in 'An Outpost of Progress'
illustrates this theme of the disintegration of those cut off from their
'clan': 'To the sentiment of being alone of one's kind, to the clear
perception of the loneliness of one's thoughts, of one's sensations—
to the negation of the habitual, which is safe, there is added the
affirmation of the unusual, which is dangerous; a suggestion of
things vague, uncontrollable and repulsive, whose discomposing

intrusion excites the imagination and tries the civilized nerves of the wise and foolish alike' (OP 89). Just as Freud depicts the threat of the foreign in *Totem and Taboo*, so Conrad implies that the foreign is threatening to the fragile sense of identity of his Europeans. As so often occurs in Conrad, the detachment from the tribe, the 'memory of people like them, of men that thought and felt as they used to feel', introduces the danger of atavism:

> It was not the absolute and dumb solitude of the post that impressed them so much as an inarticulate feeling that something from within them was gone, something that had worked for their safety, and had kept the wilderness from interfering with their hearts. The images of home; the memory of people like them, of men that thought and felt as they used to think and feel, receded into distances made indistinct by the glare of sunshine. And out of the great silence of the surrounding wilderness, its very hopelessness and savagery seemed to approach them nearer, to draw them gently, to look upon them, to envelop them with a solicitude irresistible, familiar, and disgusting.   (OP 107–8)

As in *Heart of Darkness*, this deterioration is marked as a function of spatial movement; as Kayerts and Carlier are drawn away from the European community they are drawn 'nearer' to the 'surrounding wilderness'.

'No Warning Voice'

In *Heart of Darkness*, Marlow imagines the African imperial experience as a fiendish social experiment, in which man is detached from his culture and freed from the constraints of civilization. Recalling the theme of 'An Outpost of Progress', man in Western society, says Marlow, is intricately bound up in a web of customs, laws and expectations that do not apply elsewhere:

> You can't understand? How could you—with solid pavement under your feet, surrounded by kind neighbours ready to cheer you or to fall on you, stepping delicately between the butcher and the policeman, in the holy terror of scandal and gallows and lunatic asylums—how can you imagine what particular region of first ages a man's untrammeled feet may take him into by the way of solitude—utter solitude without a policeman—by the way of silence—utter silence, where no warning voice of a kind neighbour can be heard whispering of public opinion. These little things make all the difference.   (HD 49–50)

Freed from these external impositions on his behaviour, man might degenerate atavistically to the 'region of first ages' where no restrictions are placed upon him. For Marlow, then, outer constraints such as the fear of police and, perhaps more importantly, of the opinion of one's peers, are the greatest restrictions on man's behaviour. In *Lord Jim*, too, Conrad's French Lieutenant stresses that ethics are not a product of internal mechanisms which can fail one (as in Jim's 'impulse' to jump), but rather of external limitations: 'Man is born a coward ... But habit—habit—necessity—do you see?—the eye of others—voila' (*LJ* 147). Thus, even the higher moral attributes such as altruism which lead one to act heroically, can be the result of a social and external code. Society dictates even our apparently selfless acts. As T. H. Huxley speculated, 'It is needful only to look around us, to see that the greatest restrainer of the anti-social tendencies of men is near, not of the law but of the opinion of their fellows'.[29] Only in Patusan does Jim becomes cognizant of this social imperative, the pull of community and of communal expectations. Ironically, he discovers the importance of community only in a society where his actions are not fully understood. Jim moves from an egocentric sense of self-preservation on the Patna to a communal sense of sacrifice; but even the self-sacrifice must be enacted in a social context—before the whole tribe. It is worth recalling here what was said early about man's dependence on the implicit and often subconscious signs and responses he receives from his peers: 'The total gamut of sensory cues that are reflected or mirrored back from the other help to stabilize the individual's sense of identity; without a relatedness to another human being, one's sense of identity collapses.'[30] The same may be said of one common version of Victorian ethics—people relied on others to mirror back cues as to expected behaviour. The difficulty occurs in the case of an isolated individual—a Kurtz, a Kayerts or Carlier, a Willems—who has no reliable mirror of his behaviour.

Thomas Carlyle, whom Ian Watt has convincingly demonstrated as an important influence on Conrad's thought, complained in 'Signs of the Times' that morality in society depended largely upon external restrictions rather than on any innate sense of ethics:[31]

[29] Huxley, *Evolution and Ethics*, 24.   [30] Wengle, 8.
[31] See Watt, *Conrad in the Nineteenth Century*, 149–51.

Again, with respect to our Moral condition: Here also he who runs may read that the same physical, mechanical influences are everywhere busy. For the 'superior morality', of which we hear so much, we too would desire to be thankful: at the same time, it were blindness to deny that this 'superior morality' is properly rather an 'inferior criminality', produced not by great Virtue, but by greater perfection of Police; and of that far subtler and stronger Police, called Public Opinion. This last watches over us with its Argus eyes more keenly than ever; but the 'inward eye' seems very heavy with sleep. Of any belief in invisible, divine things, we find as few traces in our Morality as elsewhere. It is by tangible, material actions that we are guided, not by inward and spiritual.[32]

Marlow's belief in the importance of police, and of the police called 'Public Opinion' might well have derived, in part, from this famous essay. This passage from Carlyle also highlights the issue of what might be termed the secularization of ethics. Carlyle laments that morality has become a matter of external controls rather than internal ones, and blames this change on the secularization of his age, the reliance on 'tangible material considerations' rather than 'inward and spiritual' ones. The restraint which Marlow upholds, Carlyle finds to be largely absent in his age; 'Self-denial, the parent of all virtue, in any true sense of that word, has perhaps seldom been rarer'.[33] Deprived of these societal constraints, and lacking self-denial, the 'parent of all virtue', it is not surprising that a man like Kurtz should degenerate so rapidly.

Darwin argued in *The Descent of Man* (1871) that 'there is another and much more powerful stimulus to the development of the social virtues, namely, the praise and blame of our fellow men, (. . .) primeval man at a very early period would have been influenced by the praise and blame of his fellows'.[34] Conrad also seems to have believed that human beings are intimately bound up within a web of societal expectations, the constraints of community, and the fear of praise and blame that Darwin cites as the basis of ethics. The logical extension of this argument is that when these constraints are removed, degeneracy is likely. Much later, in *Under Western Eyes*, the question is posed, what ethical system a man can depend on when divorced from these considerations of societal

[32] Thomas Carlyle, 'Signs of the Times' (1829), in *Critical and Miscellaneous Essay*, 7 vols. (Reprinted London: Chapman & Hall, 1869), ii. 249.
[33] Ibid.
[34] Charles Darwin, *The Descent of Man and Selections in Relation to Sex* (1871), 2 vols. (Reprinted London: John Murray, 1891), i. 164.

conformity: 'Did it ever occur to you how a man who had never heard a word of affection or praise in his life would think on matters on which you would think first with or against your class, your domestic tradition—your fireside prejudices?' (*UW* 61). In other words, human beings are intensely tribal, caught up within the sub-cultures of class, family, etc.; detribalization or exile—the fate of the individual who dwells only on the margins of society— calls into question the whole idea of ethics. Conrad's degenerates— Almayer, Willems, Kayerts, Carlier, and Kurtz—not surprisingly, are social outcasts who, deprived of their social context, quickly become decivilized. This sense of atavism arising from cultural dislocation often depends on an implicit adherence to cultural or ethnic solidarity, a theme that has already been discussed at some length.

Long Ascent, Quick Descent: Maudsley and Moral Insanity

In Victorian scientific circles, the proposition that higher moral instincts would have been among the last acquired during the course of natural selection sustained a large following. Extending the theory to degeneration, then, the last acquired characteristics seemed to be most readily lost. Scientists applied recapitulation theory to moral as much as to embryological development. The inversion of evolution, degeneration, led to a corresponding inversion of ontogeny and phylogeny. The Italian criminologist and moral historian, Rafaele Garofolo, who broke away from orthodox Lombrosanism to develop a theory of 'natural crime', began his *Criminologia* (1885) with a study of the evolution of the moral sense. Although not apparently widely known in Britain until the translation of his later work in 1914, Garofolo may be viewed as a representative figure. 'Influenced by Darwin and Spencer,' as the criminologist De Quiros says, 'he ends with this formula for natural crime: "an offense against the fundamental altruistic sentiments of pity and probity in the average measure possessed by a given social group." '[35] Garofolo's work is of interest here because he, like so many of his contemporaries, viewed altruism as being at the centre

[35] Bernando de Quiros, *Modern Theories of Criminality*, trans. Alfonso de Salvio (London: Heinemann, 1911), 29.

of all theories of moral evolution. The 'fundamental altruistic sentiments of pity and probity' are those most rapidly lost by the criminal. Crime, asserted Garofolo, represented an impairment of 'moral sense resembling an ethical degeneration through retrogressive selection, which would make man lose his best qualities acquired slowly through a long evolution'.[36] This statement characterizes a common idea in Victorian histories of ethics—that degeneration would proceed recapitulatively: 'Atavism, then, considers the criminal as retrograde. Phylogenetically, he has been detained in the human or prehuman evolution; ontogenetically, his arrest has taken place in childhood, granted the parallelism between the evolution of the individual and of the species according to F. Muller or of Haeckel.'[37]

Perhaps the clearest statement of this inversion of moral evolution is in Victorian psychologist Henry Maudsley's *Body and Will* (1883). Maudsley (1835–1918) was one of the most influential Victorian medical psychiatrists, 'one of the most remarkable names in contemporary mental science'.[38] Nordau alluded to Maudsley's work in *Degeneration*;[39] Darwin quoted him in the *Descent of Man*;[40] and Tylor referred to him at the beginning of *Primitive Culture*.[41] Certainly, many affinities exist between Nordau's and Maudsley's works. Drawing upon the term 'moral insanity' which Prichard had coined in *A Treatise on Insanity* (1835),[42] Maudsley developed a theory of atavistic morality in *Responsibility in Mental Disease* (1874); he defined a condition in which all of the higher attributes of morality deteriorated and base egoistic instincts arose:

Notwithstanding prejudices to the contrary, there is a disorder of the mind, in which, without illusion, delusion or hallucination, the symptoms are mainly exhibited in a perversion of those mental faculties which are usually called the active and moral powers—the feeling, affection, propensities, temper, habits, and conduct. (. . .) He has no capacity of true moral feeling; all his impulses and desires, to which he yields without check, are egoistic; his conduct appears to be governed by immoral

---

[36] Bernando de Quiros, 31   [37] Ibid. 42
[38] Ibid. 8. Pick writes that Maudsley 'was certainly the Victorian psychiatrist most widely read and quoted in Italy, France, and Germany at the time'. Pick, 205. Saveson has suggested Maudsley as a source for Conrad's *Secret Agent*. Cf. Saveson, 118–26 and *passim*.
[39] Nordau, *Degeneration*, 18, 255.   [40] Darwin, *Descent of Man*, i. 24.
[41] Tylor, *Primitive Culture*, i. 1.   [42] See Pick, 203.

motives, which are cherished and obeyed without any evident desire to resist them.[43]

In *Lord Jim*, Marlow makes the connection between extreme egoism and moral insanity which Maudsley insisted upon in speaking of Gentleman Brown: 'reflecting how much certain forms of evil are akin to madness, derived from intense egoism, inflamed by resistance, tearing the soul to pieces, and giving factitious vigour to the body' (*LJ* 344). Nordau refers favourably to Maudsley's *Responsibility in Mental Disease*:

That which nearly all degenerates lack is the sense of morality and of right and wrong. For them there exists no law, no decency, no modesty, (...) When this phenomenon is present in a high degree, we speak of 'moral insanity' with Maudsley; there are, nevertheless, lower stages in which the degenerate does not, perhaps, himself commit any act which will bring him into conflict with the criminal code, but at least asserts the theoretical legitimacy of crime; seeks, with philosophically sounding fustian, to prove that 'good' and 'evil,' virtue and vice are arbitrary distinctions; goes into raptures over evildoers and their deeds; professes to discover beauties in the lowest and most repulsive things; and tries to awaken interest in, and so-called 'comprehension' of, every bestiality. The two psychological roots of moral insanity, in all its degrees of development, are, firstly, unbounded egoism, and, secondly, impulsiveness.[44]

In *Body and Will*, Maudsley applied the idea of biological degeneration to the pathology of individuals. 'His work signals a wider development within Victorian social commentary, the confluence of a medical-psychiatric theory of degeneration, a Darwinian theory of evolutionary regression and a positivist theory of criminal inheritance, all of which in turn flowed into a wider current of concern about the pathology of the city and modernity.'[45] Maudsley explored the notion of degeneracy in many of his works: *Body and Will*, *Life in Mind and Conduct*, *Body and Mind*, and *Organic to Human*. Following Lombroso, Maudsley believed in physiological stigmata associated with degeneracy: 'Without doubt the character of every mind is written in the features, gestures, gait, carriage of the body, and will be read when, if ever, the extremely fine and difficult language is accurately learnt.'[46] An avowed

---

[43] Henry Maudsley, *Responsibility in Mental Disease* (London: Henry King, 1874), 171–2.
[44] Nordau, *Degeneration*, 18–19.   [45] Pick, 203.
[46] Maudsley, *Life in Mind and Conduct*, 54.

hereditarian and evolutionst, he believed that the individual is inextricably bound up in his hereditarian acquisitions, 'linked in a chain of causation which renders it impossible he should ever transcend himself'. This chain, moreover, Maudsley believes, can 'reach an indefinitely long way back in an ancestral past'.[47] Recalling the theme of the vestigial remains of primitivism, which has already been mentioned, he asserted that man 'is living his forefathers essentially over again', a re-enactment that includes the most primitive aspects of his heritage: 'the vicious or virtuous ancestral quality, imbued as silent memory in his nature may leap to light on the first stimulus'.[48] This extreme form of biological determinism recalls, in an oblique way, Marlow's dictum that 'the mind of man is capable of anything—because everything is in it, all the past as well as all the future' (HD 38).

In a chapter of Body and Will entitled 'The Pathology of Will, Concerning Degeneration', Maudsley argued that morality is the apex of cultural evolution, and thus thought that one must look for the sign of descent from that high point:

we must occupy ourselves with the most highly developed state of man, since the earliest and most subtle signs of degeneration can be fixed only in the most fully developed specimens (. . .) the region of moral feeling which, representing the highest reach of evolution, is the consummate efflorescence of human culture—that will be the first to exhibit the signs of impairment.[49]

Inverting Haeckel's theory that ontogeny recapitulates phylogeny, Maudsley argues that the process of degeneration in individuals replicates degeneration in the species. The degeneration of the individual parallels in miniature the degeneration of mankind. Since morality is the last acquired characteristic, it seems natural to Maudsley that it will be the first lost: 'That conscience is at best being a late, is still a precarious possession is shown by its quick and easy downfall under the sudden stress of a great catastrophe in every civilized community, and by its swift effacement in individuals and peoples.'[50]

Maudsley argues that the moral sense is not a permanently fixed instinct in man, but on the contrary, that anthropology demonstrates its variability:

[47] Maudsley, Body and Will, 26.   [48] Ibid. 29.   [49] Ibid. 243.
[50] Maudsley, Life in Mind and Conduct, 139–40.

Like all organic matter, it is plastic and exhibits a circumstance-suiting power; and therefore it varies in its sanctions in different nations, societies, sects, casts, individuals, in a way that a thoroughly formed and fixed instinct, like the instinct to walk upright, does not. Why should not a savage steal when he wants fed, or kill his mother when she is old and useless, or sell his sister's children, since it seems the most natural and proper thing in the world to him? Tis the categorical imperative of reason, the instinct of right in him.[51]

Maudsley and Lubbock both rely implicitly upon the Lamarckian notion that acquired characteristics may be passed on as a biological inheritance. But as the development of morality depends upon acquired characteristics, so conversely the acquisition of immoral characteristics could just as easily be passed on to another generation. Just as Lamarck argued that climatic changes altered species characteristics, so, in Maudsley's view, do changes in climate or culture propel physiological and psychological changes in man. The implications here seem straightforward, for if, as Maudsley says, the moral instincts are not fixed, and, as Lubbock argues, are not 'natural', then the degeneration of moral feelings is a distinct possibility.

The savage nature of man, according to Maudsley, was encapsulated in the brain of the modern. Like Lombroso, Maudsley believed that this atavistic section of the brain influenced the behaviour of criminals and degenerates. There is, he argued,

truly a brute brain within the man's; and when the latter stops short of its characteristic development as human—when it remains at or below the level of an orang's brain, it may be presumed that it will manifest its most primitive functions, and no higher functions (. . .) some very strong arguments in support of Mr. Darwin's views might be drawn from the field of morbid psychology. We may, without much difficulty, trace savagery in civilization, as we can trace animalism in savagery; and in the degeneration of insanity, in the unkinding, so to say, of the human kind, there are exhibited marks denoting the elementary instincts of its composition.[52]

Man's evolutionary inheritance, in other words, was manifested in his later development; and the stages of evolution could be traced without reference to his current state. As a writer in the *Fortnightly Review* phrased the problem in 1894: 'our modern life still retains quite sufficient vestiges of the old barbarous condition, and the

---

[51] Maudsley, *Body and Will*, 267. [52] Maudsley, *Body and Mind*, 52–3.

stages that succeeded it'.[53] The degenerate clearly represented an earlier and more primitive level of humanity, before the higher attributes of morality had been successfully acquired. The degenerate lay somewhere between the 'orang' and the 'primitive'.

Like Nordau later, and also anticipating Freud, Maudsley views unleashed egoism as a primitivistic force threatening society. During the course of degeneration, he argues, the altruistic or sympathetic instinct, which has been built up in man as the last product of the evolution of morality, would be displaced by egoism. 'At a higher level still', wrote Maudsley, 'with the social egoistic instincts in pretty full activity, there will be an entire absence of the altruistic instincts, accompanied it may be by a great deal of cunning intelligence.'[54] Maudsley called this process the 'desocialization of the individual', as well as degeneracy. The term desocialization is particularly resonant here, for what Maudsley and others viewed as the principle characteristic of the degenerate was his inability to function within society. Deprived of the intricate web of social custom and expectations that controlled the lives of 'civilized' people, the Victorians believed that man would degenerate. This theme is particularly relevant to Kurtz's decline.

In the study of ethics, altruism and sympathy were often viewed as being tentatively balanced against egoism and self-interest, and solidarity opposed to individualism. Clearly, Conrad's early works chart the oscillations of these contrasting sides of human nature; this theme has been viewed as central in his work.[55] Henry Maudsley again provides an interesting parallel here, and helps us to situate Conrad's views in an historical context. In a very Conradian manner, Maudsley writes that 'the moral aim of the individual everywhere is to find out the just mean between his personal rights and the duty claims of the society to which he belongs—to *reconcile individuality with solidarity, egoism with altruism*' (italics mine). Again, on the balance of these powers in society, he writes similarly: 'No society could probably exist long in which everybody made a complete renunciation of self, any more than a society could exist in which nobody made any self-renunciation: the problem in the particular case is to reconcile individuality

---

[53] Ludwig Buchner, 'The Origin of Mankind', *Fortnightly Review*, 61/320 (January 1894), 82.

[54] Maudsley, *Body and Mind*, 252.

[55] One of the first reviewers of *Lord Jim* remarked on this as the central theme: 'the soul of a dreamer, rising, under affliction, to ever higher flights of altruism and self-sacrifice'. Sherry, *Critical Heritage*, 125.

with solidarity—to find the just mean between egoism and altruism, a mean which must vary according to the individual nature and the conditions of society.'[56] These two statements seem to be an apt summation of the ethical patterns of *Heart of Darkness* and *Lord Jim*. As Conrad wrote later in a letter to the *New York Times* on 2 August 1901:

Egoism, which is the moving force of the world, and altruism, which is its morality, these two contradictory instincts of which one is so plain and the other so mysterious, cannot serve us unless in the incomprehensible alliance of their irreconcilable antagonism. Each alone would be fatal to our ambition. For, in the hour of undivided triumph, one would make our inheritance too arid to be worth having and the other too sorrowful to own.[57]

The sense of the irreconcilable antagonism and tentative balance between the warring forces of altruism and egoism here clearly resembles Maudsley's conception.

In Maudsley's view, the societal instincts were more fragile because they were secondary. The egoistic instinct remained strong even in social man, and would surface under extreme pressure. The following passage provides a fascinating gloss on Jim's actions:

Self being basic, always divulges and asserts itself in the last resort when the individual comes into violent encounter with the elemental facts of nature, physical or human. Then all the latest vestures of shams, hypocrisies, conventions, reserves, formalism, are rudely stripped off; the restraints patiently woven in the interests of the species rent to pieces by the selfishness of human ferocity of the individual. Thence, too, the hideous exhibitions of human ferocity in crises (. . .) when the fundamental instincts burst out with brutal violence (. . .).[58]

Faced with the 'elemental facts of nature, physical or human' restraints are thrown off.[59] Jim's instinct to jump is one example of what Maudsley refers to as the realization of an elemental fact of physical nature. Under such conditions, the acquisitions of higher morality are shed: 'Principles won't do. Acquisitions, clothes, pretty rags—rags that would fly off with the first good shake' (*HD* 38).

[56] Maudsley, *Life in Mind and Conduct*, 81.
[57] *Collected Letters of Conrad*, ii. 348.
[58] Maudsley, *Life in Mind and Conduct*, 149.
[59] Conrad sometimes accepted this stereotype of so-called primitives as unrestrained. For example, in *Almayer's Folly*, he writes of the 'unrestrained fierceness of natures as ignorant of culture as their own immense and gloomy forests' (*AF* 38).

Kurtz and Retrogressive Metamorphosis

The degeneration of Kurtz in *Heart of Darkness* occurs along very similar lines to those patterns which Maudsley and other Victorian thinkers outlined. Kurtz functions not merely as a morally retrograde individual character, nor even as a psychoanalytic portrait of the pathology of unleashed egoism, but as a familiar emblem to the Victorians of what might be called reverse or inverse Darwinism. In *Evolution and Ethics*, Huxley made the point that too often his contemporaries attached connotations of progress or betterment to the term 'evolution', while, in fact, it was a neutral word which could just as easily signify 'retrogressive metamorphosis'.[60] In Kurtz, all of the developmentalist and progressionist theories are profoundly challenged. In what Conrad and many of his contemporaries would have seen as a natural reversal of the evolutionary process, following Maudsley, Nordau, and others, Kurtz sheds all the higher moral sensibilities, which have become ingrained social instincts in man. The 'instincts' of sympathy and altruism disappear. Upon reading Kurtz's report for the 'International Society for the Suppression of Savage Customs', Marlow is shocked when he finds 'at the end of that moving appeal to every *altruistic* sentiment it blazed at you, luminous and terrifying, like a flash of lightning in a serene sky: "Exterminate all the brutes"' (*HD* 51, italics mine). Here the notion of altruism, which the Victorians cherished so greatly, and which was at the base of many of the theories of ethical evolution, is utterly subverted. The Victorians were fascinated with the idea that ontogeny recapitulates phylogeny. Degeneration is really just an extension of that idea to the moral and social spheres. If the development of the individual recapitulates the evolution of the species, the argument went, then the degeneration of the individual reverses that process as the individual rapidly loses the higher moral attributes which are evolutionary legacies.[61] When the last of the social instincts has finally degenerated, then the very first

[60] Quoted above.
[61] The idea that degeneration recapitulated in reverse form the process of evolution is summarized by Topinard. He repeats a common anthropological belief, that the degeneration of savage tribes from a higher level of culture could be studied as a model for evolution: 'Happily for us, the degenerate groups stand us in excellent stead for reconstructing the probable course of evolution of the first man, for retrogression is, by privilege, of inestimable value, being a retracing of the steps through which progression has passed.' Topinard, 156.

acquired instinct, the instinct of walking upright, goes as well. The physiological features which Darwin, Huxley, and others believed marked man out as different from apes also disintegrates, and the upright man has become once more an animal, 'crawling on all fours' (*HD* 64). The image of regression taken to the extreme is the natural extension of the theory of degeneration. Maudsley says in *Body and Will* that 'no one in walking seems to entertain the notion of going on all fours'.[62] Nevertheless, even this final degeneration is not inconceivable according to the paradigm of degeneracy as the reversal of evolution.

The idea of widespread moral and cultural degeneration, as we have seen, was not limited to Nordau's theories. Many other Victorian thinkers believed that civilization would eventually degenerate, and that the current problems only presaged the future disintegration of civilization. The foreshortening of the period of humanity's advance perpetuated this sense of pessimism. Anthropology, palaeontology, and archaeology had all demonstrated the human species' origin and successive development to be of a highly attenuated nature in relation to the geological time-scale. The *homo sapiens* was a comparatively recent inhabitant of the earth and his progress in civilization, though amazing, could not have been but an aberration. If it occurred, it was argued, decline could be rapid and unstoppable.

In part, this pessimism stemmed from common apocalyptic belief in a second ice age, a theory which derived from Kelvin's 'Second Law of Thermodynamics'.[63] This notion prompted Conrad's bleak conclusion that reason 'demonstrates (. . .) that (. . .) the fate of a humanity condemned to perish from the cold is not worth troubling about. If you take it to heart, it becomes an unendurable tragedy. If you believe in improvement, you must weep, for the attained perfection must end in cold, darkness, and silence'.[64] Another passage from a letter of 1897 shows that for Conrad this remained a deep anxiety. He writes to Cunninghame Graham again of the 'eternal decree that will extinguish the sun, the stars one by one, and in another instant shall spread a frozen darkness over the whole

[62] Maudsley, *Body and Will*, 252.

[63] Ian Watt quotes Edward Carpenter, writing of this view of the physical universe: 'one of its properties was that it could run down like a clock, and would eventuate in time in a cold sun and a dead earth—and there was an end of it'. Watt, 152.

[64] Quoted Watt, 153.

universe'.[65] Maudsley takes this image of the cooling earth and applies it to the idea of human degeneracy. If man had indeed, as the developmental anthropologists argued, progressed from a universal primitive state to his current peak in contemporary Western civilization, then the converse would also be true. Given the importance of accidents of time and place, and of climatic change in Darwin's theory, man might be expected to deteriorate along the same lines. Paul Topinard posited this reversal of the evolutionary process when he wrote bleakly: 'The end, so far as we are concerned, we know. Our earth will cease to be habitable. It will grow cold, will doubtless lose its atmosphere, its humidity, and will resemble our present moon. Evolution from having been progressive, will become stationary, then retrogressive.'[66] Maudsley, too, envisaged a cultural atavism prevailing after a second ice age:

The nations that have risen high in complexity of development will degenerate and be broken up, to have their places taken by less complex associations of inferior individuals (. . .) a few scattered families of degraded human beings living perhaps in snow huts near the equator, very much as Esquimaux live now near the Pole, will represent the last wave of the receding tide of human existence before its final extinction.[67]

In cultural degeneration, Maudsley asserts, the falling off is invariably greater in those cultures which have risen highest. Thus he believed that degeneration would produce savages like those which he saw around him in primitive cultures, but savages who would be all the more barbarous because they were produced by the reversal of the highest form of evolution:

Not that humanity will retrograde quickly through the exact stages of its former slow and tedious process, as every child now quickly goes through them; it will not in fact reproduce savages with the simple mental qualities of children, but new and degenerate varieties with special repulsive characters—savages of a decomposing civilization, we might call them—who will

---

[65] *Collected Letters of Conrad*, i. 243.   [66] Topinard, 261.
[67] Maudsley, *Body and Will*, 320. T. H. Huxley writes, in a passage with which Conrad may have been familiar: 'If what the physical philosophers tell us, that our globe has been in a state of fusion, and, like the sun, in gradually cooling down, is true, then the time must come when evolution will mean adaptation to an universal winter, and all forms of life will die out, except such low and simple organisms as the Diatom of the arctic and antarctic ice, and the Protococcus of the red snow.' 'Struggle for Existence in Human Society', *Evolution and Ethics*, 199.

be ten times more vicious and noxious, and infinitely less capable of improvement, than savages of the most primitive barbarism; social disintegrates of the worst kind, because bred of the corruption of the best organic development, with notions and properties virulently anti-social.[68]

This passage goes along with what Maudsley said about the degeneration of individuals producing antisocial variants, but often with a cunning intelligence. Maudsley's dark musings here seem prescient of the sort of interpretation that the twentieth century has put upon the savagery of modern man, most notably on the Holocaust. Regression would not re-enact the evolutionary process in reverse; it would lead to something much worse.

What Possible Restraint?

Henry Maudsley's whole theory of moral development and reversion is analogous to Conrad's treatment of Kurtz, who is the archetypal Maudsleyan degenerate—a highly cultured and sophisticated individual who becomes when he reverts to savagery far worse than the so-called primitives around him. He knows 'no restraint, no faith, no fear' (*HD* 66). The cannibal crew, though lower in the Victorian anthropological hierarchy, are apparently progressing in culture, for they have at least developed some of the early products of morality as construed by Victorian scientists and philosophers—discipline and restraint, as well as the virtues of community. Discipline and restraint marked two of the most important facets of the Victorian evolution of ethics. For example, Huxley wrote in *Evolution and Ethics*:

the practice of what is ethically best—what we call goodness or virtue—involves a course of conduct which, in all respects, is opposed to that which leads to success in the cosmic struggle for existence. *In place of ruthless self-assertion it demands self-restraint*; in place of thrusting aside, or treading down, all competitors, it requires that the individual shall not merely respect, but shall help his fellows; its influence is directed, not so much to the survival of the fittest, as to the fitting of as many as possible to survive. It repudiates the gladiatorial theory of existence.[69]

[68] *Body and Will*, 321.
[69] Huxley, *Evolution and Ethics*, 81–2, italics mine.

Conrad suggests this theme of developing restraint as a concomitant of societal evolution when Marlow wonders why the starving
crew did not attack and devour the passengers. Hungry as they are,
such an act would appear to be instinctive—indeed, one of the most
primal instincts—that of self-preservation. Instead, Conrad implies,
morality has obtruded in the course of evolution. 'Restraint!'
Marlow muses.

What possible restraint? Was it superstition, disgust, patience, fear—or
some kind of primitive honour? No fear can stand up to hunger, no
patience can wear it out, disgust simply does not exist where hunger is; and
as to superstitions beliefs, and what you might call principles, they are less
than chaff in the breeze (. . .) And these chaps, too, had no earthly reason
for any kind of scruple. Restraint! I would as soon have expected restraint
from a hyena prowling among the corpses of a battlefield. But there was the
fact facing me—the fact dazzling, to be seen, like the foam on the depths of
the sea, like a ripple on an unfathomable enigma.   (HD 43)

For 'primitive honour' or 'principles' here moral development or
evolution might be substituted. Marlow cannot unravel the mystery
but also cannot deny the presence of restraint, nor its implications.
Even in the presence of apparently overwhelming instincts, restraint
intercedes to prevent action. He believes that the so-called primitive
men have not yet acquired characteristics through a Lamarckian
evolutionary inheritance because, in Victorian terms, 'They still
belonged to the beginnings of time, had no *inherited experience* to
teach them as it were' (HD 43, italics mine).

   The belief that 'primitive' people were utterly unrestrained seems
to have been among the most widely distributed stereotypes in
writings on non-European cultures; therefore, it is all the more
striking that Conrad's story works against the stereotype.
Christopher Herbert has explored this theme of savage cultures, in
the view of early nineteenth-century ethnographers, as exemplify-
ing the characteristics of what Durkheim called *anomie*. As one
representative explorer in Polynesia put it, among 'primitive' peoples, 'the passions of man are more openly and strongly developed,
and his actions, generally speaking, under much less restraint'.[70]
Herbert writes: 'Focusing their attention on such themes, nineteenth-century observers portrayed the Polynesian savage in the
conventional imagery that has played so important a role in the

----

[70] Quoted in Herbert, 161.

social thought of the last two centuries: that of the figure of bound-less, exorbitant, uncontrollable desires . . . which in the idiom of Prichardian psychology was called 'moral insanity', and in that of Durkheimian sociology was to be called anomie'.[71] Herbert cites numerous examples of this view of 'savages' as embodiments of unrestrained desire or *anomie*, and concludes that 'the trope of absent boundaries to desire and the idea of "savages" as vessels of unchecked carnal passions form the governing and catalyzing prin-ciples of this whole project of ethnographic research'.[72] The idea was so widely dispersed in E. B. Tylor's time that he felt obliged to refute it in his work, *Anthropology*. His comment seems particu-larly applicable to *Heart of Darkness*:

It must not be supposed that in any state of civilization a man's conduct altogether depends on his own moral sense of right and wrong. Controlling forces are at work even among savages. (. . .) Explorers of wild countries, not finding the machinery of police they are accustomed to at home, have sometimes rashly concluded that savages live unrestrained at their own free will. We have already noticed that this is a mistake, for life in the uncivil-ized world is fettered at every turn by chains of custom.[73]

Tylor also remarks, in another analogous passage that has interest-ing implications for *Heart of Darkness*, that even amongst 'sav-ages', 'Public opinion is already a great power'.[74] What both Marlow and Tylor intimate here goes far beyond the Victorian belief in the prevalence of 'taboos' among so-called primitive people. Rather, the implications of this passage impact upon the growing modern conception of 'culture' as a system of restraints or constraints, which are invisible but nonetheless powerful checks on people's behaviour in 'civilized' as much as in 'savage' cultures. The solidarity of the *Gemeinschaft* is what enforces such restrictions; thus, the African crew's ability to restrain themselves seems to be bound up with the fact that they are part of a community. Malinowski writes in *Argonauts of the Western Pacific* that one of the principal goals and benefits of ethnography is in its discernment of laws and customs in 'primitive' cultures which earlier travellers

---

[71] Herbert, 160.   [72] Ibid. 161.

[73] E. B. Tylor, *Anthropology*, 408–9. D. H. Lawrence wrote similarly much later, drawing on anthropological sources: 'The wild Australian aborigines are bound up tight, tighter than a China girl's foot, in their few savage conventions.' Lawrence, 'The Good Man', in *Phoenix: The Posthumous Papers of D. H. Lawrence*, 752.

[74] Tylor, *Anthropology*, 409.

had viewed as chaotic: 'Ethnology has introduced law and order into what seemed chaotic and freakish. It has transformed for us the sensational, wild and unaccountable world of 'savages' into a number of well ordered communities, governed by law, behaving and thinking according to consistent principles.'[75]

That restraint had become an innate quality in 'modern' societies was a common, though not universal, belief in Conrad's time. Usually in modern civilization, as Tylor implies, the obvious constraints are external ('not finding the machinery of police they are so accustomed to at home'), so that there is no need to face the possibility of unrestrained liberty. Yet, other hidden codes govern behaviour in both 'civilized' and 'primitive' societies: 'Among the lessons to be learnt from the life of rude tribes is, how society can go on without the policeman to keep order. (. . .) Without some control beyond the mere right of the stronger, the tribe would break up in a week, whereas in fact savage tribes last on for ages.'[76] Tylor's answer is that not all constraints on people's behaviour are external: 'whether a custom is useful or not, and even when its purpose is no longer known, once established as a custom it must be conformed to'.[77]

Truly unrestrained liberty, or the release which is summed up in the term *anomie*, is perhaps only possible when one is isolated from one's own culture and set down in the midst of an 'alien' culture. In this context, a person's identity, his status as a creature of culture is severely challenged. He has three primary choices: to maintain his own sense of culture even in the midst of the unfamiliar (a common response in colonialist endeavours); to adapt to the new culture (going native), which implies an adoption of the cultural norms of that society; or to reject the entire idea of societal constraints and become a self-directed renegade, subject to the restraints of *no* culture. Clearly, Kurtz chooses the third option, and in so doing, his fragile identity collapses. Kurtz is the apogee of the notion of a European who abandons himself utterly to a state of unbounded desire: 'I saw the mystery of a soul that knew no restraint, no faith, and no fear, yet struggled blindly with itself' (*HD* 66).[78] Kurtz's degeneration is described in terms of spatial disorientation ('he had kicked himself loose of the earth . . . he had kicked the very earth to pieces' *HD* 65). As he observes Kurtz, Marlow feels unsure whether

[75] Malinowski, *Argonauts*, 9–10.   [76] Tylor, *Anthropology*, 405.
[77] Ibid. 409.   [78] On *anomie*, see Herbert, *passim*.

he himself 'stood on the ground or floated in the air' (*HD* 65).
Marlow's imagery when he speaks of Kurtz as 'lying at the bottom
of a precipice where the sun never shines' (*HD* 68) seems to be
prefigured in Durkheim's definition of *anomie* as 'an insatiable and
boundless abyss'.[79]

Societal evolution, Conrad implies, in a manner that parallel's
Huxley's theories traced above, is contingent upon the obedience to
laws and customs dictated by a sort of implicitly understood social
contract. Man gives up some of his individual liberties in order to
acquire peace of mind, and in order to allow him to acquire and
secure his property. The colonial system, however, radically
decontextualizes the individual, and undercuts the sense of cultural
norms. This is where the challenge to cultural identification becomes clear. Placed in the 'heart of darkness', free from the bounds
of law and custom which restrain people, the social contract is
suspended, and cultural identifications may break down. People
might then degenerate rapidly. The writer of *Regeneration: A Reply
to Max Nordau* (1895) had summarized Nordau's fear of the
'realization of bestial propensities now kept in check only by law,
police, and public opinion'.[80] The idea of the lack of restraint in
primitive cultures was not uncommon. One of the distinctions
made by many writers between African and European cultures was
in the lack of a legal system, an obvious external restraint. Brodie
Cruickshank, the Gold Coast colonist quoted in the first chapter,
argued that 'the proneness of the African to evil assumed the
character of an undeviating instinct, to which the absence of any
sufficient legal constraint give the utmost scope'.[81] The natural
extension of this argument to colonists rendered it unsurprising
that Europeans should degenerate in contact with 'unrestrained'
natives. Distinctions among various kinds of constraints had not
yet been clearly made.

An Enemy of Progress

Kurtz's fall is made to seem even more decadent due to the high
level of culture he has ostensibly attained. Despite moments of
cultural relativism, most Victorian anthropologists were assured of

---

[79] Durkheim, *Suicide*, 247–8. Quoted in Herbert, 70.
[80] Anon., *Regeneration*, 31.   [81] Cruickshank, ii. 3.

the moral inferiority of 'primitive' cultures in relation to Europe: 'On the whole, then, it appears to me that the moral feelings deepen with the gradual growth of a race.'[82] If, in general, civilized man proved morally superior to 'primitive' man, then the repulsiveness of degeneration to the Victorians was the more pronounced. Similarly, Nordau seemed to be all the more enraged by the degeneration of the modern artist or literary figure because he placed art so high in the hierarchy of culture. Like Maudsley, Nordau viewed the ethical development of society as a constant increase of discipline and restraint in man, and believed that the arts ought to be allied with this restraining tendency. Marlow's demigods, discipline, restraint, and the deliberate belief to which he clings when faced with Kurtz's primitivism, are precisely the qualities which Nordau also advocates as the saviours of society:

Progress is possible only by the growth of knowledge; but this is the task of consciousness and judgment, not of instinct. The march of progress is characterized by the expansion of consciousness and the contraction of the unconscious; the strengthening of the will and the weakening of the impulsions; the increase of self-responsibility and the repression of reckless egoism. He who makes instinct man's master does not wish for liberty, but the most infamous and abject slavery, (. . .) and he who places pleasure above discipline, and impulses above self-restraint, wishes not for progress, but for retrogression to the most primitive animality.[83]

Nordau's writing provides an interesting contemporary commentary on *Heart of Darkness*, for most of the manifestations of Kurtz's degeneration are precisely those which Nordau outlines. Finally, Kurtz, 'satiated with primitive emotions', surrendering to 'forgotten and brutal instincts, monstrous passions' (*HD* 65) and utterly devoid of discipline and restraint, sinks into the 'most primitive animality' which Nordau describes.

At the centre of the study of Kurtz's degeneration, and of the theme of degeneracy generally in Victorian culture, lay the idea that man carries with him residual primitivism which may break out at any time. For example, Huxley argued that the same characteristics which raise man above the animals, his cunning and rapacity, were never fully sublimated to civilized instincts: 'For his successful progress throughout the savage state, man has been largely in-

---

[82] Lubbock, *Origin of Civilisation*, 307.　　　[83] Nordau, *Degeneration*, 554.

debted to those qualities which he shares with the ape and the tiger.'[84] 'After the manner of successful persons', he continues, 'civilised man would gladly kick down the ladder by which he had climbed', and see the ape and tiger die; and the intrusion of these 'boon companions of his hot youth into the ranged existence of civil life' proves a constant source of embarrassment to him.[85] In the end, Kurtz represents the final degeneration back to what the Victorians perceived as an early evolutionary level of the amorality of the ape and tiger. Nordau also uses animal imagery to portray the degradation of the degenerate. He reviles Nietzsche's 'freely-roving lusting beast of prey' with this admonition: 'Get you gone from civilization! Rove apart from us! Be a lusting beast of prey in the desert. (. . .) There is no place among us for the lusting beast of prey; and if you dare return to us, we will piteously beat you to death with clubs.'[86] Again, consider Huxley's warning for civilization, which closely parallels Nordau's: 'The animal man, finding that the ethical man has landed him in such a slough, resumes his sovereignty, and preaches anarchy; which is, substantially, a proposal to reduce the social cosmos to chaos, and begin the brute struggle for existence once again.'[87]

The concern over the possibility of the reversal of cultural progress manifested itself in a common call in the Victorian period for a return to 'morality', 'restraint', 'work', and 'discipline', concepts which Conrad's Marlow would have advocated. Nordau writes:

The criterion by which the true moderns may be recognized and distinguished from impostors calling themselves moderns may be this: Whoever preaches absence of discipline is an enemy of progress; and whoever worships his 'I' is an enemy of society. Society has for its first premise neighbourly love and self-sacrifice; and progress is the effect of an ever more rigorous subjugation of the beast in man, of an even tenser self-restraint, an even keener sense of duty and responsibility.[88]

Here Nordau sets up the degenerationist/progressionist debate as the very arbiter of 'modernity'. Progress is defined as a subjugation of the beast in man, the growth of altruism or sympathy, and the abnegation of egoism in favour of societal responsibility. While

[84] Huxley, *Evolution and Ethics*, 50.   [85] Ibid. 52.   [86] Nordau, 557.
[87] Huxley, *Evolution and Ethics*, 215.   [88] Nordau, 560.

Nordau's didacticism may seem hopelessly naive to us now, it enjoyed a wide currency during the Victorian period when Conrad and his contemporaries struggled with the problems of moral evolution.

Bibliography

ACHEBE, CHINUA, 'An Image of Africa: Racism in Conrad's *Heart of Darkness*'. *The Massachusetts Review*, 18 (1977), 782–94. Reprinted in Robert Kimbrough (ed.), *Heart of Darkness: An Authoritative Text, Background, Sources, Criticism* (New York: W. W. Norton, 1988), 251–62.

ALLEN, RICHARD, *Malaysia, Prospect and Retrospect: The Impact and Aftermath of Colonial Rule* (London: Oxford University Press, 1968).

ANDERSON, BENEDICT R., *Imagined Communities: Reflections on the Origin and Spread of Nationalism* (London: Verso, 1991).

ANONYMOUS, *Regeneration: A Reply to Max Nordau* (London: Constable, 1895).

——, 'New Writers: Mr. Joseph Conrad'. *Bookman*, 10/50 (May 1896), 41.

——, 'Stevenson's Voyages'. *Bookman*, 10/65 (February 1897), 144.

——, 'Among Cannibals'. *Academy*, 51/1294 (20 February 1897), 228.

——, 'Edward Gibbon', *Academy*, 51/1285 (27 February 1897), 249.

——, 'Life and Death in the Niger Delta'. *Blackwood's Edinburgh Magazine*, 162/1990 (April 1898), 451–62.

——, 'The Works of Mr. Kipling'. *Blackwood's Edinburgh Magazine*, 164/897 (October 1898), 285.

——, 'The Ethics of Conquest'. *Blackwood's Edinburgh Magazine*, 164/1908 (December 1898), 849.

——, 'From the New Gibbon', *Blackwood's Edinburgh Magazine* (February 1899), 241–9.

——, 'Criminology'. *Encyclopaedia Britannica*, 11th edn (1910), vii, 465.

ARCHER, MARGARET S., *Culture and Agency: The Place of Culture in Social Theory* (Cambridge: Cambridge University Press, 1988).

ARMISTEAD, W., *A Tribute to the Negro: Being a Vindication of the Moral, Intellectual, and Religious Capabilities of the Coloured Portion of Mankind* (Manchester: William Irwin, 1848).

ARNOLD, MATTHEW, *Culture and Anarachy* (1869) (Rpt.: Cambridge: Cambridge University Press, 1969).

ASSAD, TALAL (ed.), *Anthropology and the Colonial Encounter* (London: Ithaca Press, 1975).

BAINES, JOCELYN, *Joseph Conrad: A Critical Biography* (1960) (London: Weidenfeld and Nicholson, 1969).

BAKHTIN, MICHAEL M., *The Dialogic Imagination* (Austin: University of Texas Press, 1981).

BAKER, ROBERT S., 'Watt's Conrad'. *Contemporary Literature* 22 (1981), 116–26.

BARZUN, J., *Race—A Study in Superstition* (New York: Harper & Row, 1965).

BATCHELOR, JOHN, *H. G. Wells* (Cambridge: Cambridge University Press, 1985).

——, *Lord Jim* (London: Unwin Hyman, 1988).

BATES, ROBERT H., *Ethnicity in Contemporary Africa* (Syracuse, NY: Syracuse University Press, 1973).

BENEDICT, RUTH, *Patterns of Culture* (Cambridge: The Riverside Press, 1934).

BERNSTEIN, RICHARD J., *Beyond Objectivism and Relativism: Science, Hermeneutics and Praxis* (Oxford: Blackwell, 1983).

BERTHOUD, JACQUES, *Joseph Conrad, the Major Phase* (London and New York: Cambridge University Press, 1978).

BLUMENBACH, JOHANN FRIEDRICH, *The Anthropological Treatises of Johann Friedrich Blumenbach*, trans. and ed. Thomas Bendyshe (London: Longman, 1865).

——, *A Manual of the Elements of Natural History* (London: W. Simpson & R. Marshall, 1825).

BOAS, FRANZ, *Essays on Primitivism and Related Ideas* (Oxford: Oxford University Press, 1948).

BOCK, MARTIN, *Crossing the Shadow-Line: The Literature of Estrangement* (Columbus: Ohio State University Press, 1989).

BOLT, CHRISTINE, *Victorian Attitudes to Race* (London: Routledge & Kegan Paul, 1971).

BOOTH, WILLIAM, *In Darkest England and the Way Out* (London: Carlyle Press, 1890).

BRANTLINGER, PATRICK, *Bread and Circuses: Theories of Mass Culture as Social Decay* (Ithaca: Cornell University Press, 1983).

——, *Rule of Darkness: British Literature and Imperialism, 1830–1914* (Ithaca: Cornell University Press, 1988).

BREWSTER, EARL, *D. H. Lawrence: Reminiscences* (London: Heinemann, 1934).

BRIDGEWATER, PATRICK, *Nietzsche in Anglosaxony* (Leicester: Leicester University Press, 1972).

BROWN, DENNIS, *The Modernist Self in Twentieth-Century English Literature. A Study in Self-Fragmentation* (New York: St. Martin's, 1989).

BUCHAN, JOHN, 'No-Man's Land'. *Blackwood's Edinburgh Magazine*, 165/994 (January 1899), 2.

BUCHNER, LUDWIG, 'The Origin of Mankind'. *Fortnightly Review*, 61/320 (January 1894).

BUCKLE, HENRY, *The History of Civilization in England*, 2 vols. (London:

John Parker & Son, 1858).

BURROW, J. W., *Evolution and Society* (Cambridge: Cambridge University Press, 1965).

BURROWS, GUY, *The Land of the Pigmies* (London: Arthur Pearson, 1898).

BURTON, RICHARD, *Two Trips to Gorilla Land and the Cataracts of the Congo*, 2 vols. (London: Low, Marson, Low, & Searle, 1876).

——, *Zanzibar: City, Island and Coast*, 2 vols. (London: Tinsley Brothers, 1872).

BURY, J. B., *The Idea of Progress. An Inquiry into its Growth and Origins* (1920) (Rpt.: Chicago: Chicago University Press, 1948).

CAIRNS, A. C., *Prelude to Imperialism* (Oxford: Oxford University Press, 1965).

CAMPBELL, GEORGE DOUGLAS, *Primeval Man: An Examination of Some Recent Speculations* (London: Straham & Co., 1869).

CARLYLE, THOMAS, 'Signs of the Times' (1829). In *Critical and Miscellaneous Essay*, 7 vols., ii (Rpt.: London: Chapman & Hall, 1869).

CHAPPLE, J. A. V., *Science and Literature in the Nineteenth Century* (London: Macmillan, 1986).

CLIFFORD, HUGH, *In Court and Kampong* (London: Grant Richards, 1897).

——, *The Further Side of Silence* (New York: Doubleday, Page & Co., 1916).

——, Untitled review. *Spectator* (29 November 1902), 827–8.

CLIFFORD, JAMES, *The Predicament of Culture: Twentieth Century Ethnography, Literature and Art* (Cambridge, Mass.: Harvard University Press, 1988).

CLIFFORD, JAMES and D. MARCUS (eds.), *Writing Culture: The Poetics and Politics of Ethnography* (Berkeley: University of California Press, 1986).

COHEN, A. P., *The Symbolic Construction of Community* (London: Tavistock, 1985).

COLLINGWOOD, R. G., *The Idea of History* (Oxford: Clarendon Press, 1946).

COMMON, THOMAS, 'Human Evolution—According to Nietzsche'. *Natural Science*, 10/64 (June 1897), 393–4.

CONRAD, JOSEPH, *Dent's Collected Edition of the Works of Joseph Conrad* (London: Dent, 1945–55).

——, *Doubleday, Page and Company Canterbury Edition of the Works of Joseph Conrad*, 26 vols. (Garden City, NY: Doubleday, Page & Company, 1926).

COOK, STANLEY A., 'Religion'. In James Hastings (ed.), *Encyclopaedia of Religion and Ethics* (Edinburgh: Clark, 1918), x. 664.

COSLETT, TESS, *The 'Scientific Movement' and Victorian Literature* (Sussex: The Harvester Press, 1982).

CRUICKSHANK, BRODIE, *Eighteen Years on the Gold Coast of Africa,*

Including an Account of the Native Tribes, and Their Intercourse with Europeans, 2 vols. (London: Hurst & Blackett, 1853).

CURLE, RICHARD, *Joseph Conrad: A Study* (London: Kegan, Paul, Trench, 1914).

CURTIN, PHILLIP, *The Image of Africa: British Ideas and Action, 1780–1850* (Madison: University of Wisconsin Press, 1964).

DALE, PETER ALLEN, *In Pursuit of a Scientific Culture: Science, Art, and Society in the Victorian Era* (Madison: University of Wisconsin Press, 1989).

DARWIN, CHARLES, *The Descent of Man and Selections in Relation to Sex* (1871), 2 vols. (Rpt.: London: John Murray, 1891).

——, *Journal of Researches into the Natural History and Geology of the Countries Visited During the Voyage of the H. M. S. Beagle Round the World Under the Command of Captain Fitzroy, R. N.* (1839) (Rpt.: London: John Murray, 1902).

——, *On the Origin of Species by Natural Selection, or the Preservation of Favoured Races in the Struggle of Life* (1859) (Rpt.: London: John Murray, 1902).

DAVIDSON, BASIL, *The African Past: Chronicles from Antiquity to Modern Times* (London: Longman, 1964).

DE GOBINEAU, ARTHUR, *The Inequality of Human Races* (1853), trans. Adrian Collins (Rpt.: London: Heinemann, 1915).

——, *Moral and Intellectual Diversity of Race*, H. Hotz (ed.) (Philadelphia: Lippincott, & Co., 1856).

DE QUIROS, BERNANDO, *Modern Theories of Criminality*, trans. Alfonso de Salvio (London: Heinemann, 1911).

DRUMMOND, HENRY, *The Ascent of Man* (London: Hodder & Stoughton, 1894).

——, *Tropical Africa* (1888) (Rpt.: London: Hodder & Stoughton, 1891).

DU CHAILLU, PAUL, *Adventures in the Great Forest of Equatorial Africa and the Country of the Dwarfs*, 2 vols. (London: Murray, 1890).

——, *Explorations and Adventures in Equatorial Africa: with Accounts of the Manners and Customs of the People, and of the Chase of the Gorilla, Crocodile, Leopard, Elephant, Hippopotamus, and other Animals*, 2 vols. (London: Murray, 1861).

EAGLETON, TERRY, *Criticism and Ideology* (London: NLB, Humanities Press, 1976).

ELLIS, HAVELOCK, *The Criminal* (1890) (Rpt.: London: Walter Scott, 1891).

EVANS-PRITCHARD, EDWARD E., *Social Anthropology* (London: Cohen and West, 1951).

FABIAN, JOHANNES, *Time and the Other: How Anthropology Makes its Object* (New York: Columbia University Press, 1983).

FAIRCHILD, H. N., *The Noble Savage: A Study in Romantic Naturalism*

(Oxford: Oxford University Press, 1928).

FERGUSON, ADAM, *An Essay on the History of Civil Society* (Dublin: 1767).

FERRI, ENRICO, *Criminal Sociology* (London: T. Fisher Unwin, 1895).

FLEISCHMANN, AVROM, *Conrad's Politics: Community and Anarchy in the Works of Joseph Conrad* (Baltimore: Johns Hopkins University Press, 1967).

FORSTER, E. M., *Abinger Harvest* (New York: Harcourt, Brace & Co., 1936).

FOX, RICHARD G. (ed.), *Recapturing Anthropology: Working in the Present* (Santa Fe: School of American Research Press, 1991).

FRAZER, JAMES G., *The Golden Bough: A Study in Magic and Religion* (1890), 12 vols. (Rpt.: London: Macmillan, 1917).

——, *Lectures on the Early History of Kingship* (London: Macmillan, 1905).

——, 'Robertson Smith'. *Fortnightly Review*, 60/330 (June 1894), 789–807.

FRELICH, MORRIS (ed.), *The Relevance of Culture* (New York: Bergin & Garvey Publishers, 1989).

FROBENIUS, LEO, *The Childhood of Man: A Popular Account of the Lives, Customs and Thoughts of the Primitive Races*, trans. A. H. Keane (London: Seeky & Co., 1909).

——, *The Voice of Africa: Being an Account of the Travels of the German Inner African Exploration Expedition in the Years 1910–1912*, 2 vols., trans. Rudolph Blind (London: Hutchinson & Co., 1913).

FURNHAM, ADRIAN and STEPHEN BOCHNER, *Culture Shock: Psychological Reactions to Unfamiliar Environments* (London: Methuen, 1986).

GALTON, FRANCIS, *Hereditary Genius, an Inquiry into its Laws and Consequences* (1869) (Rpt.: London: Watts & Co., 1950).

GANS, ERIC, *The End of Culture: Toward a Generative Anthropology* (Berkeley: University of California Press, 1985).

GEERTZ, CLIFFORD, 'The Impact of Culture on the Concept of Man'. In J. R. Platt (ed.), *New Views on the Nature of Man* (Chicago: University of Chicago Press, 1965).

——, *The Interpretation of Cultures* (New York: Basic Books, 1973).

——, *Local Knowledge: Further Essays in Interpretive Anthropology* (New York: Basic Books, 1983).

——, *Works and Lives: The Anthropologist as Author* (Stanford: Stanford University Press, 1988).

GLASSMAN, PETER J., *Language and Being: Joseph Conrad and the Literature of Personality* (New York: Columbia University Press, 1976).

GOMME, GEORGE LAWRENCE, *Folk-Lore Relics of Early Village Life* (London: Macmillan, 1883).

GOONETILLIKE, D. C. R. A., *Joseph Conrad: Beyond Culture and*

Background (London: Macmillan, 1990).

GOULD, STEPHEN JAY, *The Mismeasure of Man* (London: Pelican, 1984).

GOULD, TONY, *In Limbo: The Story of Stanley's Rear Column* (London: Hamish Hamilton, 1979).

GRAVER, LAWRENCE, *Conrad's Short Fiction* (Berkeley and Los Angeles: University of California Press, 1969).

GREEN, MARTIN, *Dreams of Adventure, Deeds of Empire* (New York: Basic Books, 1979).

GREEN, T. H., *Prolegomena to Ethics* (1883) (Rpt.: Oxford: Oxford University Press, 1924).

GUERARD, ALBERT, *Conrad the Novelist* (Cambridge, Mass.: Harvard University Press, 1958).

GURKO, LEO, *Joseph Conrad: Giant in Exile* (New York: Macmillan, 1962).

GUTKIND, PETER CLAUS WOLFGANG (ed.), *The Passing of Tribal Man in Africa* (Leiden: Brill, 1970).

HAGGARD, H. Rider, *Allan Quartermain* (1887) (Rpt.: Mattituck, NY: Ameron House, 1983).

HAWKINS, HUNT, 'Conrad and Congolese Exploitation'. *Conradiana*, 13/2 (1981), 94–100.

——, 'Conrad's Critique of Imperialism in *Heart of Darkness*'. *PMLA*, 94/2 (1979), 286–99.

——, 'Joseph Conrad, Roger Casement, and the Congo Reform Movement'. *Journal of Modern Literature*, 9 (1981), 65–80.

HAWTHORN, JEREMY, *Joseph Conrad, Language, and Fictional Self-Consciousness* (London: Arnold, 1979).

——, *Joseph Conrad: Narrative Technique and Ideological Commitment* (London: Edward Arnold, 1990).

HAY, ELOISE KNAPP, *The Political Novels of Joseph Conrad* (Chicago: University of Chicago Press, 1963).

HEGEL, GEORG WILLIAM FRIEDRICH, *Lectures on the Philosophy of World History* (1822–30) (Rpt.: Cambridge: Cambridge University Press, 1980).

HERBERT, CHRISTOPHER, *Culture and Anomie: Ethnographic Imagination in the Nineteenth Century* (Chicago: University of Chicago Press, 1991).

HEWITT, DOUGLAS, '*Heart of Darkness* and Some "Old and Pleasant Reports"'. *Nineteenth Century Fiction*, 38 (1987), 374–5.

HINDE, SIDNEY LANGFORD, *The Fall of the Congo Arabs* (London: Methuen, 1897).

HOBSON, J. A., *Imperialism: A Study of Social Pathology* (1902) (Rpt.: London: Allen & Unwin, 1938).

HOWELL, NANCY, *Surviving Fieldwork: A Report of the Advisory Panel on Health and Safety in Fieldwork* (Washington, D. C.: American Anthropological Association, 1990).

HUNT, JAMES, Untitled. *The Anthropological Review*, 8 (1870).

HUNTER, ALLAN, *Joseph Conrad and the Ethics of Darwinism* (London: Croom Helm, 1983).

HUXLEY, LEONARD (ed.), *Life and Letters of Thomas Henry Huxley*, 2 vols. (London: Macmillan, 1900).

HUXLEY, T. H., *Evolution and Ethics and Other Essays*, vol. ix of *Collected Works*, 9 vols. (London: Macmillan, 1894).

JACOB, GERTRUDE L., *The Raja of Sarawak. An Account of Sir James Brooke, K. C. B., L. L. D., Given Chiefly Through Letters and Journals*, 2 vols. (London: Macmillan & Co., 1876).

JAMESON, FREDERICK, *The Political Unconscious: Narrative as a Socially Symbolic Act* (Ithaca: Cornell University Press, 1983).

JAMES S. JAMESON, *Story of the Rear Column of the Emin Pasha Relief Expedition*, Mrs. J. S. Jameson (ed.) (London: R. H. Porter, 1890).

JARVIE, I. C., *Thinking about Culture: Theory and Practice* (Drodecht: Reidel, 1986).

JEAN-AUBRY, GÉRARD (ed.), *Joseph Conrad: Life and Letters*, 2 vols. (Garden City, NY: Doubleday, Page & Co., 1927).

Johnson, Bruce, 'Conrad's Impressionism and Watt's "Delayed Decoding"'. In Ross C. Murfin (ed.), *Conrad Revisited: Essays for the Eighties* (Birmingham, Ala.: University of Alabama Press, 1985), 51–70.

——, *Conrad's Model of Mind* (Minneapolis: University of Minnesota Press, 1971).

JONES, GARETH STEDMAN, *Outcast London: A Study in the Relationship between Classes in Victorian Society* (1971) (Rpt.: London: Penguin, 1984).

KALLAM, G. D., *Africa in English Fiction 1874–1939* (Ibadan: Ibadan University Press, 1968).

KARL, FREDERICK R., *Joseph Conrad. The Three Lives* (New York, Farrar, Straus & Giroux, 1979).

KARL, FREDERICK and LAWRENCE DAIRES (eds.), *Collected Letters of Joseph Conrad* (Cambridge: Cambridge University Press, 1983).

KEESING, ROGER M., 'Not a Real Fish: The Ethnographer as Insider Outsider'. In Philip R. DeVita (ed.), *The Naked Anthropologist: Tales from Around the World* (Belmont: Wadsworth, 1992).

KERSHNER, R. B., 'Degeneration: The Explanatory Nightmare'. *Georgia Review*, 40 (1986), 416–44.

KIERKEGAARD, SØREN, *Either/Or*, 2 vols., trans. Howard V. Hong and Edna H. Hong (Princeton: Princeton University Press, 1987).

KIERNAN, V. G., *The Lords of Human Kind: Black Man, Yellow Man, and White Man in an Age of Empire* (1969) (Rpt.: New York: Columbia University Press, 1986).

KINGSLEY, CHARLES, *The Roman and the Teuton* (1864) (Rpt.: London: Macmillan, 1887).

KINGSLEY, MARY H., *Travels in West Africa* (London: Macmillan, 1897).
——, *West African Studies*. London: Macmillan, 1901.
KIRSCHNER, PAUL, *Conrad: The Psychologist as Artist* (Edinburgh: Oliver & Boyd, 1968).
KNOX-SHAW, PETER, *The Explorer in English Fiction* (New York: St. Martin's Press, 1986).
KRENN HÉLIENA, *Conrad's Lingard Trilogy: Empire, Race, and Women in the Malay Novels* (New York: Garland Publishing, 1990).
KRISTEVA, JULIA, *Nations Without Nationalism*, trans. Leon S. Roudiez (New York: Columbia University Press, 1993).
KUKLICK, HENRIKA, *The Savage Within: The Social History of British Anthropology, 1885–1945* (Cambridge: Cambridge University Press, 1991).
KUPER, ADAM, *The Invention of Primitive Society: The History of an Illusion* (London: Routledge & Kegan Paul, 1988).
KURELLA, HANS, *Cesare Lombroso: a Modern Man of Science*, trans. M. Eden Paul (London: Rebmen, Ltd., 1911).
LANG, ANDREW, *Myth, Ritual and Religion* (1887), 2 vols. (Rpt.: London: Longman, 1899).
——, 'Mr. Kipling's Stories'. In *Essays in Little* (New York: Charles Scribner's Sons, 1891).
LANKESTER, E. RAY, *Degeneration: A Chapter in Darwinism* (London: Methuen, 1880).
LAWLESS, ROBERT, VINSON H. SUTLIVE, MARIO D. ZAMORA (eds.), *Fieldwork: The Human Experience* (New York: Gordon & Breach Scientific Publishers, 1983).
LAWRENCE, D. H., 'Au Revoir, U. S. A.'. In Edward McDonald (ed.), *Phoenix: The Posthumous Papers of D. H. Lawrence* (1931) (Rpt.: London: Heinemann, 1961).
——, *Studies in Classic American Literature* (1923) (Rpt.: London: Penguin, 1987).
LEAVIS, F. R., *The Great Tradition* (New York: New York University Press, 1967).
LECKY, W. E., *A History of European Morals from Augustus to Charlemagne* (London: Longman, 1869).
LEVENSON, MICHAEL, *A Genealogy of Modernism* (Cambridge: Cambridge University Press, 1984).
——, *Modernism and the Fate of Individuality: Character and Novelistic Form from Conrad to Woolf* (Cambridge: Cambridge University Press, 1991).
LEWIS, GORDON K., *Slavery, Imperialism, and Freedom: Studies in English Radical Thought* (New York: Monthly Review, 1978).
LEWIS, I. M., *Social Anthropology in Perspective: The Relevance of Social Anthropology* (1976) (Rpt.: London: Penguin, 1981).

LIVINGSTONE, DAVID, *Last Journals of David Livingstone, in Central Africa, from 1865 to his Death*, 2 vols. (ed.) Horace Waller (London: John Murray, 1874).

LOMBROSO, CESARE, *Crime: Its Causes and Remedies*, trans. Henry B. Horton (London: Heinemann, 1911).

——, *Criminal Man* (London and New York: Putnam's, 1911).

——, *The Man of Genius*, trans. and ed. Havelock Ellis (London: Walter Scott, 1891).

LOMBROSO, CESARE and WILLIAM FERRERO, *The Female Offender* (London: T. Fisher Unwin, 1895).

LUBBOCK, JOHN, *Origin of Civilisation* (London: Longman, 1876).

——, *Pre-Historic Times* (London: Williams & Norgate, 1865).

LUKÁCS, GEORG, *The Theory of the Novel* (Cambridge, Mass.: M. I. T. Press, 1971).

LÜTKEN, OTTO, 'Joseph Conrad and the Congo'. *London Mercury*, 22/127 (May 1930), 40–3.

——, 'Joseph Conrad and the Congo'. *London Mercury*, 22/130 (August 1930), 350–1.

——, 'New Writers: Mr. Joseph Conrad', *Bookman*, 10/56 (May 1896).

MACDONALD, ARTHUR, *Criminology* (New York: Funk & Wagnalls, 1893).

MCCLURE, JOHN A., *Kipling and Conrad: the Colonial Fiction* (Cambridge, Mass.: Harvard University Press, 1981).

MCLAUCHLAN, JULIET, 'The Value and Significance of *Heart of Darkness*' (1983). In Robert Kimbrough (ed.), *Heart of Darkness: An Authoritative Text, Background, Sources, Criticism* (New York: Norton, 1988), 375–91.

MCLENNAN, J. F., *Studies in Ancient History* (1876) (Rpt.: London: Macmillan, 1886).

MAHOOD, M. M., *The Colonial Encounter: A Reading of Six Novels* (London: Rex Collings, 1977).

MALINOWSKI, BRONISLAW, *Argonauts of the Western Pacific: An Account of Native Enterprise and Adventure in the Archipelagoes of Melanesian New Guinea* (1922) (Rpt.: New York: E. P. Dutton & Co., 1950).

——, *A Diary in the Strict sense of the Term* (New York: Harcourt, Brace & World, Inc., 1967).

MAUDSLEY, HENRY, *Body and Will: Being an Essay Concerning Will in its Metaphysical, Physiological and Pathological Aspects* (London: Kegan, Paul, Trench, 1883).

——, *Life in Mind and Conduct* (London: Macmillan, 1873).

——, *Responsibility in Mental Disease* (London: Henry King, 1874).

MEYER, BERNARD, *Joseph Conrad: A Psychoanalytic Biography* (Princeton: Princeton University Press, 1967).

MEYERS, JEFFREY, *Joseph Conrad: A Biography* (New York: Scribnes,

1991).

MILLER, CHRISTOPHER, *Blank Darkness: Africanist Discourse in French* (Chicago: University of Chicago Press, 1985).

MILLER, J. HILLIS, *The Poets of Reality: Six Twentieth Century Writers* (Cambridge, Mass.: Belknap Press of Harvard University, 1965).

MITCHELL, ARTHUR, *The Past in the Present: What is Civilisation?* (Edinburgh: David Douglas, 1890).

MOREL, E. D., *King Leopold's Rule in Africa* (1904) (Rpt.: Westport, Conn.: Negro Universities Press, 1970).

——, *Red Rubber* (London: T. Fisher Unwin, 1907).

MORGAN, LEWIS HENRY, *Ancient Society* (London: Macmillan, 1877).

MORTON, PETER, *The Vital Science: Biology and the Literary Imagination* (London: George Allen & Unwin, 1984).

MURFIN, ROSS C., 'The New Historicism and *Heart of Darkness*'. In Ross C. Murfin (ed.), *Heart of Darkness: A Case Study in Contemporary Criticism* (New York: St. Martin's Press, 1989).

NAIPAUL, V. S., *Finding the Center: Two Narratives* (New York: Knopf, 1984).

NAJDER, ZDZISLAW (ed.), *Conrad's Polish Background: Letters to and from Polish Friends* (London: Oxford University Press, 1964).

——, (ed.), *Conrad: Under Familial Eyes*, trans. Halina Carroll-Najder (Cambridge: Cambridge University Press, 1983).

——, *Joseph Conrad: A Chronicle*, trans. Halina Carroll-Najder (New Brunswick: Rutgers University Press, 1983).

NISBET, ROBERT A., *History of the Idea of Progress* (New York: Basic Books, 1980).

NORDAU, MAX, *Degeneration* (1895) (Rpt.: London: Heinemann, 1920).

NOTT, JOSIAH, *Two Lectures on the Natural History of the Caucasian and Negro Races* (Mobile, Ala.: Dade & Thompson, 1844).

O'HANLON, REDMOND, *Joseph Conrad and Charles Darwin: The Influence of Scientific thought on Conrad's Fiction* (Edinburgh: Salamander Press, 1984).

ORWELL, GEORGE, 'Shooting an Elephant'. In *Inside the Whale and Other Essays* (1936) (Rpt.: London: Penguin, 1957).

PÁLSSON, GÍSLÍ, 'Introduction: Going Beyond Boundaries'. In Gísli Pálsson (ed.), *Beyond Boundaries: Understanding, Translation and Anthropological Discourse* (Oxford: Berg, 1993).

PARRY, BENITA, *Conrad and Imperialism: Ideological Boundaries and Visionary Frontiers* (London: Macmillan, 1983).

PEACOCK, JAMES L., *The Anthropological Lens: Harsh Light, Soft Focus* (Cambridge: Cambridge University Press, 1986).

PEARSON, CHARLES H., 'An Answer to Some Critics'. *Fortnightly Review*, 60/320 (August 1893).

PHILMUS, ROBERT M. and DAVID Y. HUGHES (eds.), *H. G. Wells: Early Writings in Science and Science Fiction* (Berkeley: University of California Press, 1975).

PICK, DANIEL, *Faces of Degeneration: A European Disorder, c.1848–1918* (Cambridge: Cambridge University Press, 1989).

PRICHARD, JAMES, *Researches into the Physical History of Mankind*, 5 vols. (London: Longman, 1831–7).

RASKIN, JONAH, *Mythology of Imperialism* (New York: Random House, 1972).

RETINGER, J. H., *Conrad and his Contemporaries* (New York: Roy Publishers, 1943).

RIDLEY, HUGH, *Images of Imperial Rule* (London: Croom Helm, 1983).

ROBINSON, RONALD and JOHN GALLAGHER, with ALICE DENNY, *Africa and the Victorians: The Official Mind of Imperialism* (1962) (Rvd.: London, Macmillan, 1981).

ROMANE, J. G., *Mental Evolution in Man, the Origin of Human Faculty* (London: Kegan, Paul, Trench, 1888).

RUTHVEN, K. K., 'The Savage God: Conrad and Lawrence'. *Critical Quarterly*, 10 (1968), 39–54.

RUTTER, OWEN, *British North Borneo: An Account of its History, Resources and Native Tribes* (London: Constable & Co., 1922).

SAID, EDWARD, *Culture and Imperialism* (New York: Knopf, 1993).

——, *Joseph Conrad and the Fiction of Autobiography* (1966) (Rpt.: Cambridge, Mass.: Harvard University Press, 1968).

——, *Orientalism* (New York: Pantheon, 1978).

SANDISON, ALAN, *The Wheel of Empire* (London: Macmillan, 1977).

SAVESON, JOHN E., 'Conrad's Attitude to Primitive Peoples'. *Modern Fiction Studies*, 16 (1970), 163–83.

——, *Joseph Conrad: The Making of a Moralist* (Amsterdam: Rodopi NV, 1972).

SCHWARZ, DANIEL R., *Conrad: 'Almayer's Folly' to 'Under Western Eyes'* (Ithaca: Cornell University Press, 1980).

SEDGWICK, HENRY, *Outline of the History of Ethics* (1886) (Rpt.: London: Macmillan, 1954).

SEIDEL, MICHAEL, *Exile and the Narrative Imagination* (New Haven: Yale University Press, 1986).

SHAFFER, BRIAN W., *The Blinding Torch: Modern British Fiction and the Discourse of Civilization* (Amherst, Mass.: University of Massachusetts Press, 1993).

SHAW, GEORGE BERNARD, *Man and Superman: A Comedy and a Philosophy* (1903) (Rpt.: London: Penguin, 1957).

——, *The Sanity of Art: An Exposure of the Current Nonsense about Artists Being Degenerates* (London: Constable & Co., 1911).

SHERRY, NORMAN (ed.), *Conrad: the Critical Heritage* (London: Routledge & Kegan Paul, 1973).

——, *Conrad's Western World* (Cambridge: Cambridge University Press, 1971).

SORLEY, W. R., *The Ethics of Naturalism* (Edinburgh and London: Blackwood's, 1885).

SPENCER, HERBERT, *The Data of Ethics* (London: Williams & Norgate, 1879).

SPINDLER, LOUISE S., *Culture Change and Modernization: Mini-Models and Case Studies* (New York: Holt, Rhinehart & Winston, 1977).

STEPHEN, LESLIE, *The Science of Ethics* (London: Smith, Elder & Co., 1882).

STANLEY, H. M., *The Congo and the Founding of its Free State: a Story of Work and Exploration*, 2 vols. (London: Law, Marston, Searle, & Rivington, 1885).

——, *Life and Finding of Dr. Livingstone* (London: Dean & Son, 1880).

STEVENSON, ROBERT LOUIS, *The Beach of Falesá: Being The Narrative of a South Sea Trader*. In *Island Nights' Entertainment* (1892), Vailima edition of the works of R. L. Stevenson, 26 vols., vol. xv (Rpt.: London: Heinemann, 1922).

——, *The Ebb Tide: A Trio and a Quartette* (1896), Vailima edition, vol. xviii (London: Heinemann, 1922).

——, *In the South Seas* (1891), Vailima edition, vol. xvi (London: Heneimann, 1922).

STOCKING, GEORGE W. Jr., 'Empathy and Antipathy in the Heart of Darkness'. In Regna Darnell (ed.), *Readings in the History of Anthropology* (New York: Harper & Row, 1974).

——, 'History of Anthropology'. In *Observers Observed: Essays on Ethnographic Fieldwork*, vol. i of *History of Anthropology* (Madison: University of Wisconsin Press, 1983).

——, 'The Ethnographer's Magic: Fieldwork in British Anthropology from Tylor to Malinowski'. In *Observers Observed: Essays on Ethnographic Fieldwork*, vol. i of *History of Anthropology* (Madison: University of Wisconsin Press, 1983).

——, *Race, Culture and Evolution* (London: Collier-Macmillan, 1968).

——, *Victorian Anthropology* (London: Macmillan, 1987).

STREET, BRIAN V., *The Savage in Literature: Representations of 'Primitive' Society in English Fiction, 1858–1920* (London: Routledge & Kegan Paul, 1975).

STUTFIELD, HUGH M., 'Tomyrotics'. *Blackwood's Edinburgh Magazine*, 157/956 (June 1895), 833–9.

SYMONDS, J. A., *Stella Fregelius* (London: Macmillan, 1906).

SZEKELY, LADISLAO, *Tropical Fever: The Adventures of a Planter in Sumatra* (New York: Harper & Brothers, 1937).

TALBOT, EUGENE S., *Degeneracy, Its Causes, Signs, and Results* (London: Walter Scott, 1898).

TAYLOR, W. COOKE, *The Natural History of Society in the Barbarous and Civilized State: An Essay Towards Discovering the Origin and Course of Human Improvement*, 2 vols. (London: Longman, 1840).

THATCHER, DAVID S., *Nietzsche in England, 1880–1914: the Growth of a Reputation* (Toronto: University of Toronto Press, 1970).

THORBURN, DAVID, *Conrad's Romanticism* (New Haven: Yale University Press, 1974).

TILLE, ALEXANDER, 'Preface' to Friedrich Nietzsche, *A Genealogy of Morals, Poems* (London: T. Fisher Unwin, 1899).

TÖNNIES, F., *Community and Association* (1887), trans. C. P. Loomis (Rpt.: London: Routledge & Kegan Paul, 1955).

TOPINARD, PAUL, *Science and Faith: Man as an Animal and Man as a Member of Society*, trans. Thomas McCormack (London: Kegan, Paul, Trench, 1899).

TORGOVNICK, MARIANNA, *Gone Primitive: Savage Intellects, Modern Lives* (Chicago: University of Chicago Press, 1990).

TURNER, VICTOR W., *On the Edge of the Bush: Anthropology as Experience* (Tuscon: University of Arizona Press, 1985).

TURNER, VICTOR W. and EDWARD M. BRUNER (eds.), *The Anthropology of Experience* (Urbana: University of Illinois Press, 1986).

TYLOR, E. B., *Anahuac* (London: John Murray, 1861).

—— , *Anthropology: An Introduction to the Study of Man and Civilization* (London: Macmillan, 1881).

—— , *Primitive Culture, Researches into the Development of Mythology, Philosophy, Religion, Art, and Custom*, 2 vols. (London: John Murray, 1871).

VAN MAANEN, JOHN, *Tales of the Field: On Writing Ethnography* (Chicago: University of Chicago Press, 1988).

VOGT, CARL, *Lectures on Man*, James Hunt (ed.) (London: Longman, 1864).

WAGNER, ROY, *The Invention of Culture* (Englewood Cliffs, NJ: Prentice-Hall, 1975).

WAITZ, THEODOR, *Introduction to Anthropology*, trans. J. Frederick Collingwood, 2 vols. (London: Longman, 1863).

WALLACE, ALFRED RUSSEL, *The Malay Archipelago* (New York: Harper & Brothers, 1869).

WATT, IAN, *Conrad in the Nineteenth Century* (Berkeley: University of California Press, 1980).

WATTS, CEDRIC, *A Preface to Conrad* (London: Longman, 1982).

—— (ed.), *Heart of Darkness and Other Tales* (Oxford: Oxford University Press, 1990).

WELLS, H. G., 'The Extinction of Man'. *Pall Mall Gazette*, 59 (25

September 1894), 3.

WELLS, H. G., 'On Extinction'. *Chambers's Journal,* 10 (30 September 1893), 623–4.

——, 'Human Evolution: Mr. Wells Replies'. *Natural Science: A Monthly Review of Scientific Progress,* 10 (May 1897), 244.

——, 'Morals and Civilisation'. *Fortnightly Review,* 61 (February 1897), 263.

——, *The War of the Worlds.* In *The Invisible Man, The War of the Worlds, and A Dream of Armageddon,* The Atlantic Edition of the Works of H. G. Wells, 24 vols., vol. iii (London: T. Fisher Unwin, 1924).

WENGLE, JOHN L., *Ethnographers in the Field: The Psychology of Research* (Tuscaloosa: University of Alabama Press, 1988).

WHATLEY, RICHARD, *Introductory Lectures on Political Economy* (London: B. Fellowes, 1831).

——, 'The Origin of Civilisation' (1854) In *Lectures Delivered Before the Young Men's Christian Association from November 1854 to February 1855* (Rpt.: London: Nisbet, 1879).

WHITE, ANDREA, *Joseph Conrad and the Adventure Tradition: Constructing and deconstructing the imperial subject* (Cambridge: Cambridge University Press, 1993).

WILEY, P. L., *Conrad's Measure of Man* (Madison: University of Wisconsin Press, 1954).

WILLIAMS, RAYMOND, *Culture and Society, 1780–1950* (New York: Columbia University Press, 1983).

——, *Marxism and Literature* (Oxford: Oxford University Press, 1977).

WILLIAMS, THOMAS RHYS, *Field Methods in the Study of Culture* (New York: Holt, Rinehart & Winston, 1967).

WOLF, ERIC, *Europe and the People without History* (Berkeley: University of California Press, 1982).

Index

Abyssinia 55
Academy 166, 191
Achebe, Chinua 43–4, 204
Africa 14, 18, 21–4, 28–30, 32, 33–5, 37, 39, 43–4, 46, 48–9, 53–4, 60, 62, 65, 69, 72–7, 83, 88–91, 98–9, 108, 110–18, 120, 122, 126, 128–34, 139–41, 166–7, 172, 174–7, 199–205, 207–9, 225, 227
Aïssa 145, 146, 148–50, 187–8
Allen, Grant 125
Almayer, Kaspar 16, 141–4, 151, 203, 213
Almayer, Nina 141–4, 203
Anthropological Society of London 103, 122
Arctic 165
Armistead, William 113
Arnold, Matthew 97
Ashanti 110
Assad, Talal 74
Australia 110

Beagle 137
Belgium 209
Benedict, Ruth 187
Benin 76
Bernstein, Richard J. 70
Bichat, M. F. X. 101
Blackwood, William 107
Blackwood's Edinburgh Magazine 82, 89, 102–4, 106, 118, 156, 165, 193
Blumenbach, J. F. 103, 159
Bobrowski, Tadeusz 160–1
Bolt, Christine 140
Bongola 167
Bookman 155
Borneo 4, 80, 141–3
Bowen, Eleanore 139
Brantlinger, Patrick 151
Brewster, Earl 68
Brinton, Daniel 134
Broca Paul 159
Brodsky, Joseph 16
Brooke, James 80–1

Brown, Dennis 204
Brown, Gentleman 163, 186–7, 215
Brussels 201
Buchan, John 118–19, 125
Burrows, Guy 89, 166, 172
Burton, Richard 22, 29, 30
Button, Jemmy 138

Caesar, Julius 113
Campbell, George Dougal 119
Camper, P. 158
Carlier 95, 128, 209–11, 213
Carlyle, Thomas 81–3, 118, 211–12
Casement, Roger 128
Charcot, J. M. 174
Chesson, Wilfred Hugh 142
Cicero 112
Clifford, Hugh 37, 75, 89, 94, 125, 148–50
Clifford, James 2, 32, 54, 57, 66, 93–6, 186
Congo 4, 7, 15, 28–9, 40, 49, 53–5, 61–3, 81–91, 100, 114, 123, 126–8, 130, 134, 141, 166–7, 172, 178, 202
Conrad, Joseph 1–5, 7–10, 13–55, 58, 60–9, 74–6, 79, 80–96, 98–100, 102–10, 112–23, 125, 126–34, 139, 140–56, 159–61, 163–4, 165–74, 176–8, 180, 182–3, 185–90, 192–7, 199–200, 202–13, 215, 218–21, 223–7, 229–30
   Works:
      Almayer's Folly 4, 7, 16, 26, 41, 43, 50, 124, 141–4, 203;
      'Amy Foster' 16–19, 20;
      'Congo Diary' 54, 130;
      'Falk' 165–6, 168–72;
      'Geography and Some Explorers' 28; *Heart of Darkness* 4, 7–9, 13–15, 20, 23, 27–8, 30–1, 33–7, 39–41, 43–4, 46–55, 57, 61–4, 69–70, 74, 76, 82–6, 88, 90–6, 102–3, 105–6, 108, 111, 118–21, 123, 125–9, 131–2, 134, 138–40,

Conrad, Joseph (*cont.*):
  145, 154, 160, 163, 167–8,
  173–4, 176–8, 189, 196,
  199–200, 202–4, 208–10,
  219–21, 223–8; *Lord Jim* 4, 7,
  19, 48–50, 61, 75, 82, 84–5,
  98, 120, 163–4, 172–4, 177,
  183–7, 190, 203, 211, 215,
  219; *An Outcast of the
  Islands* 4, 7, 16, 17, 39, 50,
  129, 141, 143–8, 150–2, 187–8;
  'An Outpost of Progress'
  87–8, 93, 128–9, 208–10; *The
  Mirror of the Sea* 117, 203;
  *The Nigger of the
  'Narcissus'* 37–9, 41, 58, 185;
  Nostromo 5, 7; *Notes on Life
  and Letters* 82; *A Personal
  Record* 61; *The Rescue* ('The
  Rescuer') 50–2, 81; *The Secret
  Agent* 7, 206; *Under Western
  Eyes* 212–13; 'Upriver
  Book' 54; *Victory* 11, 13,
  14; *Youth* 37
Cracow 160–1
Crèvecoeur, Hector Saint John de 68
Cruickshank, Brodie 22, 33–5, 39,
  40, 44, 227
Curtin, Phillip 130, 135
Curzon, Martin 148–50
Cuviers, George 72–3

Dahomeh 110
Daily News 142
Darwin, Charles 34, 81, 83, 85, 103,
  116, 132, 134, 137–8, 155, 157–8,
  161–2, 168, 170–1, 179, 181–4,
  189, 193, 212–15, 217, 221–2
Davies, Robertson 181
Da Vinci, Leonardo 82
De Gobineau, Arthur 101–2, 108
De Gourmont, Remy 189
De Quiros, Bernando 213
Devray, H. 178
Drummond, Henry 22, 35, 44, 83,
  131, 134, 180, 194
Dublin 77
Du Chaillu, Paul 22, 130, 177
Durkheim, Emile 153–4, 172–3,
  224–5, 227
Dyaks 205–6

Eagle and the Serpent 193

Eagleton, Terry 82
Ellis, Havelock 154, 163, 174–5
Erebus and Terror 165
Eskimoes 135
Evans-Pritchard, Edward 47, 62–6

Fabian, Johannes 74
Ferguson, Adam 100–1
Firth, Raymond 56
Ford, Ford Madox (Hueffer) 37
Forster, E. M. 44
Fortnightly Review 104, 155, 217
Foster, Amy 16–18
Franklin, John 165
Frazer, James George 69, 181
Freud, Sigmund 208, 210, 218
Frobenius, Leo 60, 65, 74
Fuegians 34, 135, 137–8

Gall, J. 159
Galton, Francis 131–3
Garnett, Edward 44, 123, 126, 142,
  193
Garofolo, Rafaele 172, 213–14
Germany 98, 153, 157, 194
Geertz, Clifford 2–3, 15, 56–8, 65,
  98, 187, 202
Gibbon, Edward 101, 104–7
Gomme, George Lawrence 114
Goorall, Yanko 16–19, 21, 32
Graham, Gabriella Cunninghame 189
Graham, R. B. Cunninghame 39,
  189, 193, 222
Green, T. H. 180
Gurko, Leo 15

Haddon, A. C. 59
Haeckel, Ernst H. P. A. 157, 214,
  216
Haggard, H. Rider 125
Harlequin 36, 47
Hegel, Friedrich 75–6, 101, 194
Henty, G. A. 136
Herbert, Christopher 173, 224–5
Hesiod 100
Hewitt, Douglas 165
Heyst, Axel 10
Hinde, Sidney L. 29, 166–7
Hobson, J. A. 131–1, 147
Hunt, James 134
Huxley, T. H. 9, 10, 82, 112, 159,
  165, 171, 180–1, 183, 193, 195,
  211, 220, 223, 227–9

Jacob, Gertrude L.   80
Java   81
Jim, Lord   19, 48, 49, 50, 61, 120,
    177, 183–8, 211, 219
Jorgenson   51

Karl, Frederick R.   160
Kayerts   87–8, 95, 128, 209–11, 213
Kelvin, William Thomson   221
Kierkegaard, Søren   1, 2
Kingsley, Mary H.   23, 90, 207–8
Kipling, Rudyard   50, 83, 105, 125
Knox, Robert   133
Kopernicki, Izydor   160–1
Kristeva, Julia   198
Kubary, Jan Stanislaus   66–7
Kurella, Hans   155
Kurtz   6, 9, 16, 31, 37, 46–7, 49, 52,
    55–6, 61–7, 69, 70–1, 83–4, 86, 91–
    2, 94–5, 120–1, 126–7, 129, 134,
    150, 154–5, 164–5, 168, 173–8,
    192, 200–1, 212–13, 218, 220, 223,
    225–9

Lamarck, Chevalier de   81, 190, 211,
    217, 224
Lang, Andrew   24–6
Lankester, E. Ray   87
Lawrence, D. H.   3, 68–9
Lecky, W. E.   179
Leopold II, King   73, 89, 166
Levenson, Michael   31–2
Lèvy – Strauss, Claude   66
Liberty   155
Lingard   51, 61, 81, 146, 148
Lombroso, Cesare   9, 154–5, 157,
    165, 169, 172–4, 206, 213, 215
Lubbock, John   24, 77–8, 80, 82–3,
    103, 109, 176–7, 182, 217
Lukács, Georg   31
Lütken, Otto   126–7

Macaulay, Thomas Babington   114
MacDonald, Arthur   174
Maclay, Nikoai Miklouho   66–7
McLennan, J. F.   77, 79, 103, 182
McLintock, Leopold   165
Maine, Henry   77, 103
Malaysia   4, 51, 75, 80–1, 141, 143–
    4, 146, 148–51, 177, 186–7, 205–7
Malinwoski, Bronislaw   55–9, 63–6,
    68, 93–4, 138, 225
Marlow   14, 19, 20–1, 23, 24, 27–8,

30–41, 44–7, 52–3, 55, 61–3, 65,
    69, 70–1, 75, 83–4, 86–9, 92–5, 98,
    106, 110–12, 116, 118, 123, 129,
    134, 138, 140, 160, 164, 169–70,
    172–3, 176–7, 183–7, 190, 199–
    204, 208, 210–12, 215, 220, 224–9
Marryat, Frederick   113
Maudsley, Henry   10, 87, 169–70,
    180, 182, 184, 214–23, 228
Mayhew, Henry   206
Melville, Herman   3
Menander   17, 63
Mexico   68
Meyers, Jeffrey   145
Mitchell, Arthur   8, 81, 104, 115
Morgan, Lewis   77
Morel, B. A.   154, 157–8, 174
Morel, E. D.   127
Morrison, William Douglas   161
Müller, Friedrich Max   214

Nation   152
New York Times   10, 219
New Zealand   110
Nietzsche, Friedrich   157, 176, 188–9,
    191–5, 229
Nordau, Max   9, 138–9, 152, 153–8,
    164, 169, 174, 191–4, 206, 214–15,
    218, 220–1, 227–30
Nott, Josiah   128, 133, 145

Oberg, Kalervo   52–4, 139
Orwell, George   54
Outlook   193

Papua-New Guinea   66–7
Park, Mungo   29
Parry, Benita   70
Patna   185, 211
Patusan   48–9, 50, 61, 75, 186, 211
Peacock, James L.   32, 98
Pick, Daniel   5, 6, 7, 96
Poland   61, 96
Polynesia   224
Poradowska, Marguerite   54
Prichard, James   110, 214, 225

Ribot, T.   174
Rimbaud, Arthur   55
Rivers, W. H. R.   59
Roman Britain   111–19, 130–1
Romanes, J. G.   180–1
Ruskin, John   73

Shaw, George Bernard 155–6, 162
Said, Edward 25–6, 34, 74, 94, 97, 198–9
Samoa 152
Sanderson, Helen 193
Saturday Review 155
Saveson, John E. 143
Schopenhauer, Arthur 189
Sedgwick, Henry 180
Shaffer, Brian W. 97
Slade Lectures 73
Sorley, W. R. 180
South America 4, 75, 205
South Pole 165
Speaker 143
Speke, John Hanning 29
Spencer, Herbert 161, 170, 179, 213
Spurzheim, C. 159
Stanley, Henry M. 22, 29, 73–4, 83, 91
Stein 47
Stephens, Leslie 179
Stevenson, Robert Louis 26, 148, 151–2
Stocking, George W., Jr. 55–7, 66–7, 181
Street, Brian 142
Sumatra 81
Symonds, J. A. 6
Szekely, Ladislao 46

Tahiti 110
Talbot, Eugene S. 154
Tanner, John 162
Tarde, Gabriel de 175
Tarzan 120

Taylor, W. Cooke 77–8, 167–8
Thames 111
Thomas, Brook 109, 110
Tille, Alexander 191
Tönnies, Ferdinand 196, 205
Topinard, Paul 180, 189, 222
Trobriand Islands 56–7
Turner, Victor 2
Tylor, E. B. 5, 24, 43, 69, 77–9, 82–3, 96, 97–8, 103, 108–9, 120–1, 135, 141, 143, 180–2, 214, 225–6

Van Maanen, John 60–1, 69
Virchow, Rudolf 164

Waitz, Theodor 74, 103, 121–4, 128–9, 136, 184, 188
Wallace, Alfred Russel 144, 159, 205–6
Wallace, William 194
Warris, Dain 190
Watt, Ian 41, 86, 129, 211
Wells, H. G. 9, 18, 84–6, 143, 162, 180, 182
Wengle, John L. 19, 49, 50, 147
Whatley, Richard 77–8
Willems 16, 49, 143–50, 187–8, 211, 213
Williams, Raymond 92
Wiltshire, John 151
Wittgenstein, Ludwig 61
Wyndham 51, 52.

Zagorski, Karol 130
Zulu 125